SHAMANISM AND THE MYSTERY LINES

'Ley Lines', Spirit Paths, Out-of-Body Travel & Shape-shifting

Paul Devereux

quantum

LONDON • NEW YORK • TORONTO • SYDNEY

quantum

An imprint of W. Foulsham & Co. Ltd,
The Publishing House, Bennetts Close,
Cippenham, Slough, Berkshire, SL1 5AP, England

ISBN 0-572-02664-1

Paul Devereux was editor of *The Ley Hunter*
magazine (1976–96), and is Director of The
Dragon Project Trust. For many years the
Dragon Project has been studying energy
effects at ancient sites by instrumental
monitoring as well as the use of
dowsers and psychics. He has conducted
his own research at sites in Britain, the USA
and Egypt. His lecturing and broadcasting
commitments in Britain, America and Europe
bring him in contact with other researchers on
a worldwide basis. He currently lives and
works in the Cotswolds, England.

Printed in Great Britain at St Edmundsbury Press Ltd, Bury St Edmunds, Suffolk

CONTENTS

INTRODUCTION TO THE
2000 EDITION

This book was originally published in Britain in 1992, with various foreign editions appearing in the following year. What appears in this reprint edition is the original text, but with a small number of minor changes and repairs, plus this updating introduction.

I have written many books, but *Shamanism and the Mystery Lines* perhaps more than any of the others was truly revolutionary in nature, and like any such work, it presents a different way of thinking about a subject, in this case 'leys' or 'leylines', and this inevitably creates a disturbance to fixed ideas. People react differently to such a challenge: some feel liberated and excited by the change of perspective, others stubbornly resist it or studiously ignore it, while many try to absorb the new message and graft it to their existing belief structures so as to not risk any conceptual shocks that might oblige them actually to think differently. *Shamanism and the Mystery Lines* received all these responses, plus a few more. One of the biggest surprises to me in the years since the book was first published has been to find that there is more acceptance of at least parts of the thesis it expounds among some academics than there has been among some of those of a more 'New Age' persuasion. This is a reversal of the situation at the outset of the great ley revival of the 1960s, when it was the energetic 'New Agers' who were making the running, and the academic establishment that was fiercely resistant.

Well, here we go again, eight years on. It is generally reckoned that a new theory takes about 15 years to establish itself, so with this reprint edition we are about halfway through that assimilation process – that makes you, brave reader, still a pioneer! I urge you to read every word, because there were misconceptions on numerous people's parts the first time around. In going through the work in detail again while preparing this introduction, I have been surprised at the range of material and connections of information in these pages that even I, the author, had forgotten about! It is time for us all to revisit *Shamanism and the Mystery Lines*.

Enter within

What does the book deal with? First of all, it provides a brief but authentic history of the whole 'leyline' story. In the course of this, the book points out the fallacies that have arisen in the subject. This is contentious, because some people still want to believe in those fallacies, and some people still make their livings peddling them. And who am I to claim they are fallacies? Well, I have lived through them and believed in them, and had to make the painful effort of dispensing with them, otherwise I would have to have closed down my critical faculties. The book then goes on to look at physically real ancient lines on the landscape, from Europe to the Americas. These various kinds of ground markings and features are the real 'leylines' – genuine archaeological mysteries. It is these that this work then goes on to probe. This enquiry finds such mystery lines, whether great earthen avenues laid down in Neolithic Britain, or mysterious straight lines marked on American deserts, to be associated with one or both of two themes: the spirits of the ancestral dead, and the ancient practice of shamanism, the tribal religious and healing activity that involved the use of trance ecstasy. We also find that the linking of spirits of the dead with both visible and invisible roads and tracks survived up to the medieval period in Europe. The book shows that these two themes of spirits of the dead and the spirits of out-of-body – that is, entranced – shamans seem to spring from the same basic complex of archaic beliefs.

Criticisms and developments

While the book was being written, new information was coming in about shamans and the use of paths, and about spirit ways and death roads in Old Europe – see the notes on page 230, for instance. In the years subsequent to the book's publication, more has been learned about the death roads of Continental Europe, and a link has been made between these and church ways or funeral paths as occur in Britain. How these features relate to the conceptual (i.e. invisible) spirit ways, is at present unclear and requires more work. We do now know, however, that there are ancient traditions of the spirits of shamans in trance treading specific physical paths in the actual landscape: this happens in Nepal, for instance, where certain places and certain paths are associated with the shaman's spirit. There is some as yet unclear evidence of similar traditions in Siberian shamanistic societies, too, but further research is required on this. In addition, there is now archaeological evidence indicating that the idea of spirits walking the land goes back to at least Neolithic times in Europe: rock art in Scandinavia shows footprints leaving Bronze Age and Neolithic cemeteries and walking off into the surrounding landscape. Some of the feet appear to be shod in *hel*-boots – special footwear worn by the newly dead in Norse tradition. (See my *The Sacred Place*, Cassell.) What can be said is that, overall, the new evidence that has come to light since the writing of *Shamanism and the Mystery Lines* tends to support the basic arguments the book presents.

After almost a decade, I would naturally now write a different work – all theories have to be modified. I would play down some aspects and place greater emphasis on others. For example, I would now slightly reduce the insistence on associating straight line features with only the *spirit flight* of the shaman when in out-of-body trance and broaden that into *any* form of believed locomotion while in the spirit world. (This invariably seems to have involved flying, floating, or walking slightly above the ground, however.)

5

One thing that seems to have been poorly understood by some critics of the original work, is that in a shamanistic society, the visionary and mythic world is *projected out onto the landscape*. This is fully understood by anthropologists who study such people, and is not some idiosyncratic notion that I am trying to sell to the reader. The ancient mind was out there in front of the eyes as much as behind them.

Another misunderstanding seems to have been that the book argues for a universal system of shamanic lines. This is not the case: such features occur in places around the world, but they were not the remnants of one single system. Rather, they were varied cultural expressions of universal traits in human experience. It is a different argument. Also, it might be worth clarifying for this edition that many of the linear features such as the death roads of Holland and elsewhere, as described in the text, were not *in themselves* shamanic, but it is suggested that the ancient blueprint they were derived from did originate in such a source.

On page 188 I state that there are two kinds of shamanic landscape – those characterised by straight-line features of one sort or another, and those that have giant effigies emblazoned on them, either in the form of desert engravings, as at Nazca, Peru, or in the form of effigy mounds, as in the north-central United States. This statement was only partially correct: it is now clear that there was a *third* kind of shamanic landscape, namely one in which large-scale, abstract, wandering lines and enclosures were laid out on the ground using various methods. Examples occur on the floor of Death Valley in California, for instance. The ethnological evidence now suggests that these were 'symbolic landscapes' used by rival shamans during magical battles. The lines represented features such as mountain ranges which could protect the shaman. So the emphasis on *straight* lines in this book is not meant to imply that is all there is, it is simply that the straight line was book's the main subject coming at it as it does from the 'leyline' perspective.

In due course, I will be writing a major new work on the whole topic, taking all constructive criticisms and new evidence on board. In the meantime, elements of the thesis are updated piecemeal in various other works of mine – such as *The Illustrated Encyclopedia of Ancient Earth Mysteries* (Blandford, UK, Sterling, USA, 2000).

Practical work

One of the joys of 'ley hunting' has been that it was great excuse for getting out into the countryside and seeking alignments between ancient monuments, or dowsing across fields trying to pick up 'energy lines'. One complaint about *Shamanism and the Mystery Lines* was that it took this fun away. It does not do so, of course – it simply redefines the nature of the activities involved. So in British and Continental landscapes there are funeral paths and death roads to find and trace in the field. Such mapping is important, because these features are at risk of disappearing from the cultural record. Along with this fieldwork, there is much library work to be done in finding references to these features, and the folklore attached to them. And, you can even try dowsing for them – in this case the results will not be a matter of belief or mere assertion. It is also intriguing to visit the 'cursus' features or Neolithic earthen avenues described in Chapter 2. The vast majority of visitors to Stonehenge, for instance, never know about the nearby cursus there, which is well marked along its length with signs by the National Trust. It is an enthralling experience walking along such features, looking for the visual clues that might reveal the answer to their mystery. There are also stone alignments, and, yes, occasional alignments of sites, to hunt for. It is only 'leylines' that have died (because the term has been devalued to the point of uselessness by being subjected to too many fantasies), not alignments. In the Americas, there are ancient Native American lines as described in Chapter 3, to find and trace. A great place to start is Chaco Canyon, New Mexico. Books that will help you with all this kind of practical work include my own *The New Ley Hunter's Guide* (Gothic Image, 1994).

Ironically, *Shamanism and the Mystery Lines* actually *added* another kind of activity – the study of the inner visionary world that gave rise to the physical shamanic landscapes. The best way to try to experience this is through the use of lucid dreaming, described in the final part of the book. I undertook special research and co-wrote, with my wife, *The Lucid Dreaming Kit* (Tuttle, USA; Connections, UK), so that anyone could develop the ability to enter this remarkable state of consciousness. You can go alignment hunting with the virtually the same realism in the lucid dream state as you can in the great outdoors!

Moving on

It is time now to get into the book proper. For the genuinely interested reader, here is a new starting point, and new revelation. What you will not find here are invented histories about the ancient past – no spacemen or Atlanteans – but what you *will* find is a story that is about our actual human heritage. In the end, I suppose, it is all down to a matter of philosophy – one either engages in modern fantasies about the past, or one wants to know what ancient people actually thought and did – how they saw the world. This book is guided by that latter philosophy.

PREFACE

This book explores the mystery surrounding ancient alignments of sites or 'leys'. This exploration includes stone rows,
prehistoric linear earthworks and straight lines or tracks in
archaic landscapes in many parts of the world. What I believe to
be the solution to that mystery is presented here; it has come
together only slowly, increment by increment, over years of
inquiry, pondering and insight. In my first flush of interest in
'ley hunting', I had no inkling how far-reaching the study
would become for me, and where it would lead. From early
simplistic and naive notions, the subject now incorporates
some very sophisticated material, as this book will demonstrate.
The outcome of this development is therefore not some
carefully-groomed, fixed personal agenda: it is as much a
surprise to me as it will be to the reader. It is, as we shall see, at
once both simple and complex.

Many people have heard of the word 'ley', but ideas as to
what the term refers to vary dramatically. Typically, a
mainstream archaeologist will dismiss the whole concept as a
fallacy. At some levels, such a view is, actually, correct – I am
more aware of that than the archaeologists. If they allow their
prejudices to be tested against this book, however, they will
experience the delightful surprise of finding some rich and
authentic lines of inquiry.

At the other extreme, there are those who are convinced that
'leylines' are lines of energy, forming etheric configurations
over the whole landscape; indeed, over the whole globe. These
energy lines can be 'felt'; they can be located by dowsing (water

9

witching or divining; radiesthesia). To such people, leylines take on spiritual overtones. As this book will reveal, there is indeed a (surprisingly) long history of associating lines with power of various perceived kinds, but it will also show that far from being 'spiritual', this is in fact a process of making exoteric much subtler; inner matters. To refer to the numinosity one can experience from nature, from the land, as 'earth energy', to think of ancient landscape lines as channels of 'energy' or 'spiritual force' instead of being the expressions of a deep experience of the human mind, is to make . . . a mistake.

The third type of person with preconceived ideas about leys is the purist ley hunter, who wants a back-pack, a map, a picnic lunch and the great outdoors. And very healthy such an activity is, too. But the sighting of an old church spire across the fields, perhaps lining up with some distant earthworked hill, while evocative, only goes so far. Likewise, the endless pencil-plotting of lines on maps eventually becomes a circular exercise. It is excellent, even necessary, to undertake this work, but unwise to remain for ever at that stage.

Old Alfred Watkins, the man who gave the term 'leys' to perceived ancient alignments, thought he was uncovering the remnants of prehistoric traders' tracks. That theory, too, is firmly put away in this work. Though there are paths and tracks in some cases, they were not simply for traders.

Many others of this work's readership will be those who have vaguely heard about leys, and are simply curious. They may, perhaps, most readily of all be able to accept what these pages reveal; they will not have to struggle so much with fixed ideas and prejudices. I have believed in everything to do with leys in my time, I have plotted them on maps, dowsed them (or convinced myself that I did), surveyed them in the field and tramped through the countryside along what I preceived as authentic alignments of sites. I have been on the moors, the mountains and the deserts. At some point or other, I have taken on board every notion. My personal progress through the whole subject has been at times a painful one of stripping away cherished ideas.

Because the findings expressed within these covers will be, for some controversial, I feel I have to do something I have never considered necessary in years of writing books, and that is to present my credentials.

I became fascinated with the idea of leys in the mid-1960s, as far back as anyone now alive and truly active in the field. The subject has been a constant source of interest and study for me ever since. In 1976, in addition to being an active researcher, I took over as editor of *The Ley Hunter*. As the editor of any specialist journal tends to do, I assembled over the years the kind of specialised library few people can afford, and became informed in certain relevant topics. As editor, one meets the researchers, the people who are actually doing things in the subject area; one constantly receives news of the latest developments. One becomes informed in a way that is not otherwise easily possible.

As an editor, one also receives the mail, the endless correspondence. Over enough years, this reveals certain patterns in people's thinking; it becomes noticeable, pre-dictable even, at what levels of information (and lack of) they are tempted to begin speculating, and then tenaciously cling to the questionable beliefs that result.

While there are certainly individuals considerably more informed than me on specialist areas of alignment research, such as archaeologists studying lines in the Americas, or 'Earth Mysteries' colleagues researching mediaeval alignment patterns, I am quite confident that — through the accidents of fate rather than any innate ability on my part — no one has currently a greater comprehensive knowledge of the whole field of ancient alignments than myself, nor (perhaps even more importantly) the fallacies inherent within it.

The concepts worked through in this book, therefore, come from an informed author who has paid his dues. There are, alas, no university chairs in ley research, or *alignment studies* as I would prefer to call it, and many people write on the subject who are, frankly, insufficiently informed or who are simply peddling a pet notion. There is no 'quality control' as there is in the academic world. Nevertheless, like any other subject, proficiency in alignment studies nowadays requires time, application, knowledge of the literature, clear thinking and ongoing research.

Finally, the subject of leys *per se* is dealt with here in only the first chapter. The important factors are dealt with and a summary of the current scene provided. For more lengthy discussion, the reader is referred to *Lines on the Landscape* (Hale, 1989) by Nigel Pennick and myself. My concern here has been to get on with the fresh material as swiftly as possible. What results is an extraordinary detective story.

So, if you have definite ideas as to what a ley or leyline is, be prepared to experience a change. Whatever one's views on the subject, this book will provide an approach to the enigma that will surprise and challenge.

Paul Devereux

PART ONE
THE HISTORY

CHAPTER 1

THE RISE OF A HERESY

It was Alfred Watkins of Hereford who gave the term 'ley' to alignments of ancient sites. It was he who, in the 1920s, provided the most complete early vision of a linear pattern of apparently great antiquity still discernible in the landscape. This vision was viewed as a heresy by the mainstream archaeologists and scholars of the day. But Watkins' ideas, to which we will return shortly, did not arise out of a vacuum.

Straws in the wind

Observations of alignments of various types of monuments seem to have accompanied the growing interest in antiquarianism that developed in the eighteenth century. Viewed as a whole, the process is rather akin to a person awakening in unfamiliar surroundings from a deep sleep, taking a while to get things into focus and trying to understand what the situation is that they have awoken to.

We probably do not know of all those people in relatively modern times who believed they saw the remnants of old alignments (this is particularly true of researchers who wrote up their findings in languages other than English), but certainly one of the first was the British antiquarian, William Chapple. In 1778, he noted that the main avenue of stones at a megalithic ('large stone') prehistoric site at Drewsteington in Devon aligned to a dolmen (a megalithic 'box' of upright slabs and a capstone dating to the New Stone or 'Neolithic' age) some distance away.

14

A strand of interest that ran through antiquarianism was a romantic interest in the Druids. One such antiquarian was the Reverend Edward Duke, who, in 1846, proposed that Stonehenge and Avebury, some 20 miles (32 km) apart, were on a straight line that also included a stone circle and two prehistoric earthworks. Duke saw these sites as being points on 'orbits' radiating out from Silbury Hill, the great Neolithic mound in the Avebury complex, representing a terrestrial model of what he supposed to be the Druidic earth-centred (geocentric) view of the solar system. Silbury represented the Earth, Avebury henge was on the solar orbit, and, at the furthest extremity, Stonehenge stood on the orbit of Saturn.

In his book, *Traditions of De-Coo-Dah*, published in the 1850s, Indian trader William Pidgeon described his journeys through parts of the American Midwest. He gave an account of his association with an old Indian sage, De-coo-Dah, and his

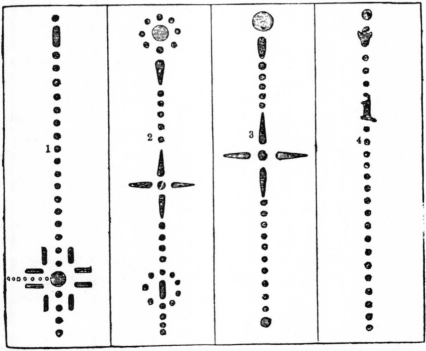

Figure 1. One of William Pidgeon's 'lineal ranges' of Amerindian earthworks, shown in four stages.

studies of some of the many old Indian mounds and monumental earthworks of the region. From his surveys of 449 Indian mounds, Pidgeon came to the conclusion that many of them lay in alignments, or 'lineal ranges' as he called them: 'the lineal ranges were designed as and constructed for national or international landmarks and boundaries.' Pidgeon's book has been dismissed as effectively a work of fiction by scholars, but John Michell has commented that Pidgeon's 'artless accounts of his rambles among the native peoples and monuments of old America have an authentic ring.'[1]

In 1870, William Henry Black gave a lecture on 'Boundaries and Landmarks' to an archaeological gathering in Hereford, Alfred Watkins' home city. He spoke of 'great lines' formed by alignments of sites and landmarks which he had at that time been studying for some 50 years. He attributed such alignments to Roman origin.[2]

The last two decades of the nineteenth-century saw a flurry of alignment-related snippets in various papers and publications in Britain. In an 1882 paper for Herefordshire's Woolhope Club, G.H. Piper noted an alignment of prehistoric stone and earthwork sites to a prominent local peak. The following year, W. T. Watkin published an account of alignments of mounds in Lancashire, which, typical of his time, he ascribed to Roman surveying. In 1889, Joseph Houghton Spencer published a paper in *The Antiquary* called 'Ancient Trackways in England' in which he extended ancient straight forest tracks and parkland 'drives' into their surrounding landscapes. He claimed these extended lines passed through ancient sites, beacon hills and road junctions. He considered the lines, a combination of track segments and sight-lines, to be the remnants of some archaic system of long-distance signalling. At some point in the 1890s, if not earlier, Colonel Johnston, director at the time of the Ordnance Survey, discovered during field survey work that Stonehenge, the hilltop of Old Sarum to the south, containing remains of Iron Age and medieval usage, Salisbury Cathedral and the Iron Age hilltop earthwork of Clearbury Ring fell on a straight line. (It was later claimed by

16

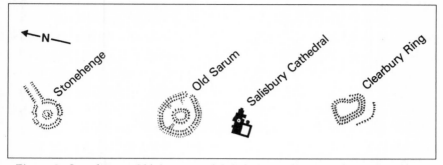

Figure 2. Stonehenge, Old Sarum and Salisbury Cathedral align to the edge of the earthworks called Clearbury Ring. This alignment has been rediscovered and presented in modified forms for nearly a century. (After Ian Thomson)

German researcher, Josef Heinsch — see below — that the discovery of this line assisted in increasing the accuracy of the Ordnance Survey.) Magnus Spence, a schoolmaster on Orkney, the group of islands off the northern coast of Scotland, published a small book in 1894 detailing the alignments between some of the major Neolithic sites there, such as the chambered mound of Maeshowe, the Ring of Brogar and the Stones of Stenness. He associated these with astronomical alignments. Astronomy was another major theme in antiquarianism that came into greater prominence at this time due to the work of Sir Norman Lockyer, editor of the science journal *Nature*, and F. C. Penrose on the astronomical orientations of Greek and Egyptian temples. In 1896, A. L. Lewis published research showing that all the then known stone circles in the western half of Bodmin Moor, Cornwall, fell accurately into line with the main, prominent hills of the region.

In 1904, F. J. Bennett published an article in the *South Eastern Naturalist* which described supposed 'meridional' (north–south) alignments between megaliths in Kent. He had heard of Duke's line linking Avebury and Stonhenge, and this seems to have sparked off his studies. He also proposed a version of the Stonehenge–Old Sarum–Clearbury Ring line. *The Old Road*, by Hilaire Belloc, was published the same year, and was a popular volume of its day. Though not dealing specifically with alignments, Belloc discussed prehistoric roads in general and their traces in pilgrimage routes and ridgeways. He noted how, on its way from Winchester to Canterbury, The 'Old Road' passed immediately alongside 13 existing or ruined churches. Belloc observed that the Old Road would tend to go straight, even up and over hills, because it belonged to a time before wheeled traffic, which has to negotiate steep terrain. He had visited America, and it is clear from his book that he was aware of the straight Indian tracks (see Chapter 3).

As a result of his and Penrose's work in studying astronomical orientations at ancient temples in various countries, Lockyer turned a similar eye on Britain's megalithic monuments. In 1906, he published *Stonehenge and Other British Stone Monuments Astronomically Considered*. In a second edition in 1909, he noted that astronomical sight-lines from Stonehenge passed through features in the surrounding landscape. He perceived Stonehenge as being involved in a triangular arrangement of alignments, one of which was the Old Sarum — Clearbury Ring line yet again. Apparently, Lockyer's interest in this line had been raised by Colonel Johnston.

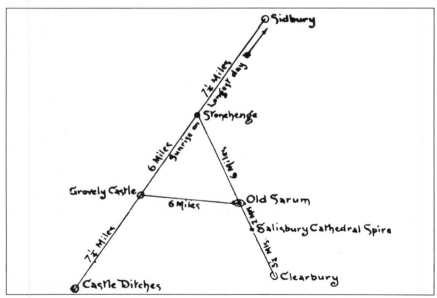

Figure 3. Lockyer's plan of alignments involving Stonehenge and surrounding hilltops containing prehistoric earthworks.

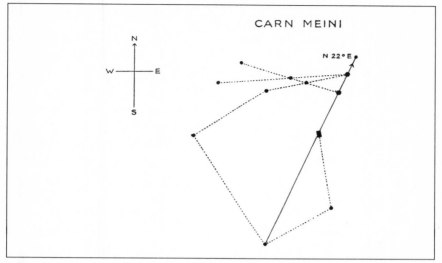

Figure 4. W. Done Bushell's sketch of alignments of standing stones on Carn Meini in the Preseli Hills of Wales.

In 1908, Sir Montagu Sharpe published research on a grid of alignments in Middlesex, marked by churches, named mark-stones and earthworks. Like others before him, he assumed the pattern was a remnant of the Roman Survey. In 1909, Alfred Devoir published a paper in a German archaeological journal on astronomical alignments he had discovered among the megaliths of the Carnac region of Brittany. In 1910, James G. Wood noted the intervisibility of ancient mounds and their alignments to prehistoric earthworks in the Welsh border area. In 1911, Alice Dryden, a folklorist working in the central English county of Leicestershire, commented that she felt that the legend of a tunnel between two standing stones, the St John's Stone in Abbey Fields, Leicester, and the Humber Stone three miles distant, was in fact a folk memory of an astronomical alignment between the monuments. (Alfred Watkins similarly claimed that folklore involving tunnels was a reference to alignments.) In the same year, the Reverend W. Done Bushell noted alignments between standing stones in the Welsh Preseli Hills.[4] In his *The Green Roads of England* of 1914, R. Hippisley Cox noticed that Bronze Age tumuli (mounds) aligned to the

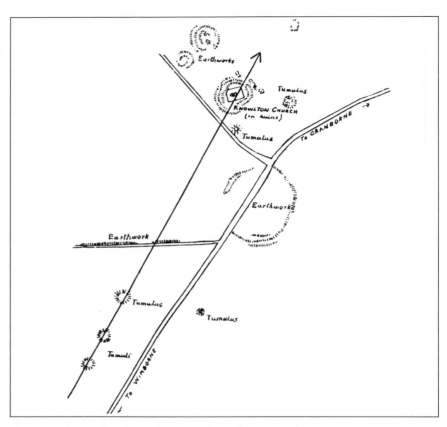

Figure 5. Hippisley Cox's drawing of an alignment of Bronze Age mounds with the Neolithic henge at Knowlton, Dorset.

Neolithic henge monument of Knowlton in Dorset. In 1915, Ludovic MacLellan Mann published accounts of 'geometrical relationships' between prehistoric cairns (stone mounds), standing stones and prominent topographical features.

With these and other observations, it can be seen that the idea of archaic alignments was thoroughly aroused by the time Alfred Watkins made his discovery of 'leys'.

The ley heresy

On the sunny afternoon of 30 June, 1921, Watkins was perusing a map of Herefordshire in his car while parked at Blackwardine in that county. The 66-year-old businessman, inventor, miller, photographic pioneer and public figure suddenly saw that a set of hilltops and ancient places fell into a straight line. The late Allen Watkins, Alfred's son, said that 'scales fell' from his father's eyes and he saw 'in a flash' that in prehistory trackways had been laid out in straight lines by surveyors using a line-of-sight system. 'The whole plan of The Old Straight Track stood suddenly revealed.'[5] Alfred Watkins knew his unspoilt Welsh Border countryside with extraordinary intimacy; his lifetime of travelling around it had seemingly primed his subconscious perception of its embedded linear patterns. He naturally realised that the original prehistoric tracks had long since disappeared, and all that remained were some of the markers laid out along them. He described his vision of the Old Straight Track thus:

> ... imagine a fairy chain stretched from mountain peak to mountain peak, as far as the eye could reach ... it touched ... the earth at a number of ridges, banks, and knowls. Then visualise a mound, circular earthwork, or clump of trees, planted on these high points, and in low points in the valley other mounds ringed with water to be seen from a distance. Then great standing stones brought to mark the way at intervals, and on a bank leading up to a mountain ridge or down to a ford the track cut deep so as to form a guiding notch on the skyline ... Here and there and at two ends of the way, a beacon fire used to lay out the track ... All these works exactly on the sighting line.[6]

Sighting from one hilltop, peak or ridge to another (called 'initial points' by Watkins), the track was laid out using a system of staves or rods. A great many years later, archaeologist R. J. C. Atkinson was to confirm from his own field experience that a line ranged out in such a way could be expected to have an error of only one metre in 50 km.[7]

Watkins' etymological investigations led him to suggest that an early English word for the prehistoric surveyor had been 'dodman' and that the country name for a snail, 'Hoddyman Dod', related to this because of the creature's horns being like the surveyor's rods. (This is the origin of *The Ley Hunter* journal's cartoon snail, 'Dod'.) These same studies led him to

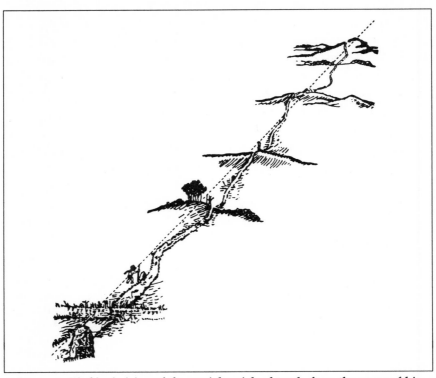

Figure 6. Watkins' vision of the straight, sighted track, from the cover of his 1927 The Ley Hunter's Manual.

the 'ley' term for the alignments, the remants of the old straight tracks, which he felt must have had a name, at least by Celtic (Iron Age) times. He suggested it 'perhaps was akin' to the Welsh *llan*, meaning sacred enclosure, which he claimed shared a similar etymological development with ley. Although ley is now most often interpreted as meaning a field put to grass, a meadow, pasture or cleared glade, Watkins noted rock outcrops, islets and hills with the name too. He considered that the meadow inference derived from strip clearance along some forest stretches of the old straight tracks. He also found associations with 'light' in the history of the word ley — its origins seem to be in the Latin verb *lucere*, to shine, which, interestingly, also gives the Latin *lucus*, a grove. Other words frequently found as place-name elements along leys also had links with light, especially black and cole. Black may seem difficult to associate with light, but Watkins found it has a root which also got into terms like 'bleach', to whiten. And cole/coal may be a black substance, but does it not give off brilliance when burnt? Watkins surmised that such associations went back to the use of beacon fires for surveying purposes.

Whether or not 'ley' was suitable as the ancient name for the old straight tracks, Watkins argued that it did not affect the reality of the features themselves. Nevertheless, he must have come to feel uneasy about the use of the ley term, for modern researcher Jonathan Mullard has determined that Watkins used the word only for a limited number of years in the 1920s, after which he stuck with 'old straight track' or 'archaic track'.[8] He may have been nearer the mark than he thought, however, for recent work by Alan Wharam has uncovered the facts that *laia* was used in legal English, at least, until the seventeenth century as meaning 'a roadway in a wood', and in French the word still relates to such features. It seems the word was also cognate with others meaning 'street' throughout Europe.[9] Belgian researcher Francois Geysen also notes that a word, *lei*, 'well known around Antwerp', was used on old maps to refer to roads going straight to a church or chapel (personal communication).

Whatever the truth about their ancient name, Watkins was of the opinion that the old alignments recorded a system of traders' tracks, appearing first in the Neolithic period, and then developing over the millenia 'on past the Roman occupation into a period of decay'. In addition to natural topographic features like hilltops (often those which became beacon points in Elizabethan times because of their special intervisible nature) and prehistoric mounds, standing stones, and earthworks, Watkins found certain other kinds of ancient sites recurring on the lines he now began to research earnestly throughout his home landscape. These included, amongst others, old (pre-Reformation) churches and crosses, castle sites, holy wells, ancient and named crossroads. He also kept finding distinctive boulders along the lines he studied. He was sure they were part

23

of the original ley survey, and consequently called them 'markstones'. He also remarked on certain classes of tree groupings at eye-catching points on the alignments. Although he was fully aware that the trees were relatively modern, he wondered if the history of the actual clumps might have gone back much earlier, their perpetuation being caused by natural seeding. Nevertheless, he stressed that such clumps had only secondary value as ley marker points.

Watkins explained the presence of Christian churches on what were supposed to be prehistoric lines by arguing that over time certain markers took on special or sacred significance. It is known, for example, that in Celtic times, if not earlier, road junctions were considered sanctified places — and Watkins considered ancient crossroads to be possible ley marker points. Such special spots evolved into various kinds of shrines, ultimately to be Christianised by a cross or a church. There is certainly considerable documentation and excavational evidence for this in Europe as a whole, and to a limited degree in Britain. It was a process clearly approved and prescribed by the early Church. Castles occurred on some lines, Watkins reasoned, because they were placed at high points commanding wide views for military purposes, a factor equally important to

Figure 7. The Chapelle des Sept-Saints, Brittany, a dramatic example of a Christianised prehistoric site. The current seventeenth-century church fabric, replacing earlier churches, embraces a Neolithic dolmen. (After A. de Mortillet)

the earlier ley surveyors. Watkins listed numerous medieval castles in which pre-Norman remains had been unearthed. He also pointed out that the word 'castle' not only meant fortification, but had been used earlier to denote prehistoric earthworks.

The ley discoverer gave a paper on his findings to the Woolhope Naturalists' Field Club, of which he was a prominent member, in September 1921. The following year he published *Early British Trackways*, essentially the text of his Woolhope Club paper. In 1925, he published his main work on leys, *The Old Straight Track*. This was richly illustrated using his photographic skills during the intensive fieldwork which had followed his initial insight, adding to his already extensive pictorial record of the Welsh border country, and which is now a recognised archaeological, architectural and sociological treasure. *The Ley Hunter's Manual* came out in 1927, and *Archaic Tracks Round Cambridge* in 1932.

Watkins was yet another to note the Stonehenge–Old Sarum–Clearbury Ring alignment, and claimed he had not previously known of Lockyer's version. He did admit knowledge of some of his predecessors' linear musings, however, and must have been told of W. H. Black's Woolhope Club paper given when he was a teenager, though he never said so. By 1922, we know he was slightly aware of the existence of straight Amerindian tracks through a newspaper article (he had also read Belloc's work).

During his ley hunts the old Herefordian found evidence of his leys in old towns, the alignments being invariably focused on the ancient churches, a cathedral or key crossroads within them. In his native city of Hereford, he discovered that the straight stretch of Broad Street, which links All Saints church at one end and the cathedral at the other, could be extended to the north of the city to pass through three ancient churches, and to the south through an ancient ford in the River Wye to another old church. He found several similar lines in London, one of which involved the ancient crossroads of Trafalgar Square and the course of The Strand, and another passed through St Paul's

Cathedral (built on ancient foundations on the 'initial point' of Ludgate Hill). In Oxford, he noted that lines of churches crossed through the Carfax, at the Roman central crossroads of the city. It was the site of the old market place too, and he obtained plenty of evidence throughout the land that ancient market places (also often the traditional locations of seasonal fairs, wayside preaching and open-air courts) were literally *mark*-ets, their mark stones sometimes still surviving.

In the countryside, Watkins found mounds, churches, old stones, ancient crossroads and hilltops aligning. A particularly interesting example involved the prehistoric hilltop earthworks of Sutton Walls in Herefordshire. Watkins had stood in a notch between the main earthworks and an outlying mound, and saw, as can be verified to this day, the pointed spire of Marden Church aligning with the square tower of Wellington Church. In the other direction, the line continues to Sutton St Nicholas Church. A year after this discovery, Watkins was approached by a countryman who informed him that during ploughing a dark linear mark had appeared in the field next to the Sutton Walls. It could be 'one of your old roads' the old fellow suggested. (When a field is ploughed, any underlying disturbed soil, such as eroded earthworks, a building's foundation or the course of a road, can show up as a dark stain.) Watkins quickly went to the location and saw that the dark plough-mark 'plainly went to the notch from which I had sighted over the churches'.

Although Watkins did not think of his leys as being primarily astronomical alignments, he nevertheless did observe that a few seemingly had significant celestial orientations.

Watkins sought 'proof by spade' of his old straight tracks whenever the opportunity arose, so when the sewerage system was being laid in Hereford, he took advantage of the ditches and workmen involved to see if evidence could be found of tracks deeply buried on some of his map lines. He was at least sometimes successful, as his photographs record.

The Straight Track Postal Portfolio Club was formed in 1926 in response to Watkins' work, and research and viewpoints

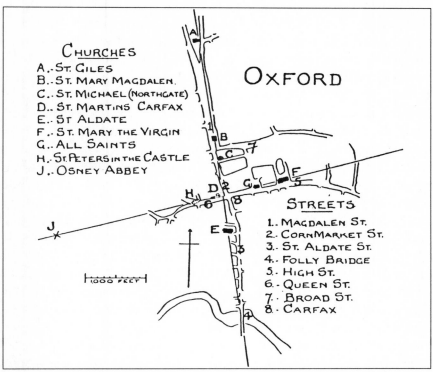

Figure 8. Alfred Watkins' drawing of church alignments in Oxford.

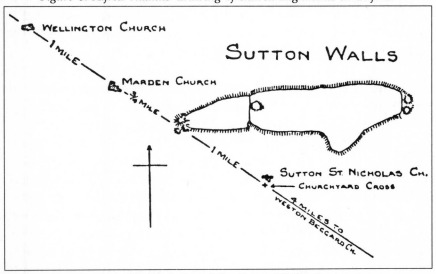

Figure 9. Watkins' plan of the Sutton Walls alignment.

27

would be circulated by post amongst the members, to be collated by the secretary, Major F. C. Tyler. Every so often, members would meet for a picnic at a ley marker point. It was nationally acknowledged that Watkins had spawned a new outdoor hobby — ley hunting.

But despite Watkins' distinguished reputation, and his success in other aspects of archaeology — such as correctly predicting where the medieval walls of Hereford had been and cataloguing the ancient wayside crosses of the county — his ley theory fell foul of the orthodoxy. O. G. S. Crawford, founder-editor of the august archaeological journal, *Antiquity*, refused a paid advertisement for *The Old Straight Track*, and poured scorn on the ley theory. Another archaeologist said the theory was 'not only nonsense, but damned nonsense'. Indeed, it was damned, in the sense of excluded. The very idea of ancient Britons surveying alignments clashed with the then overriding belief in the 'ascent of Man'. Also, there was at the time little archaeological awareness in Britain of linear features like the Neolithic cursuses (Chapter 2), or the old straight tracks of the Americas (Chapter 3). There was thus no perceived precedence for Watkins' notions. It is perhaps a sign of the gradual, though still grudging, change in attitude towards Watkins that Ron Shoesmith, head of the Archaeology Unit in Hereford, could acknowledge in 1990 that Watkins had 'the trademark of the great archaeologist'.[10]

Watkins died in 1935, and the Straight Track Club folded in the late 1940s. Boxes containing its archives are held in Hereford library.

A German interlude

There was a curious parallel in Germany with the British alignment work. Nigel Pennick has suggested that a 1909 article in a German journal by Alfred Devoir, a French researcher who had studied astronomical lines at the Carnac stones, Brittany, and who had been in touch with Lockyer, 'laid the foundation for what may be called the "German School" of alignment studies'.[11] Also, Lockyer's work was written up in Germany by a surveyor called Albrecht, and this duly influenced Johann Leugering, a Catholic priest, who, in 1920, sought astronomical alignments in his native Westphalia. He began to collaborate with a regional planner called Josef Heinsch (see below). In the 1920s, Wilhelm Teudt was independently studying German alignments which he called *heilige Linien*, holy lines. His work seems to have started with a study of the curious rock-hewn chapel atop one of the strange limestone pinnacles near Detmold called the Externsteine. This chapel has a circular window that admits sunbeams on midsummer morning. Teudt found there were horizon marker sites visible from the chapel giving various alignments. He went on seeking his holy lines amongst ancient chapels, sanctuaries and hermitages, wayside crosses, castles, ancient places of assembly and other locations throughout north Germany. John Michell describes Teudt's ideas:

> According to Teudt the astronomical relationships of these places arose from their former use in connection with the ancient round of festivals. From the place of assembly the people would look for the sun in the direction of a known landmark on the horizon. This was both an act of spiritual invocation and a practical method of reckoning the calendar ... In time the distant landmarks themselves became sacred, and festivals were held there, creating a need for another horizon mark in line with the two earlier sites. So developed the system of holy places, strung out in straight lines across the German heartland like, in Teudt's phrase, 'pearls on a thread'.[12]

Teud published his findings and ideas in 1929. He was a German chauvinist, relished the arrival of Hitler on the scene, and became involved in an SS project to turn the Externsteine into a Nazi cult centre.

Heinsch was a much different kind of man, and he ultimately fled Germany. He conducted his work on ancient linear patterns in Germany in 'fruitful collaboration' with Leugering, and in pilot studies in England, France and the Middle East. He concluded that from the Stone Age 'large tracts of land were already being accurately divided and surveyed'. His researches uncovered recurring measurements in the distances involved in the landscape geometry, which covered ancient sacred sites and boundary marks. Furthermore,

> Because of the general conservative retention of pagan religious sites, and their occupation by churches, chapels and mosques ... the pattern is recognisable in its main features even today, and gives a characteristic local stamp to the structure of a country or landscape.[13]

The 'fundamental triangulation of the country' was based on 30° and 60°, and the diagonals of a square and double square amongst other geometrically-significant angles. The

> ... base line of this system of orientations links two important sacred sites which are found to occur regularly: (a) the holy hill in the west, originally associated chiefly with Moon-worship and in Christian times often dedicated to Our Lady and (b) to the east of this on 84° or 96° (a six-degree deviation north or south of due east) the former solar site, in Christian times often dedicated to St John the Baptist.[14]

He found abundant evidence of his geometrical relationships in the 'old landscape arrangement near Munich'. In France, Chartres Cathedral, the remarkable Gothic edifice on its most ancient hilltop site, dedicated to St Mary, was a lunar position. An 84° line links the cathedral with the solar site now marked by the church of Nognt-le-Paye, 6.5-km distant. Southwest of Chartres, another lunar holy hill is marked by Notre Dame des Chatelliers, which has its solar site 84° to the east at the church of Ermenonville-le-Grande. In all, Heinsch found 36 convincing examples of his orientations within a 25-km radius of Chartres. In England, he noted Lockyer's triangle around Stonehenge, and he was another to show particular interest in the Stonehenge–Old Sarum–Clearbury Ring Line. He found the Odry stone circles in Poland, sites near Jerusalem, and many more areas to display his linear pattern.

Heinsch felt that the underlying principles of the old linear patterns could play 'a not unimportant role in the formation of a *new science of landscape arrangement* suited to the needs of modern communities'. This seems to have been the first call for a modern version of geomancy (sacred geography).

In the early 1930s, A. Röhrig published work on a grid-like arrangement of alignments over part of Germany, using all the

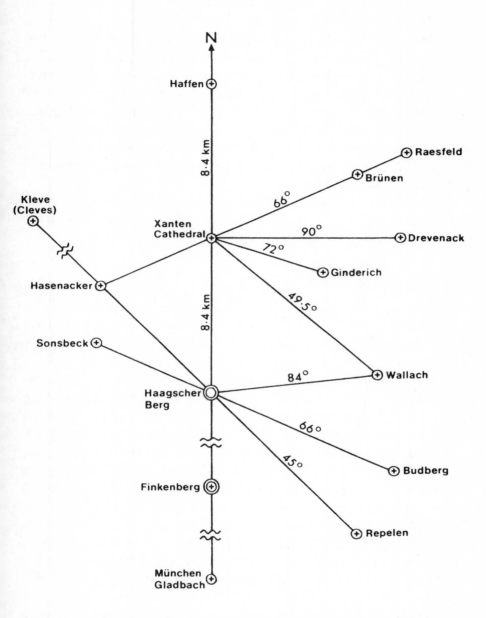

Figure 10. Heinsch's claimed ancient landscape pattern marked by old sites in the countryside around Xanten and the Haagscher Berg, Germany. (Michael Behrend after Josef Heinsch)

typical Watkinsian range of sites as mark points. In the same decade, August Meier studied alignments around Lemgo in Lippe involving churches and 'holy hills'. Between 1940 and 1943, papers by Kurt Gerlach in the Nazi journal, *Germanien* argued the case for alignments marked by churches of the tenth to twelfth centuries. Their purpose was 'similar to that of Watkins' leys: to provide lines of communication and guide travellers across the landscape'.[15] Gerlach considered that the lines had been laid out by Benedictine monks 'as part of the German empire's efforts to bring civilization to the pagans of the north and east'.[16]

Because of the association of some alignment studies with Nazism, the entire range of material was discouraged in Germany after the Second World War.

The great ley hunting revival

In correspondence shortly before the Straight Track Club was wound up in 1948, a couple of the surviving members wondered if Heinsch could be contacted. This came to nought, however, and the club duly ceased its activities.

Interest in leys waned, and it was only Egerton Sykes' The Avalon Society, and the activities of isolated individuals writing up their alignment work in scattered specialist publications — even school magazines — that kept the flame glimmering at all. The subject's fortunes changed, however, in 1961, through the person of an ex-RAF pilot called Tony Wedd. This man was a freethinker, a critic of materialism, and a man with both artistic and technical abilities.[17] He had read a library copy of Watkins' *The Old Straight Track* in 1949, and a few of his own ley hunts convinced him of the validity of Watkins' theory. Wedd became interested in 'flying saucers', or UFOs, and developed the belief that telepathic contact with Space People was possible. In 1960, a psychic visiting Wedd's home in Kent found a spot of 'magnetic force' nearby, where an old sycamore tree was growing. The psychic claimed she was receiving information from a space entity called Attalita. In this communication she was informed about 'lines of force', and Wedd and friends traced twelve such lines in the Kent countryside finding some examples of Watkinsian ley marker points falling on these lines (though these were primarily tree clumps, which Watkins had warned were weak evidence). Wedd further noted that some of these locations figured in local UFO reports, and he assumed from that time that the occupants of the flying saucers 'knew about leys'. Two UFO books particularly impressed Wedd. One was Aime Michel's *Flying Saucers and the Straight Line Mystery* (1958) in which the French author put forward the observation that during a 1954 UFO wave or 'flap' in France, low-level or landed UFOs fell into straight-line patterns he called 'orthotenies' in any 24-hour period (now discredited). The other work was Buck Nelson's *My Trip to Mars, the Moon and Venus* (1956). Nelson was an American UFO 'contactee', and he claimed that he had flown in alien spaceships. Nelson said that the flying saucers travelled along 'magnetic currents'. To Wedd, the matter was simple: Watkins leys and Michel's orthotenies were one and the same, and the lines were channels of magnetic force that the UFOs used. In 1961, Wedd published a pamphlet, *Skyways and Landmarks*, expounding on his ideas.

I have no interest in attempting to justify such notions, what matters here is that this bizarre mental alchemy was the spark that rekindled interest in the subject of alignments once more in Britain, a process that has had considerable impact far outside that country. A teenager called Philip Heselton got to know Wedd in 1961, and he was the initial catalyst in making leys the foundation of what has since come to be called, variously, 'Earth Mysteries', 'geomancy', 'alternative archaeology', or 'ancient mysteries', a wide-ranging, multi-disciplinary area that has emerged from the study of ancient sites and landscapes.[18] Heselton states that he first heard about leys from Wedd:

> I was fired with his enthusiasm and ... ordered *The Old Straight Track* from the library. From this, I learned more about leys and immediately got out the local map to try and find one for myself...
>
> A schoolfriend, Jimmy Goddard, was similarly inspired and together we formed The Ley Hunters Club. With the help of Tony

33

Wedd and Egerton Sykes I tried to contact surviving members of the Straight Track Club . . . Several did respond . . .

Allen Watkins agreed to be President of the club and spoke at its inaugural meeting in November 1962 . . .

We started a small newsletter to which, in 1965, we gave the title *The Ley Hunter*: it is still flourishing, over a quarter of a century later. Jimmy gave a series of talks, including one which was attended by John Michell and Paul Devereux. He started their interest in the subject . . . Many others were brought into the subject during the 1960s, including Anthony Roberts, Nigel Pennick and Paul Screeton.

The subject also expanded greatly in scope from that of the study of leys . . . [19]

In the Sixties there was a general rebirth of interest in occultism along with leys, UFOs, and a multitude of other formerly ignored or 'taboo' topics, and the fledgling area of Earth Mysteries began to cook in the seething conceptual cauldron of the psychedelic decade. Simultaneously, archaeology was undergoing traumas and revolutions, with the recalibration of the radiocarbon dating method destroying academic models of the diffusion of civilisation and technology, revealing that megalithic sites in western Europe were older than had been thought. Further, serious research by Alexander Thom and others was published showing what a vital element astronomical orientation had been in prehistoric sacred megalithic monuments, and this also had a bearing on landscape alignment studies in general. The 'alternative' view emerged that the remote past was a great repository of potential revelation for the modern mind.

John Michell brought his erudition to the subject area of leys and UFOs in articles in 'underground' publications and *The Flying Saucer Vision* (1967), but his *The View Over Atlantis* of 1969 proved to be a truly seminal work and seeded much of the later developments, both valid and spurious, in the ley hunting and Earth Mysteries field. Also in 1969, Paul Screeton took over editorship of the *The Ley Hunter*, which had become briefly defunct. In 1970, *The Old Straight Track* enjoyed a new edition (and has been in print more or less continuously ever since). From the late 1960s and into the 1970s various specialist and underground publishing ventures appeared which extended the available literature on geomantic matters. Notable amongst these were the efforts of John Nicholson (Cambridge Voice; Arcana), Anthony and Jan Roberts (Zodiac House) and Nigel Pennick (Cambridge Voice; the Institute of Geomantic Research). These people republished classic texts on Feng shui, for instance. This was an ancient Chinese system for the optimum placing of houses and tombs, balancing the influences of the earth and the heavens (and is still practised in Hong Kong, Singapore, Taiwan). The Victorian missionaries who encountered it wrote several books and papers on the subject. They used the term 'geomancy', meaning 'sacred geography', to describe Feng shui, and it was this century-old definition of the word that the 'new geomants' came to employ. (In strict terms geomancy means divination by casting patterns of soil.) Again, The Institute of Geomantic Research was largely responsible for translating the German alignment material (above) and putting it once more in circulation. From early on in the 1960s until his death in 1990, Tony Roberts revived interest in 'Atlantean traditions', fairylore, and advanced the concept of 'geomythics', the interaction of mythic reality with the topography of ancient sacred landscapes.

The new alignment research blossomed. In 1974, John Michell published his detailed study of alignments between the standing stones and ancient crosses of the Land's End district at the westernmost tip of Cornwall.[20] He had extended some of Lockyer's suggested astronomical lines in the region, and found them to continue on across country marked by megaliths. A classic alignment which emerged from this work was a most precise, three-mile line stretching from the stone circle of Boscawen-un, marked by five standing stones.

I took over editorship of *The Ley Hunter* from Paul Screeton in 1976. The UFO connection gradually died away (though is still occasionally resurrected by an outdated journalist or some gauche newcomer to the subject area). It has been replaced to some degree by the general theory of 'earth lights', which sees exotic natural light phenomena as being produced by processes within the earth itself and occurring in the same types of terrain as those favoured by the builders of certain kinds of sacred sites.[21,22] Research into energies at sites, particularly by the Dragon Project (founded in 1977, and now a trust), has identified the possible deliberate use of natural geophysical energies and geological factors.[23]

The new ley hunters made a constant attempt to discover further alignments, and to check over known, claimed ones. A landmark in this process was *The Ley Hunters Companion* (1979) by Ian Thomson and myself. Preparing for the book, we had gathered over 300 claimed leys that either had already been published or were sent to us by enthusiasts. On studying them on large-scale maps, it was found that the vast majority were highly suspect: sites were not accurately aligned, lines were so long something would appear on them just by chance, or 'markers' included questionable features like farm houses. On the basis of the residue, plus some new lines, fieldwork was conducted throughout England. It was realised that for a line 'on the ground' to have any sort of reasonable claim to being a deliberate feature, preparatory map lines had best be under 10 miles in length, include at least five valid marker sites (three or four markers, perhaps, in very short alignments of a mile or two), and had to be checked with at least prismatic compass and 1:25,000-scale map in the field, backed up with local archive research. Lines drawn on a map had to be with a sharp, H-grade pencil and long (preferably clear plastic) straightedge, on a scale of not less than 1:50,000. Even then, the line-width would represent about 11 yards/metres on the ground.[24]

New standards in alignment accuracy slowly became the required norm.

While Watkins' contention that old churches on leys marked sites of pagan sanctity has been maintained by modern ley hunters, new research has indicated that there may also have been deliberate alignment schemes in the historical period. One way this would occur, obviously, is by churches being placed on Roman or Saxon street grids in ancient towns. In some cases, as in Oxford (see above) it seems churches may

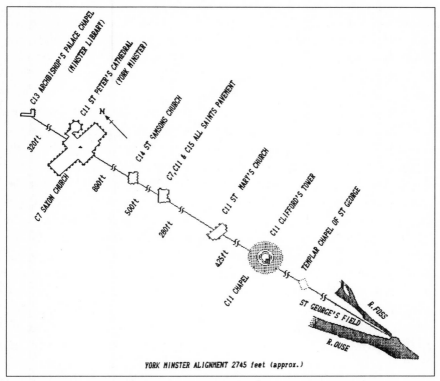

Figure 11. *The York 'corridor of sanctity'.* (After Brian Larkman)

have been on their own linear arrangements, related to but not identical with the street grids. In addition, more individual, specific alignments have also been detected. For example, Brian Larkman discovered a startling line cutting across the ancient city of York.[25] This alignment, which has been researched in great depth, is marked by York's seven most ancient and important churches or chapels, and passes through York Minster at the point where an earlier seventh-century church is thought to have been located. While this short, densely marked alignment could be the remnants of something earlier, it seems more realistic to suppose that it evolved during historic times. Nigel Pennick has found similar lines in Cambridge, including one which passes through nine pre-Conquest and medieval sacred sites.[26] He has also picked out some remarkable

37

alignments of pre-Fire of London churches, some containing as many as ten such sites. Like Watkins, he sees evidence of 'separate church and street grids' which date back to Saxon and even Roman times.[27]

Whether such grids relate to earlier geomantic factors can only be guessed at. A hint exists in one London line I have proposed.[28] It links the two legendary hills of the City of London, Tower and Ludgate. The line passes along the course of Cannon Street which partially marks a Roman street line. The Romans clearly thought it germane to link the two hills, for whatever reason. On Cannon Street, and thus on the line, is the London Stone, now a stump behind railings in a wall. Its origins are very ancient and obscure, but it might have been used as a 'king stone' in Saxon times (see Chapter 4). Two churches and St Paul's Cathedral also fall on the line as can be seen in Figure 12, and two of these sites mark the burial positions of at least three legendary or historical ancient British kings. The other church, All Hallows, stands on a Saxon shrine site. The Tower of London stands on the White Mount or Hill, mentioned in Bardic texts which contain at least Iron Age themes, and is associated with Celtic head worship and complex themes of sovereignty: the Head of Bran was said to have been interred there. That this line has so many kingly associations is no accident in my view, and I will be showing in Part Two the links between linearity and kingship, and the startling reasons for it.

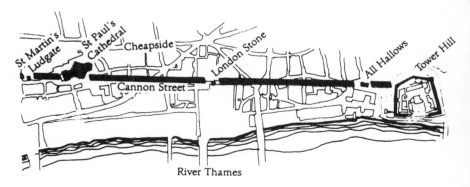

Figure 12. London's 'kingship line', linking Ludgate and Tower hills. (Author)

There is clear evidence emerging of specific medieval geomantic practice. Dutch-based researcher John Palmer, for instance, has assembled an enormous body of (as yet unpublished) documentation on a scheme of 'blue stones' used in the laying out of medieval towns in western Europe (and seemingly further afield too).[29] He has located many still-extant stones, or their former positions. They were key marker, *omphalos*, points and were associated with kingship, the Church and the judicial systems of the time.

Another example of medieval geomancy is the important study of Salisbury by Nigel Pennick. This brings us back once more to that perennial Stonehenge–Old Sarum–Salisbury Cathedral–Clearbury Ring line. Pennick has demonstrated that Salisbury has two overlapping medieval street grid patterns, and the angle of the Stonehenge–Old Sarum–Clearbury Ring line intercepts the cathedral *at the precise angle of one of the street's grids*. There can be no doubt that the medieval town planners were conscious that the cathedral was located on this line (Old Sarum and Clearbury Ring are intervisible), and its course was embedded in the city's very foundations.[30]

John Palmer and Nigel Pennick, as well as notable Belgian ley hunters such as Eugene Zimmer and Robert Dehon, the German Ulrich Magin and the Swiss Marco Bischof, amongst several others, have been generally busy studying the geomancy of continental Europe. Just one of Palmer's linear discoveries, for instance, is the remarkable 6-km-long alignment of prehistoric mounds southwest of Epe in Holland.

Then there is aerial photography. Although Watkins foresaw the significance of this, its testimony since his time has not supported the idea of a vast network of straight prehistoric tracks across the British Isles. If such a network was there, airborne survey would reveal 'crop marks', which are dark or light markings in vegetation growing over subsurface disturbance of the soil caused by former foundations, tracks, or earthworks, even when nothing is visible at ground level. These 'ghost images' are caused by variation in moisture content in the vegetation created by the disturbed soil beneath it, and can

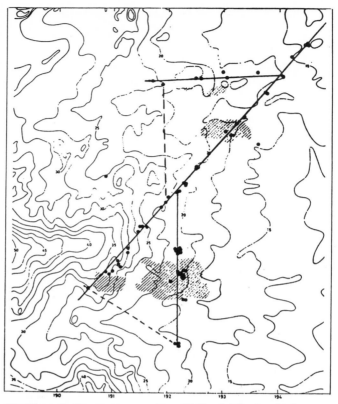

*Figure 13. Mound alignments near Epe, Holland. The hatched areas represent
'Celtic Fields'.* (John Palmer after Topographische Dienst)

show up, usually fleetingly, in specific weather conditions.
Captured on film, they are then marked on large scale maps,
and tens of thousands have now been catalogued in this
manner, the vast majority awaiting archaeological excavation.
As such markings reach back to Neolithic times, and as no
straight-track networks have shown up, Watkins' explanation
of his alignments being remnants of traders' tracks seems to be
untenable. (However, there may well be segments of alignments
that became tracks for various reasons, ritual ways and so
on.)

On the other hand, aerial archaeology in Britain *has*
confirmed large-scale linear earthworks linking mounds of

Neolithic date (roughly 5000–2000 BC in Britain), proving that there was a tradition of linearity linked with sacred sites in prehistoric Britain, and that ranging out of landscape lines by ancient Britons did in fact occur. Ley hunters have started to use this evidence, and it has become a significant development in modern alignment studies. In view of this, the following chapter is given over to these features and some of the research findings on them.

Another increasingly important strand of contemporary ley hunting research has been comparative study of old straight track systems in other parts of the world. Far and away the most important of these are the Amerindian lines, which provide a most telling avenue of enquiry as, indeed, this book will demonstrate. For that reason, this crucial material is also given its own chapter (Chapter 3).

These two developments, the study of relatively recently discovered prehistoric linear features in British landscapes and visible pre-Columbian straight tracks in the Americas, have to some extent rendered obsolete a debate between modern ley hunters and critics over much of the last two decades — the statistics of alignments. This boils down to the question: are the alignments that ley hunters find on maps chance effects, or remnants of deliberate ancient activity? Although there had been some work on this previously, and even Watkins had touched on the problem, the matter really reared its head after Michell's Land's End survey (above). Pat Gadsby and Chris Hutton-Squire produced a computer simulation of the Land's End area. They entered the grid references of all the sites used by Michell, 'nudged' them randomly with their computer creating, in effect, an artificial landscape, and tested the alignments between this artificial, randomised set and the actual lines Michell had found. If the artificial lines matched the real set, then chance would seem to be the likely explanation for the Land's End alignments. It turned out that while the computer found most of Michell's lines to be no better than chance, some seemed deliberate, while a few seemed *deliberately non-aligned*. For serious statistical consideration, however, such a test needs doing 100 times (for 'one percent' significance). But this takes a great deal of computer time, and the Land's End simulation, with its intriguing findings, was never extended further. There were also concerns about refining the selection of sites, and there remained the difficulty of making the statistical model match the reality of the situation on the ground, with factors such as intervisibility being taken into account. The Land's End material was also studied by other statisticians, but technical disagreements rendered these inconclusive as well. But in 1990, a survey of 95 extant or former menhirs (individual standing stones) in the same district by archaeologist Frances Peters (*Cornish Archaeology*, No. 29) drew the conclusion that it seemed 'the menhirs were purposely positioned along contours ... and that they were placed so that they tend to be fairly easy to see, particularly from other menhirs'. The fact that the stones were so positioned, allowing 'visibility over some distance', suggested to Peters 'a more than local significance' to the monuments.

Over the following years, Bob Forrest and Michael Behrend took on the main statistical task, challenging ley hunters on their accuracy and (sometimes) lack of thought about what they were doing, exposing the phenomenal nature of chance in such matters, and applying computerised statistical tests to specific examples of alignments. These statistical models kept shifting and being refined, so that a line that was deemed better than chance in one model would find itself no better than chance in later tests. Many ley hunters, including myself, became very frustrated at this. One example, however, that stood up to

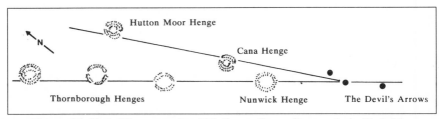

Figure 14. Tested by computer 400 times, these alignments in Yorkshire repeatedly displayed statistical significance. The line from the Devil's Arrows to the Thornborough Henges is 11 miles (18 km) long. (Schematic, not to scale)

42

everything thrown at it, was the lines from the Devil's Arrows standing stones in Yorkshire, which were to prove better than chance even after 400 computer simulations. Other lines also came out as statistically significant, but were not 'tested to destruction' with later statistical models, and thus the matter remains inconclusive, especially as Forrest has now retired from the fray.

Another way of approaching the chance problem is to see if a predictable pattern of alignments can be identified. I conducted a survey of some known lines, and realised that there was a 'holy hill' pattern showing remarkably similar characteristics. Some of these are also east–west examples. Three of the hills have ancient chalk-hill figures, possibly prehistoric, and all have prehistoric earthworks on their summits. They overlook ancient Christian holy places (which may, of course, have replaced earlier sanctified spots) at Winchester, Hereford, Guisborough, Saintbury, Cerne Abbas, Uffington and Wilmington. All the lines are only a few miles in length.

This work, like all the other strands of modern alignment research, of which only the main elements have been touched on here, requires much more development, but as it is conducted on a largely amateur basis by enthusiasts with limited resources, this happens only gradually. There is another reason, too, why the research is slow, a reason that turns off some people who could otherwise have much to contribute to the subject, and misdirects the naive enthusiasm of many who do get involved. Let us take a quick look at the culprit.

A parting of ways

The research-based element of modern alignment studies is only a small part of the current phenomenon surrounding what has come to be known as 'leylines'. From the Sixties, an element crept into thinking on the ley subject which has expanded with time until it represents the main public face of the subject, namely, that leys are lines of energy. Wedd, we saw, thought of

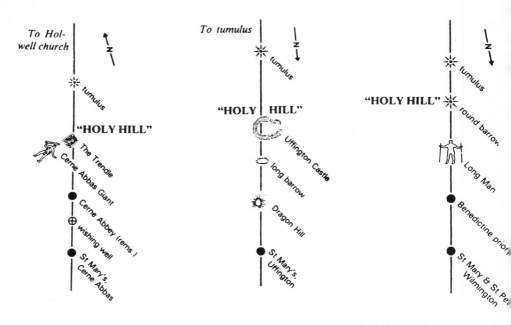

Figure 15. Seven examples of approximately north–south 'holy hill' alignments.
The top three involve hills with ancient chalk hill figures, and share very
similar configurations. The Uffington horse hill figure (next to central line above)
is now known to be Bronze Age.

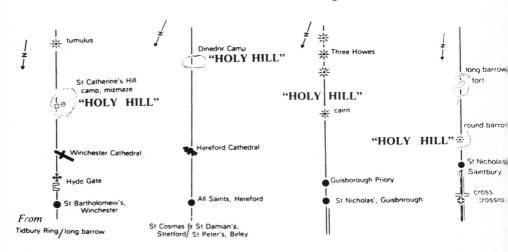

leys as magnetic paths. He got this notion initially from a psychic who spoke of 'lines of force', and secondly from his immersion in early ufology.

Wedd's psychic lady, tellingly, used the same term as the famous occultist Dion Fortune, who wrote a novel in 1936, the year after Watkins' death, called *The Goat-Foot God*. In this she referred to 'lines of force' linking ancient sites.

In 1969, Michell gave an enormous boost to the idea of leys being lines of 'magnetic current' or 'spiritual energy' in *The View Over Atlantis*. In doing this, he was clearly responding to Wedd's earlier ideas, but in addition he was subject to two other strands of influence.

One of these was the terminology used by Victorian writers on Feng shui (above), in which the energies or *ch'i* of the earth had to be brought into harmony at locations where houses or tombs were to be built. In attempting to describe these terrestrial *ch'i* energies which were symbolised by a dragon and a tiger by the ancient Chinese, the Victorians *likened* them to magnetic currents. The missionaries lived at a time when electricity and magnetism was assuming considerable importance on the intellectual stage, and they provided convenient and topical images with which to convey the idea of *ch'i*.[31] Another source of such terminology was W. Evans-Wentz' *The Fairy Faith in Celtic Countries* of 1912, in which he noted that one informant (G. W. Russell, a mystic, intellectual and agricultural engineer) claimed that fairy paths were 'magnetic arteries, *so to speak*' (my emphasis).[32] These, and other, similar analogies, typical of their age, were re-introduced by Michell into the thinking patterns of the late Sixties, when electronics was taking an almost magical high profile (recall the impact of the transistor radio, solid-state circuitry, silicon chips and space-age technology in general). This caused a subtle shift from analogy to *literalism* to occur —the lines *became* energy lines, like electrical wiring in the landscape.

This overall shift from ancient symbolism to supposed environmental lines of energy is important, and I will refer to it again much later on.

The other major influence on Michell was dowsing (water witching or divining). He was influenced by a Welsh energy dowser, John Williams (Michell; personal communication), and in his 1969 book, he referred to the posthumous book by Guy Underwood, *The Pattern of the Past*.[33] Underwood had picked up on the background of 1930s French dowsing, which claimed underground water was present beneath ancient monuments, and that there were dowsable energy grids across the landscape, and German dowsing, which claimed 'geopathological zones' (places where dowsable energies from the ground caused illness) and also that there were global energy grids (all different to the French version, and different to one another). In fact, the association between specifically leys and dowsing was first made in 1939, when Arthur Lawton, a member of the Straight Track Club, suggested that leys were part of a geometric layout of ancient sites which resulted from some 'Force ... which has not so far been classified'.[34] This force, claimed Lawton, could be dowsed. Tom Graves' modern dowsing classic *Dowsing* (1976), and *Needles of Stone* (1978), further strengthened such an association.[35] Interestingly, Graves now disowns the literalism displayed in those books.

So leys acquired some pretty vivid energy associations in the course of the modern ley-hunting revival. Because of its instant conceptual appeal, the energy idea grew faster than any other element in the new ley research. In high-tech America, reference to leys was virtually exclusively in terms of energies, and in time these notions were exported back across the Atlantic. (I have talked with some lecturers on the New Age circuit who refer to leylines in their presentations yet had no idea of the history of the subject, of Alfred Watkins, and so forth.) For a period in the mid-1970s, I doubt if there was a single ley hunter (including myself) who did not think of leys in terms of lines of energy. As the research, understanding, and experience of myself and certain colleagues evolved, however, a few of us began to see that we had a complex fallacy on our hands, the full scale and ancient origins of which will only become apparent to the reader by the end of this book.

None of this is to blame Michell for his 1969 book, of course, nor the ideas expressed in other early works; we were all trying to grapple with a complex new area of thinking at the time, and some red herrings were bound to get into the process. Today, however, when thinking and research has had time to become expanded and refined, and the history of the ideas that went into the Sixties ley revival can be unscrambled, one cannot be so charitable to those who either opt to remain uninformed, or deliberately choose to switch off their critical faculties.

We are currently left with a feedback situation, with naive or uninformed writings reinforcing one another, producing notions that are ventilated in the media, creating even less informed responses which feed in turn into further books, articles, lectures and dowsing groups. Leys as channels of 'earth energy' have become caught up with the international New Age movement, and dilettantish writers from that *milieu* have published their own pet notions and embellishments on the concept of ley energies. So now we have fantastical cosmic energy lines, planetary grids, past and future leylines which can be dowsed by time-transcending dowsers, lines of yang energy eight feet wide, energy leys that are hourglass-shaped in cross-section, energy leylines thousands of miles long, etheric ley networks that are the expression of Gaia, the living earth, and so on. Today, in some 'geomantic' quarters, the dowsing for supposed linear energies is equated with being spiritual — perhaps a somewhat sad comment on our contemporary spiritual bankruptcy. In reality, it is all psycho-showbiz.

All this would be of no concern were it not for the fact that such an image dominates the public face of geomancy in general, and alignment (ley) research in particular.

From my own experience, I am convinced that some dowsers some of the time can pick up relatively subtle environmental energies, such as ionisation, electromagnetic anomalies and so on. By the same token, however, I am equally sure that the plethora of dowsed energy lines and patterns are figments of energy dowsers' imaginations. 'Earth energy' is a buzz-phrase in popular Earth Mysteries. This in itself reveals inadequate understanding and basic commonsense thinking. There is, of course, no single entity as 'earth energy'; rather, the planet teems with countless forms of energies: gravity, geomagnetism, natural radiations, infra-red emissions, natural microwaves and other radio emissions, electrical telluric currents, ultraviolet light. Daylight, moonlight, wind, sound, all these are energies too. In addition, there are the myriad artificially-generated electromagnetic emissions of the modern world (any straight energy lines a dowser might pick up are more likely to be microwave transmission beams than 'energy leys'). So any dowser setting forth with a dowsing rod or pendulum with the idea of discovering some nebulous idea of earth energy is going to be swamped with input (even supposing he or she is truly capable of dowsing energies). Figure 16 gives diagrammatic representation of the situation. The random dots represent the seething, invisible energy environment the dowser has ventured into. The patterns show some of the typical ones claimed by energy dowsers. They have all been drawn out of the same 'data set' of dots. Thus subjective patterns can readily, and unconsciously, be drawn out of objective random information. When these unconsciously-constructed preferred patterns are published in articles and books, repeated and perhaps even used to form part of a dowsing group's dogma, they become fixed for their adherents.

The notion of a mysterious earth energy that can be dowsed and moulded into one's spiritual fantasies is a powerful vehicle for those wishing to express an anti-rational, anti-scientific sensibility. Reaction to the negative side of modern rationalism is understandable, but it might be argued that fierce — living — art, music, architecture, poetry, humanity, compassion and wholistic science are the true means of combating such contemporary ills, and that fantasy only permits, if not actually augments, the perpetuation of the malaise.

Energy dowsers want to think they are dowsing some form of spiritual, non-material *ch'i*; an unknown force. Yet a dowser cannot by definition dowse for an unknown energy: only by careful elimination could such a claim be made, and nowhere

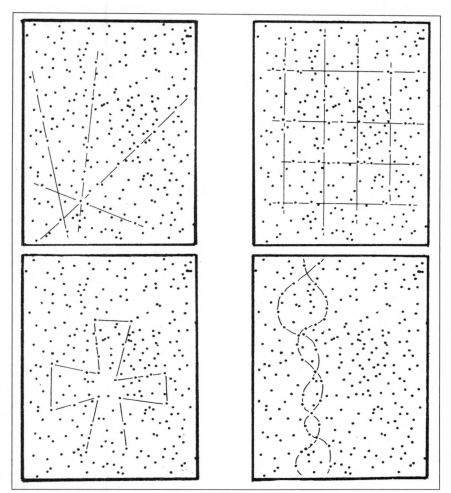

Figure 16. Which pattern would you like? The set of random dots in each frame is identical, but the patterns that can be drawn from it are virtually limitless. Similarly, a dowser seeking the bland idea of 'energies' can draw any pattern from the teeming mass of environmental energies.

does one see the research that would have to go into this. If there is a non-material field, it is more likely to be consciousness itself, and that does not run in eight-foot-wide bands through the countryside. (It is such a hypothesised mind-field, perhaps, that allows ESP to function, and the misnamed 'map dowsing' is probably a form of ESP, quite distinct to on-site dowsing.)

49

All in all, there is simply chaotic, irresponsible and inadequate thought surrounding the whole notion of energy leylines. Here, we need simply note that alignments and linear features in ancient sacred landscapes were not originally concerned with such ideas. They were not energy lines, nor, for that matter, traders' tracks. It is with the search for another understanding of the lines that the rest of this book is concerned. Alfred Watkins' flash of insight heralded the start of a journey that is to lead us across archaic landscapes, into contact with spiritual traditions as old as the human central nervous system, and into the deepest recesses of the human psyche. Authentic, noble mysteries await us, not the *ersatz* enigmas of late twentieth-century mindgames.

CHAPTER 2

OTHER LINES OF ENQUIRY

Mainstream archaeology will probably always be allergic to the term 'ley', statisticians will doubtlessly interminably query whether ley-type site alignments are chance effects, and 'energy line' enthusiasts will almost inevitably continue to need their fantasy fix. Fortunately, the person who actually wants to get to the bottom of the ley enigma has an avenue of escape from such time-wasting: there exist indisputable physical landscape lines of great antiquity not only in Watkins' home country of Britain, but at selected locations around the world. They offer literally other lines of enquiry.

It is ironic that while Watkins' ley theory, which has provided the greatest single focus on the question of ancient landscape lines in general, may never have its status resolved to universal satisfaction, these other lines, similar to, and in some cases indistinguishable from Watkins' 'leys', may help us towards the insights into the ancient mind that ley study always promised.

Although the modern ley hunter studying these physical lines will be in the company of archaeologists, archaeo-astronomers, anthropologists and other academics with their much greater resources, everyone is equal before the enigma the lines present, so anyone can, at least in theory, make a contribution.

Cursuses

The type of feature known as a 'cursus' was first recorded by William Stukeley in 1723. He noticed what has come to be

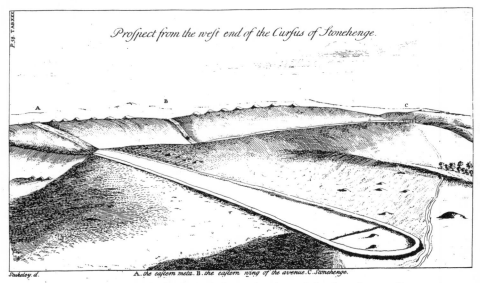

Profpect from the weft end of the Curfus of Stonehenge.

A. *the eaftern meta.* B. *the eaftern wing of the avenue.* C. *Stonehenge.*

Stukeley d.

Figure 17. One of William Stukeley's sketches of the Stonehenge Cursus.

known as the Greater Stonehenge Cursus, a linear earthwork nearly 2 miles (3.2 km) in length situated half a mile north of Stonehenge. He called it a cursus, Latin for racecourse, because that is what he thought it was. He also thought it had been built in Romano-British times, but we now know such monuments are in fact Neolithic.

Ten cursuses were discovered between Stukeley's time and 1944, but since the Second World War, largely through the advent of aerial photography, the total has leapt to around 50. Because of the erosion of ages, most of these cursuses are now invisible at ground level, and show up only as crop markings when viewed from above (see Chapter 1). They have so far been found only in Britain, where they occur from Dorset in the south to Scotland several hundred miles to the north. Their basic form is that of an extremely elongated rectangular earthwork enclosure, ranging from a few hundred metres to kilometres in length but never more than about 100 metres wide. Their ends can be square or rounded, though in some cases these are lost altogether, being so damaged or obscured they are not visible even as crop marks. Cursuses often link

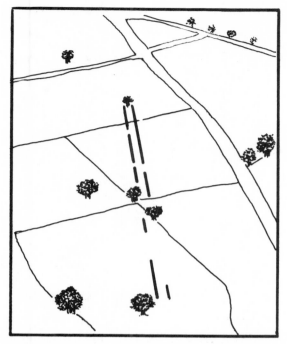

Figure 18. The crop-mark fragments of a cursus (bold lines) underlying fields near Welshpool on the Welsh border. (Redrawn after J. K. St Joseph)

Neolithic mounds, long barrows, or are associated with them. They frequently occur in core 'ritual landscapes' containing other Neolithic ceremonial monuments.

What the function of cursuses was is unknown. Few artefacts have been unearthed within them, and, in fact, they have largely been ignored by archaeologists in the past, probably because of the problems of interpretation they present. This has changed somewhat over recent years, however, and archaeologists are taking an increasing interest in cursuses.

What they tell the ley hunter clearly is that prehistoric Britons could lay out straight landscape lines, and did have some linear obsessions of a presumably ritual nature associated with certain sites, such as long barrows. The *fundamental* issue behind the ley concept is thus confirmed by the existence of cursuses. The geometric linearity, straightness, of most of them is clearly a key characteristic. A dramatic cursus, originally over

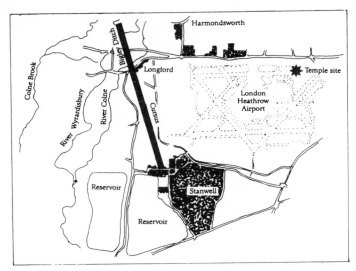

Figure 19. The course of the two-mile (3 km) long cursus (marked by the bold line) next to Heathrow airport, which itself overlays a pagan shrine.

two miles in length, was revealed as crop marks by air photography running just to the west of the runway complex at Heathrow airport (Figure 19). So straight was this feature, in fact, that archaeologists for a long time assumed that it *must* be a Roman road: only excavation in the 1980s showed its actual nature. It is an amusing coincidence that the modern runways with their precise rectilinearity should be unknowingly located so close to a prehistoric line of comparable exactitude, and which dwarfs them!

Fragmentary crop marks of another very regular cursus are to be found near Aston-upon-Trent, Derbyshire. Inside the cursus strip there are the crop marks of an oval enclosure placed against the northwest side of the cursus, four ring ditches, with one (arrowed in Figure 20) abutting one side near the southwest terminal. Archaeologists Alex Gibson and Roy Loveday noted that 'the cursus ditch appeared to be aligned on and to intersect' this ring ditch. They excavated to see if the ring ditch had been there prior to the construction of the cursus, and found that it had. The investigators found evidence to support the idea that 'the mile-long line of the cursus ditch had been

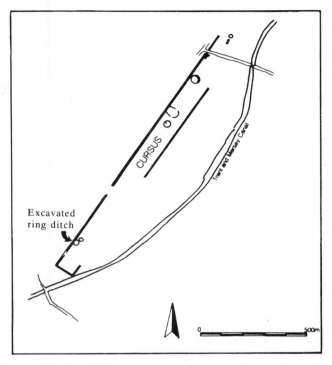

Figure 20. *The Aston Cursus, Derbyshire, with crop marks of prehistoric mounds.* (Redrawn and modified after A. Gibson and R. Loveday)

aligned to the mound.' *A long, straight line sighted on a mound* — that was the basic action of the cursus builders, and is a classic image of the ley concept. This 'respect for the ring ditch', as the archaeologists put it, seems 'a nice euphemism for geomancy' as researcher Chris Fletcher noted in *The Ley Hunter*.[2] In making special note that the other ring ditches at the cursus were 'most unusually contained almost exclusively within its interior in a spatially deliberate manner' the archaeologists were making further geomantic observations.

At another long, straight cursus at Scorton, Yorkshire, investigator Peter Topping uncovered a post-hole which he felt could represent 'the remains of some form of surveying marker'.[3] Circular crop marks just beyond the southeast end appear to have been a cluster of sites the cursus led out from. It is thought that the other (no longer visible) end was probably

55

on top of a small hill. Topping suggests a scene in which 'a system of uprights would lead the eye up the rising ground to a possible focal point . . . on the horizon'.

Clearly, we are looking at the remnants of large-scale Neolithic linear patterning in the British landscape.

Some cursuses show some irregular and curvilinear elements, especially at first glance. The Stonehenge Cursus (see Figure 22, below) initially appears to be an irregular feature, but closer observation reveals that the northern ditch is actually very straight for perhaps a mile and a half, curving only slightly to accommodate the end feature. The southern ditch gives the cursus varying width, which is what gives the irregular impression of the monument as a whole, and this is probably because it was not sighted itself, but simply ranged out from the northern ditch.

This cursus was partially excavated in the 1940s and the 1950s.[4,5] Fragments of bluestone (which forms the shorter, and original, standing stones at Stonehenge) were found clustered at one point along a ditch, and there was evidence that the interior of the cursus may have been compressed, perhaps by the pressure of feet. (In the chalk country it occupies, the cursus would have originally stood out as a brilliant white thick line against the surrounding grassland.) At the easterly end there was a pre-existing long barrow, and archaeologist R. J. C. Atkinson felt that the cursus 'was obviously aligned deliberately' on this. At the other terminus, excavations revealed an

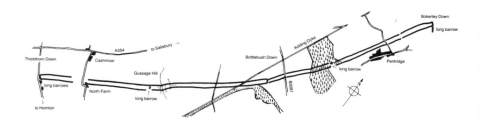

Figure 21. The Dorset Cursus, the largest yet discovered. Although it looks sinuous when viewed over its whole, vast length, many sections are in fact fairly straightly aligned. (Redrawn after R. J. C. Atkinson)

earthwork that seems to have been a copy of a long barrow. It was a *pseudo*-long barrow, built when the cursus was constructed.

The 'Dorset Cursus' is the largest known. Actually, the monument is comprised of *two* cursuses butted end to end. The combined feature runs for six miles (9.7 km) southwest (Thickthorne Down) to northeast (Bokerley or Martin Down) on Cranborne Chase, crossing Bottlebush Down. Like the Stonehenge Cursus, it is one of the few such features to be marked on Ordnance Survey maps. Overall, the monument contains an area of some 220 acres (90 hectares) and in its original state was comprised of six-and-a-half-million cubic feet (183,950 m^3) of earthworks.

The Thickthorn Down cursus was the earlier of the two, and, similarly to Stonehenge, the southwestern terminus is, even now, a high-banked earthwork, another apparent pseudo-long barrow. Very close by are actual long barrows, which either point to the end of the cursus or are co-axial with it. One of these long barrows was found to be entirely empty.

From this southwestern end, the cursus proceeds straight, and nowadays invisibly, almost to the crest of Gussage Hill, where a prominent long barrow stands, older than the cursus, now centrally placed within the cursus ditches. Atkinson commented that 'it may be inferred . . . that the latter [cursus] was aligned so as to enclose it. Certainly the long barrow, which is visible for miles around, would form an obvious sighting-mark for the alignment of the cursus, quite apart from any ritually-determined intention on the part of the cursus builders to incorporate the barrow . . .'[6] Just over the crest of Gussage Hill the line of the cursus 'wobbles'. The reason for this has been determined by Richard Bradley, the archaeologist who has studied the monument the closest. He states that this first cursus of the two was built from both ends, from Thickthorn towards the Gussage long barrow, and from the Bottlebush end towards the same point. The Bottelbush terminus was deliberately located on lower ground, Bradley suggests, because:

> . . . it meant that the long barrow now became a prominent feature on the skyline. Again the cursus was aimed at this mound, but

57

once it reached the lee of Gussage Cow Down, where the barrow was out of sight, it began to drift off course.

The second cursus commences on Bottlebush, butted onto the end of the existing terminal of the first monument, and travels up over the rise of the Down to the northeast. It seems that the rest of the cursus was constructed from the northeast end, because there seems again to have been a miscalculation as the line of the cursus staggers over the hill crest.

The northeast terminus, near Pentridge, shows up in crop marks as clean-cut and rectangular. There is a final twist in the course of the cursus at this end as if to place the terminus at the right angle, close to a long barrow. This pre-existing barrow, whose axis pointed to the location of the terminus, was actually extended in length by the cursus builders to 500 feet (152 m). Another long barrow in the vicinity also points to the end of the cursus. Some distance from this terminus, the northern bank of the cursus passes through and along the axis of another long barrow. Atkinson mused that the association with long barrows 'can hardly be fortuitous', suggesting that the cursus must in some way have been connected with 'practices intended to ensure that the benign influence of the dead was transmitted. . . to the living users of the cursus'. (These observations are important for the reader to bear in mind when we come to later chapters in our unravelling of the linear enigma.)

Bradley draws some general conclusions from his study of this huge and mysterious feature. The basic alignment of the monument was 'established by one of the ditches and its counterpart was laid out by offsets and was occasionally left unfinished'. The surveyors of the cursus found that their visibility along the ground was broken by woodland, ridges and valleys, and aligned lengths were quite short. The builders clearly had difficulty in connecting up some segments, 'but the deliberate alignments emphasise *monuments* rather than natural features', Bradley emphasises. He goes on:

> Very simply, the cursus seems to have been laid out between a number of existing long barrows, but it was not a particularly conspicuous feature in itself. It crossed a series of valleys and its

terminals were located for their views *along* the axis of the
monument; they would never have been striking from
outside. . . The importance of the ends of the cursus was
emphasised by concentrations of mounds which were either built
on the same axis as the terminals or were aligned upon them. . .
   . . . the cursus follows the spring line for almost 10 km and . . . it
reinforces the distribution of long barrows. . .
   . . . it is the alignment that matters — not the scale of the
earthwork and that alignment was meant to connect a whole series
of monuments to the dead. . . Having established that long
alignment between different monuments to the dead, the builders
of the cursus went on to create further barrows around it.[8]

'It is the alignment that matters.' Bradley has grasped the key
point, as we shall see later.

With its bank outside the ditches, the limited entrances along
its length, and its placing in the landscape, Bradley notes that
the monument must have hidden much of the activities that
went on within it: 'an element of mystery which still affects us
today'. The character of the great linear earthwork can only be
grasped when long stretches along it can be viewed, and
Bradley discovered that this was possible at only four locations:
the three termini and the Gussage long barrow. These viewing
points are inconspicuous from outside: they clearly were
meant to be used from *within* the cursus. It was noted above that
the Bottlebush Down terminus seems to have been positioned
so that the Gussage long barrow stood out on the skyline.
Bradley found that:

   . . . the same alignment. . . pointed towards the midwinter sunset.
   The alignment is over such a long distance that this phenomenon
   can still be observed today. I am not convinced by the other
   astronomical alignments which have been claimed in the cursus
   complex, but this one set the seal on the individual character of
   this monument. . . The ancestors who had been of such concern to
   the living were caught up in the forces of nature. . .
   Fewer people are celebrated by large monuments; the rest are
   archaeologically invisible. The cursus stresses the importance of
   those separate mounds, uniting them in one grand design, a
   British Avenue of the Dead, which links the positions of the
   ancestors with the movement of heavenly bodies. And yet that
   design is concealed from most of the population. Like
   archaeologists many generations later, they cannot see the real
   pattern of the cursus because it is only visible from certain specific
   points, and access to these is restricted. . .

> ...the Dorset cursus operates through the coming together of a monument to the dead and the midwinter sun.[9]

(A further, curious example of linearity in association with the Dorset Cursus was unexpectedly discovered during the more recent archaeological studies of the area, when it was found that burial mounds close to the monument had had straight avenues of wooden posts connecting them at right angles to the cursus.)

Quite apart from the interest their linear nature has for the ley hunter, cursuses may also have other alignment characteristics. In 1947, archaeologist J. F. S. Stone noted that if the axis of the Stonehenge cursus was extended eastwards the line passed through a fallen standing stone called the Cuckoo (or Cuckold) Stone, and on to the centre of Woodhenge (Figure 22). This produces an alignment two-and-a-half miles (4 km) long. It is in every sense a ley. In 1966, archaeologist D. P. Dymond[10] noted that one of the cursuses at Rudston, on the Humberside Wolds, pointed to a huge standing stone, the tallest in Britain, in the village churchyard. If the stone had been destroyed, of course, as many have, the cursus would only have been pointing at the ancient church, and that would have been discounted by the archaeologist.

If such observations were good enough for archaeologists, I reasoned, they were good enough for ley hunters. So in 1987-8,

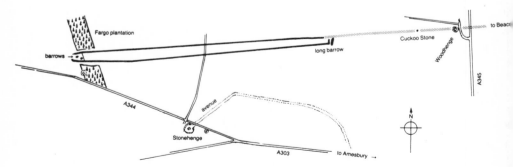

Figure 22. The (Greater) Stonehenge Cursus. The line of the northern ditch passes through a standing stone and Woodhenge to the east. The line extends 3 miles (5 km) to Beacon Hill, a typical Watkinsian 'initial point'. (After J. F. S. Stone)

60

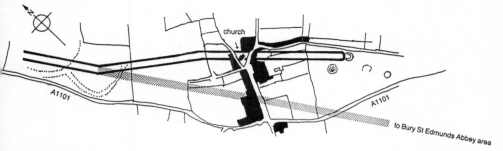

Figure 23. The three-segment cursus at Fornham-All-Saints, Suffolk. (Redrawn
after J. K. St Joseph)

I studied a sample of 25 cursuses, about half the known number
of such monuments, for similar instances of extended axiality.
Three of the monuments (including Rudston and Stonehenge)
pointed to prehistoric sites beyond one of their ends, and
twelve to ancient churches or their *llans* (sacred enclosures).
While archaeologists might have difficulty accepting the
validity of the churches as cursus 'targets', we saw in the
previous chapter how such sites could very well mark locations
of earlier sanctity, and certainly did in a number of cases. And of
course, there is the point I make about the Rudston alignment
above. The cursus at Fornham All Saints, Suffolk, was
particularly interesting with regard to this church pattern. It
was built in three straight sections, probably at different times,
each segment on a different axis. It must have disappeared from
sight at ground level thousands of years ago, yet the
southeastern section has an ancient church standing on it! In
addition, the axis of the northwestern section extended barely
three miles passes through the ancient and important Bury St
Edmunds Abbey.

Three cursuses cluster together in a small section of the Avon
valley south of Warwick; each of them points to an ancient
church. One of the churches, at Wasperton, also has a
prehistoric boundary earthwork running towards the point on
which it stands. This repeated pattern is hard to accept as
chance. The crop-mark fragment of a cursus near Lechlade,
Gloucestershire, aligns over a two-mile intervening distance of

61

open country to a solitary, ancient church at Southrop, Gloucestershire. Again, chance seems an unlikely factor.

In all, 48 per cent of the sample pointed to ancient churches. (Altogether, 64 per cent of the sample showed extended axes to prehistoric sites, ancient churches or both.) Moreover, only one cursus pointed to a modern church, and that at a distance of five miles while all the other sites were under three-and-a-half miles from their aligned cursus.

I am quite convinced that such churches mark locations that were sacred in remote antiquity, which the crop-mark cursuses still point out like ghostly fingers. Those not preserved by such happy chance have been erased from our landscapes and thus lost to us.

Reaves

Curious linear features known locally as 'reaves' have long been known of on the granite upland wastes of Dartmoor, in Devon in southern England. They are low banks comprised of loosely-assembled rocks, now often overgrown or partially covered by peat and therefore sometimes difficult to see. They can extend for several kilometres, and are of two distinct types: blocks of parallel reaves forming land divisions, and longer, single reaves, some of which are curvilinear, while others tend towards straightness. In the nineteenth century, they were usually assumed to be old tracks or causeways. Serious archaeological interest in them only commenced in the 1960s, but it was the work a decade or so later of Andrew Fleming of Sheffield University and his colleagues that really uncovered the nature of reaves.[12,13]

In brief, Fleming found that reaves were the remnants of large boundary and field or 'coaxial' systems. The field systems are on the lower slopes, and major single reaves either form divisions between valleys and community areas or form the boundaries of the high moor which seems to have been used as grazing land, and also as a ceremonial landscape, judging by the distribution of ceremonial monuments on it. Fleming found the curvilinear major reaves to follow the contours, often providing the upper limit to field systems. There were also more direct single reaves which relate radially to the centre of the moor (because they run along the watersheds between valleys), and cross-country major reaves. The archaeologist noted that the longer single reaves 'boldly cross the landscape towards invisible objectives several kilometres distant'. He found that reaves were built to varying standards of workmanship. Material from them indicated a date in the early Bronze Age, around 1600–1700 BC. Although later than many of the ceremonial monuments on the moor, the reaves sometimes included these in their lengths, and they must have provided sighting points in some cases. In other instances, however, reaves were driven through pre-existing monuments.

The picture that emerges from Fleming's research is that the Dartmoor reave layout could have been *a single episode* lasting about a century. This implies that there were Bronze Age surveyors who had a 'sense of terrain which is regional rather than strictly local'. Indeed, the reave systems unquestionably involved surveyed lines that crossed ridge and gully over large distances: they did not develop in a haphazard 'organic' fashion. In a piece of writing that would not be out of place in *The Ley Hunter*, Fleming pointed out that 'the terrain-oblivious character of the coaxial systems often means. . . that different zones within them are not intervisible,' posing awkward survey problems for the reave builders which they were obviously 'willing to tackle and able to solve'.[14] In an important passage, Fleming acknowledges that 'functional theories have their limitations':

The fact that coaxial field systems were located where food was produced does not rule out the possibility that their form had some more powerful ideological or symbolic meaning . Indeed, the terrain-oblivious character of some of these systems almost demands such an explanation. . .

What kind of concept lay behind the coaxial system? Here it is difficult to avoid the rather elusive notion of 'the ritual landscape'. . . It does seem clear that in Britain, over a period centring on the third millenium BC, there were 'core areas'. . . [which] contain 'ceremonial monuments'. . . But such monuments did not simply accumulate in these areas over the

63

centuries. Their character, their layout in relation to each other and to the terrain, the links created between them, and sometimes their orientation, all suggest the conscious creation and maintenance of a special terrain full of symbolic meaning.[15]

Fleming displays a haughty dismissiveness of leys and geomancy, yet his own words give the lie to that attitude, which is perhaps more Pavlovian than perceptive. The final sentence in the quote above, for instance, is a perfect definition of geomancy. It could not be bettered. And the idea of a 'terrain oblivious' line is surely euphemistic terminology for a ley. At any event, to stand on the reave that crosses Walkhampton Common, just south of Princetown, for instance, and see it stretching away as a straight line kilometres into the distance, certainly gives one the sense of being 'on a ley'! While we have already seen that the unrevised *totality* of Watkins' ley concept, of there once being prehistoric straight tracks all over the place, is unsafe, the fact that there were prehistoric Britons surveying long lines across country, as Fleming's own research reveals, gives much credence to the essence of Watkins' vision. That the old Herefordian may have put some now-questionable glosses on his glimpses of ancient linear aspects within the landscape does not detract from the fact that he may well have perceived an authentic imprint of prehistoric geomancy.

Ancient coaxial systems are to be found elsewhere than on Dartmoor, and from other periods of time. At Behy-Glenulra in Co. Mayo, Ireland, for example, the remains of a Neolithic system delimited by stone and earthen walls are being unearthed from bog cover, in the vicinity of a Neolithic ceremonial monument, while Iron Age and Romano-British systems have been identified in parts of England. Fleming wonders if the surveying knowledge may have been passed down by a class of priests or bards 'acting as repositories of lore and tradition, orally transmitted from generation to generation'. However, since this writing, John W. M. Peterson has challenged the idea that there was a 'tradition of regular land division [which] persisted within the British Isles for a long time, even for 2500 years'.[16] He feels the practice persisted because of its basic usefulness at a mundane level, rather than requiring a thread of knowledge handed down by 'Fleming's legendary ancestral figures'.

However that may be, the reaves on Dartmoor stand as testimony to prehistoric large-scale land concepts and surveying skills, and the consequent laying out of 'terrain oblivious' lines set towards distant and invisible targets. The basic spirit of the ley vision is thus enshrined in these physical linear remains.

Stone rows

The relatively well-preserved prehistoric landscape of Dartmoor also contains another type of linear feature — the stone row. About 60 of these have survived on the moor to a greater or lesser extent, though there were many more than this originally. They occur in single, double and multiple forms, and can be anything from a few hundred feet to a mile or two in length. The stones comprising them vary in height, but average around a yard/metre. Many rows tend towards straightness, but most either change orientation slightly or have sinuous sections. Nevertheless, a distinct linearity is their characteristic. All but a few of the extant stone rows on Dartmoor have a ceremonial monument of some kind at one end or the other

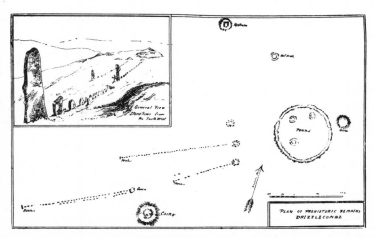

Figure 24. S. Baring-Gould's 1900 sketch and plan of the stone row complex at Drizzlecombe, Dartmoor.

(and sometimes both ends). These sites are usually tall, individual standing stones (menhirs), cairns (stone mounds) or stone circles. Examples of such arrangements can be found at Drizzlecombe, where there are three rows. One links a mound with a menhir, and another mound there also has a row running from it. The third row — which, interestingly, is double for part of its length — connects a cairn and menhir.

The rows are dated to the Bronze Age, though only one row seems to have been archaeologically excavated (on Lee Moor, 1961) and no artefacts were found. As with cursuses, archaeologists seem to shy away from the rows owing to difficulty of interpretation. Certainly, no one has yet come up with a completely satisfactory explanation for them. They are obviously ceremonial or ritual features, and I ask the reader to bear in mind their association with burial mounds or cairns and ceremonial objects like menhirs, as this will have relevance in our later investigations into the underlying nature of the mystery of prehistoric landscape lines.

Stone rows occur in other parts of England and elsewhere in the British Isles, such as isolated examples in Wales. For instance the Parc-y-Meirw (Field of the Dead) line of megaliths seems to point to the occasionally-visible tip of an Irish mountain 70 miles (113 km) across the sea, yielding a significant lunar setting position. In Scotland, there is, for example, The Hill of Many Stanes near Wick, with its 22 rows of small stones set in a fan-like arrangement. There are rows around Fermanagh in Northern Ireland, and others in the southwest of the Irish Republic.

Stone rows occur at numerous locations around the world, in the Middle East, in Kenya, and on the Malay Peninsula. Over a hundred rows exist in the Malaysian part of the peninsula, and in 1968 one was discovered in the Thai part as well.[17] It is situated next to a Buddhist monastery, Wat Mok Khalan, and contains 36 surviving stones. It is thought to mark a ritual border. The greatest concentration of stone rows in the world, however, is around Carnac-Ville in Brittany. Here thousands of stones cross the landscape in complexes of multiple rows. The major groupings are Kerlescan, which has thirteen rows, 1160 feet (354 m) in length; Kermario, with seven main lines of stones; Kerzerho where the remains of 10 alignments once well over a mile in length survive; Ménec, a complex of twelve rows linking two cromlechs (megalithic chambers) about a kilometre apart; Petite-Ménec, made up of eight straggling lines of stones, and St Barbe, Plouharnel, where there are remnants of rows once 1300 feet (400 m) long. Numerous other linear settings exist in the region, as well as a great many other megalithic sites.

These sorts of 'other lines' are noteworthy elements in the overall enigma of the linear imprint on ancient sacred landscapes. They are thus part of the core mystery which underpins the whole matter, and which we have set out to probe in this book.

CHAPTER 3

THE AMERINDIAN LEGACY

As fascinating and relevant as the physical lines described in the previous chapter are, it is to the Americas we have to go to find landscape markings that precisely match the formal aspects of Alfred Watkins' leys.

There are two aspects to the remarkable legacy the ancient Native American has left to the modern alignment researcher: a tradition of the ritual use of hallucinogens that is still accessible to modern research, and landscapes in which ceremonial straight lines, indeed old straight tracks, are still visible. These two factors taken together mean, in my opinion, that the mystery of leys, kindled in modern consciousness in the Old World, will find much of its solution in the Americas.

In this chapter, we consider just the lines. No study of the mystery of archaic straight landscape lines can be properly presented without a good look at the Amerindian lines, both for the certainty they give us that such odd artefacts were indeed created by human beings, and for the more general clues they offer us with regard to the possible solution of the mystery of the lines.

We shall make a rushed trip from north to south through much of the Americas, pausing a little longer at three locations where most research has currently been undertaken on Amerindian lines — the area around Chaco Canyon, New Mexico; the symbolic landscape around Cuzco, Peru, and the lines of Nazca, also in Peru.

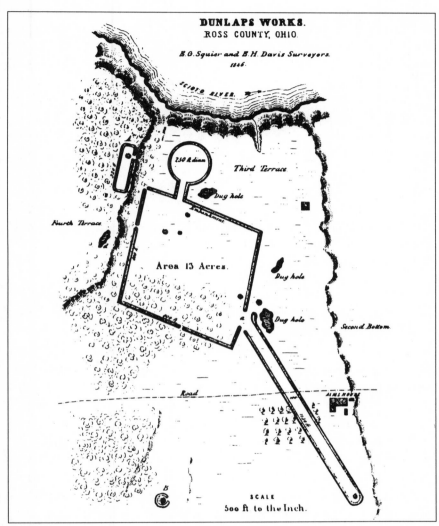

Figure 25. An example of Hopewell earthworks, surveyed by Squier and Davis in the nineteenth century.

Northern USA

The Indian culture called 'Hopewellian' by archaeologists emerged around 150 BC and flowered until around AD 500. The Hopewell culture, which may have been a religious phenomenon rather than a separate people, built imposing ceremonial

69

earthworks, distinguished by vast geometric groundplans and linear processional avenues. Many of these remarkable remains were destroyed by the incoming white settlers, but at Marietta, Ohio, the people were more enlightened, and preserved the Hopewell earthworks they found there. There, a carefully-graded ceremonial way that led up from the Muskingham River to an earthworks complex has its straight course preserved to this day by a street named 'Sacra Via'.

Because of the early settlement, industrialisation and high modern population of northern and eastern parts of the USA, only these more monumental types of Indian remains have survived. But elsewhere in the Americas, more subtle and directly ley-relevant Indian landscape markings are still visible, although many are on the verge of extinction.

California

In the Californian sierras, there are, or at least until recently, were, the remains of dead straight Indian tracks. Writing in 1950, Laetitia Sample described them thus:

> The trails of the sierra regions followed natural passes. Many trails were wide and worn a couple feet deep from long use. They could be traced long after the Indians had gone and the paths were abandoned. They seem to have gone in straight lines ... without detouring for mountains in the way.[1]

The now-extinct Miwok Indians occupied the western slope of the sierras between the Mokelumne and Fresno rivers, and an area south of Lake Tahoe. In the early decades of the century, the region was studied by S. Barret and E. W. Gifford. They noted that Miwok trails 'were usually almost airline in their directness, running up hill and down dale without zigzags or detours'.[2] *Airline in their directness* — the contents of Chapter 7 will give new significance to that telling description.

In California's Colorado Desert, early researchers found trails edged with stones and marked by cairns and 'shrines'.

The Southwest

The states of Colorado, Utah, Arizona and New Mexico comprise what is known as 'the Southwest' in the USA. There are hints in the earlier literature of straight trails in Arizona, Colorado and New Mexico, but by far the best known linear phenomena of the region are the 'Chacoan roads'. These are centred on Chaco Canyon, which is situated in semi-arid high mesa country in northwest New Mexico, within the San Juan Basin, a saucer-shaped depression about a hundred miles in diameter. The canyon is a broad, shallow, sandstone gorge which is engraved east–west across the Chaco Plateau. The northern wall of the canyon is the most abrupt, rising to about 150 feet.

The region around the junction of the four southwestern states is known as the 'Four Corners' area, and it was the cradle of an Indian people the relatively-recent Navajo call the *Anasazi*, 'Ancient Ones', who emerged in the latter centuries BC. In the eighth century AD, Anasazi 'pithouse' habitations gave way to above-ground, rectangular houses. Flat-roofed and made of mud, rock and posts, these 'pueblos' marked the beginning of the 'Pueblo Period' of Anasazi development. The pithouse became adapted into circular subterranean or semi-subterranean ritual chambers (called *kivas* by today's Hopi Indians). Chaco Canyon was one of the key Anasazi centres, where the culture reached its height, and the term 'Chacoan' is often used for this area. At Chaco the pueblos grew into multi-storied and terraced complexes or 'Great Houses', with walls, courtyards, and kivas, including Great Kivas, very large ceremonial chambers. There are nine Great Houses within Chaco Canyon itself, all constructed between AD 900 and 1115. The greatest is Pueblo Bonito, covering some three acres. In the vast landscape surrounding the canyon, some 150 Great Houses have now been identified by archaeologists.

At the height of the culture, what archaeologists refer to as the 'Bonito Phase', there was clearly extensive trade and manufacture. There was horticulture, the use of canals and dams to manage the precious water supply, rich ceremonial or religious activity, in addition to the monumental architecture. There was a ceremonial use of astronomy . . . and there were the 'roads'.

Within the canyon and for tens of miles around, there is a system of roads of striking linearity. They are not trails, but engineered features, usually 'straight as arrows', as one researcher has described them, running across country from one point to another, before changing direction then setting off straight again. The Great Houses seem to have been linked to this network, hundreds of miles of which have now been uncovered by aerial and ground study. Modern archaeologists admit that 'the factors that controlled the alignment of the roads and the position of the Great Houses are not understood'.[3] The roads are wide, usually a fairly constant nine metres (almost 30 feet), with tributary or spur roads half that width. They were bordered with earthen 'berms', rows of stones, or, occasionally, drystone walling, and their surfaces were compacted subsoil or sometimes cut to the bedrock. It is a mystery enough why a people without the wheel or horse should want such broad exact roads, yet aerial and infra-red remote sensing has also found that some lengths of road had parallel sections running alongside them, now invisible to the naked eye, and, on the 'North Road' (sometimes called 'Great North Road'), double groupings of parallel roads!

Lengths of these now almost invisible, thousand-year-old roads were recognised from at least 1879, when an army report referred to 'remarkable trails' in New Mexico 'extending as they do in a straight line from one pueblo to another. . . '. A 1901 government agent's report mentions roads at Chaco, and in the 1920s Neil Judd, a pioneer Chaco archaeologist, referred to them in his writings. In 1948, Gordon Vivian, another Chaco archaeologist, discussed the roads with a woman who recalled that 'in the old days' a wide roadway running north from the canyon 'was clearly defined in the spring or early summer because the vegetation on it was different from any other'. But it was not until the 1970s that serious work on the roads began.

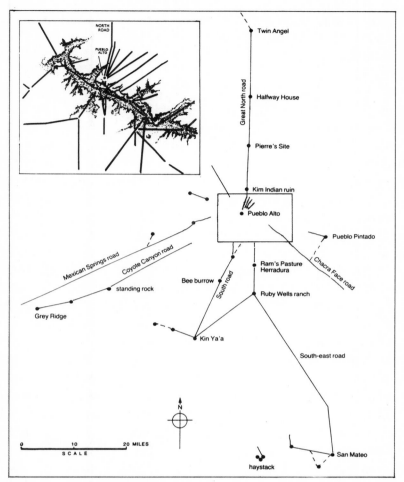

Figure 26. Map of some of the linear 'roads' around Chaco Canyon, New Mexico. Inset: detail of the canyon itself, showing deployment of the roads (bold lines) in and immediately around it.

Existing aerial photographs of the region were minutely studied, and new air pictures were taken. Although the roads showed up more clearly in the earlier photographs than in the new ones owing to differences in vegetation cover caused by climatic change and human action, the archaeologists were nevertheless amazed at the extent of the road system that emerged under their gaze, and at the exactitude of the engineering their fieldwork and excavations uncovered on the features. Even more road segments were discovered in the 1980s by state-of-the-art computer image-enhancement and infra-red techniques employed by special NASA research flights.

Where Chacoan roads on the mesa meet the rim of the canyon, they often connected with steps cut out of the living rock of the canyon walls. These stairways can be up to 25 feet (8 m) wide, and are still visible, though usually in an eroded condition. The steep angle and height of step of some of these stairways argues against an everyday usage, and they look more like the ceremonial stairs on the sides of Mesoamerican pyramids. (There are also rock stairs at Chaco which are narrower and have handholds, suggesting normal usage.)

The roads raise more questions than simple trade and mundane usage can explain. Why the apparent obsession with straightness? Why the exactitude of widths, and the width relationships between major and spur roads? Why the parallel and even double parallel sections?

Evidence from the Great Houses suggests that they were associated with the road system. They seem not to have been domestic but ceremonial. They had some rooms which did not connect with the interior of the buildings but opened out only onto the roads. Modern researchers increasingly feel that the roads had a ceremonial, religious function. This is supported by other snippets of evidence. For instance, in the 1920s Neil Judd discussed the roads with Navajo informants. We do not know all he learned, but Judd subsequently referred to the roads as 'ceremonial highways'. Certainly one Navajo elder, Hosteen Beyal, told Judd that 'they were *not really roads*, although they looked like them' (my emphasis). A Navajo legend claims that the roads are really 'tunnels' which the Ancient Ones could pass along in safety — I think this encodes a crucial memory, which I will deal with in Chapter 7. In the 1980s, Kendrick Frazier asked a Hopi Indian friend about the roads. The Indian's suggestion was that the features were symbolic, perhaps representing the migration routes of the early Anasazi. The directions of the roads so far discovered match legends in

Hopi lore.[4] Archaeoastronomer, Ray A. Williams, also refers to a Hopi tradition in which sunrise or set positions along the horizon were marked, and these became sacred places: 'Young Hopi initiates run in as straight a line as possible to the shrines and back in order to plant their prayer sticks. They follow, as it were, literally, the straight road of a beam of sunlight.'[5]

Broken pottery fragments have been found in patches stretched along some of the roads, especially near Great Houses, as at Pueblo Alto, on the northern rim of the canyon. Although some archaeologists have interpreted this as resulting from trade transport, the breaking of pottery vessels was a votive activity in many parts of the world, often associated with the dead, and it may even be that the roads *themselves* were considered holy. An example of a track being venerated is known of in France as late as the seventeenth century.[6]

The roads fell abruptly into disuse in the 1200s with the demise of the Anasazi culture, and they seem to have been little if at all used by post-Bonito Phase occupants of the area.

Archaeologists have also found a system of 'signal shrines' scattered through the landscape around Chaco Canyon. For instance, about 12 miles (19 km) north of Chaco Canyon, the North Road encounters a group of dune pinnacles. It goes directly towards one which archaeologists have dubbed El Faro (The Lighthouse) because on its summit they found a hearth on which many large fires had been lit. A kiva had also possibly existed there. Excavations revealed no evidence of the road skirting the feature, yet segments are to be found on either side of the pinnacle. A fire atop El Faro would have been visible from a great distance, including from Pueblo Alto, and it made archaeologists alert to possible signal-fire systems within the Chaco landscape.

This seems related to other findings concerning curious structures on mesa tops around the canyon. These places were minimally marked with stones, and sometimes contained bowls of beads and shells secreted in carved-out basins in the bedrock. They are so located as to have line-of-sight intervisibility with other such sites and Great Houses. So it is now pretty certain that in addition to the fantastic straight roads system there was also a complex line-of-sight communication system surrounding Chaco Canyon. NASA scientist Thomas Sever, involved with the infra-red and computer image-enhancement work at Chaco, suggests that the roads may have been designed to interface with the shrine communication system. He is sure the roads are ceremonial rather than utilitarian. He notes the instances of ritual activity indicated by the ceramic scatters, the Great Houses and other shrine sites associated with the roads, as well as the fact that *they linked specific places in the landscape rather than communities*. Sever warns that 'we should not always perceive roads as always being utilitarian; that, in short, we must not transfer our concept of modern-day roads into the prehistoric past.[7]

It is now beginning to appear that Chaco Canyon was a ritual and ceremonial centre, whose population was swollen by pilgrims at various times of the year, situated at the focus of a vast system of straight, sacred trackways, which themselves were linked to holy sites of various kinds throughout the San Juan Basin.

Mexico and Central America

Evidence of pre-Hispanic straight track systems in Mexico survives in the region around the archaeological site of La Quemada in the western state of Zacatecas. About 100 miles of Indian roads have been identified there, and dated to between AD 700–800. They were first mapped by Charles De Burghes in 1833 and again by Charles Dickson Trombold in 1974. As at Chaco, the roads seem to tend towards specific widths. The La Quemada roads are masonry structures built on the surface of the ground. This is Trombold's description of a typical road:

> Two parallel rows of stone are constructed in a straight line to the desired height and width. The area between them is then filled with rubble and capped with flagstones . . . [8]

The two wider types of road connect areas of high population density, while 'dispersed sites in marginal areas seem to be connected exclusively by "Small" roads'.

In the Yucatan Peninsula of southeastern Mexico we enter the heartland of the ancient Mayan domain. The Mayans emerged during the first century BC, but the flowering of their culture, the 'Classic Period', dated from the late third century AD, when they began working in stone, to AD 900. Remnants of the Mayan culture lasted until just after the Spanish Conquest in the sixteenth century. Even today, there are a few million Indians who still speak the Mayan languages.

The Mayans built pyramids, temples and many other buildings with remarkable masonry skills. They used ceremonial astronomy, had a highly-developed dating system involving a complex interplay of a sacred and a normal solar calendar, a sophisticated form of arithmetic and kept records by means of heiroglyphic writing on stone stelae and in plaster-coated bark paper or animal skin 'books' called Codices. These show how important the planet Venus was in the Mayan cosmology.

The Mayan sphere extended south into present-day Belize, Guatemala, El Salvador and Honduras. The culture collapsed in this southern zone for unknown reasons in the ninth century AD, and the northern Yucatan region took on greater importance. Within their sacred cities, and interconnecting them, the Mayans had straight roads called *sacbeob* (plural of *sacbe*). Most of these survive only in a fragmentary manner, and some must still await discovery within the dense rain forests of Central America. The longest-known sacbe is the 100-kilometre length that links Coba with Yaxuna in the northern part of the Yucatan peninsula not far from the famed site of Chichen Itza. Explorer Thomas Gann encountered this feature in the 1920s. He found 'a great elevated road, or causeway 32 feet wide . . . This was one of the most remarkable roads ever constructed, as the sides were built of great blocks of cut stone, many weighing hundreds of pounds . . . [It] ran, as far as we followed it, straight as an arrow, and almost flat as a rule.'

Segments of sacbeob have been discovered on the Island of Cozumel off the peninsula's northeast corner, a Mayan pilgrimage site for the worship of the moon goddess, Ixchel.

Some of these connected different settlements, the best-preserved section being between San Gervasio and the northeast coast of the island. It was mapped for over three miles (5 km). It is about five feet (1.5 m) wide and had shrines posted along it. Because of the sacbe's straightness, it was possible to predict where further sections might appear at points where visible traces had disappeared.

Colombia

The Sierra Nevada de Santa Marta on the northern coast of Colombia is the habitat of the Kogi people, who have managed to preserve the most complete example of a pre-Colombian Indian culture in all the Americas. We will have good cause to return to them in Chapter 7, but for now we need only note that their secluded area of habitation is not, as filmmaker Alan Ereira has written, simply 'a reserve for wildlife: it is a philosophical reserve, home to a society which guards the mental landscape which Europeans reworked over all the rest of America . . . the Kogi . . . maintained their world intact, with its secrets'.[9] These people have a living system of shamanism . . . and they have networks of paved tracks at least some of which are straight, which extend over the Sierra.

We will be returning to these features, and the Kogi, later on, precisely because the Kogi guard the pre-Colombian 'mental landscape', a landscape which we must try to at least glimpse, even if from a conceptual distance, if we are ever to grope towards an understanding of the straight-line mystery.

Cuzco

Cuzco, Peru, was the capital of the Inca empire, which, at its height, stretched over 2000 miles (3200 km) from Colombia in the north to Chile in the south. Cuzco was both an administrative centre and a holy city.

The Incas rose to supremacy over a number of other competing Andean tribal groups from around AD 1200 and lasted until their cultural destruction by the Spanish in the sixteenth century. The empire was ruled with absolute

78

authority by the Sapa Inca, the supreme ruler and a god-king —
the Son of the Sun. The management of the vast Inca empire
from a centralised power base was greatly assisted by a
remarkable system of roads which allowed rapid communication
and swift mobilisation of armies when required. Even the
rapacious *conquistadores* had to admit that 'nothing in
Christendom' equalled these highways. Modern researchers
have mapped some 14 000 miles (22 540 km) of an estimated
25 000 miles (40 250 km) of Inca roads. Some sections were
paved, while others, particularly in desert areas, were simply
marked out by lines of stones, which edged compressed
ground. Cairns or shrines were placed at certain points along
the routes, and wayside stations or *tampu* were located at
frequent intervals along them. These were for the *chasquis* or
messengers who would run from one station to the next, where
a simple verbal message accompanying special goods, or a
quipu (a mnemonic system comprised of a series of coloured
and knotted cords), would be handed over to the next relay.
Explorer Von Hagen noted that the Inca roads ran 'unerringly
straight'[10] between any two points, but they did deviate
sometimes to avoid obstacles. It is certain that some of these
roads were refurbished sections of older, pre-Inca tracks, [11]
which is similar to Alfed Watkins' claim that some sections of
Roman roads used more ancient courses.

But it is in the landscape around Cuzco itself that we find the
most mysterious straight lines — the *ceques*. These had a
deeply-interwoven socio-political and religious nature.

The main buildings of Cuzco were laid out to a grid pattern,
within and around which was strict social ordering. The empire
was known as *Tahuantinsuyu*, the 'Land of the Four Quarters',
and people coming to Cuzco from the far-flung regions had to
stay in certain alloted areas, reflecting where they came from in
Tahuantinsuyu. This quartering of the empire which radiated
out from Cuzco, was based on an *intercardinal* rather than a
cardinal (north–south, east–west) scheme, but this was not a
simple 'X'-pattern, because the southeast–southwest boundary
was splayed at an odd angle, making the southwest segment

wider than the southeast section. The four roads at the hub of the Inca road system left Cuzco from the present-day Plaza de Armas — which is a reduced version of the original Inca great plaza they called Huacaypata — and went out into their respective quarters. The centre of the ceque system, however, was some hundreds of metres away, at the Coricancha, which the conquering Spanish called the Temple of the Sun. In fact, the temple, where the Inca would sit on state and ceremonial occasions, was the major centre of ancestor worship 'and was related as much to the underworld as it was to the heavens'.[12] Spanish historians wrote that radiating out from this place were 41 lines or ceques. Three of Cuzco's quarters, or *suyus*, contained nine of these each, conceptually grouped in three sets of three, but the fourth, the wider southwestern quarter, had fourteen ceques.

What exactly *were* ceques? The simplest definition is that they were alignments of sacred places or *huacas*. A huaca could be a standing stone or a natural bolder or outcrop, a waterfall or spring, a bend in the river, a temple or shrine, a holy hill or cave, a sacred tree, a topographical feature, or even a bridge or battlefield site. There were apparently between three and thirteen huacas along any one ceque, and the idea has been likened to that of the knots on the string of a quipu. (The ley hunter, of course, would see it as identical to Watkins' concept.) The Spanish chroniclers identified 328 huacas along the ceques around Cuzco, stating that each represented a day of the Inca year. It was in effect a huge terrestrial calendar, but the Spanish, in addition to not bothering to understand it fully, actually destroyed a number of the huacas. Dr Tom Zuidema of the University of Illinois, who has conducted major research into the ceque system, suggested that the system was based on the sidereal lunar month of 27.3 days (the time it takes for the moon to pass from a given star in the background firmament back to that same star), because a division of 328 days by the twelve months of the Inca year gives a month of that length.

American archaeoastronomer Anthony F. Aveni has described the ceque system as 'a mnemonic device built into Cuzco's natural and man-made topography that served to unify ideas about religion, social organization, hydrology, calendar, and astronomy'.[13]

Social or kinship groups called *ayllus* had the care of specified ceques. As the ritual year rotated through the symbolic landscape, each ayllu would be responsible for preparing the holy places along their line or lines for the appropriate observances when their time came around. The water theme was a prominent one amongst the various attributes of the ceque system, and this had genealogical and thus social correlates because the water came from underground, where the ancestors dwelt. The ceques also helped to order the territorial relationships between groups, cooperative ritual and work activities, and also marriage patterns. 'In sum,' says Aveni, 'the ceque system may be considered a rather complex kinship map based upon residence and ancestor worship in a radial and quadripartite geographic framework.'[14]

Working from the descriptions of the system by the seventeenth-century Spanish chroniclers, Zuidema and Aveni have attempted to map the ceques in the actual landscape. They found the ceques did not deviate from a straight line 'by more than a few degrees', and passed over the convoluted topography of the Cuzco landscape to distant, invisible destinations. They discovered that huacas were often positioned at locations where water flow changed directions, as at the bend of a river, and that only about a quarter of the ceques had astronomical functions. Astronomical sightlines could be from a huaca on one ceque to one on another, as well as to natural skyline features. Sometimes the viewing positions would be in Cuzco itself. Now-destroyed towers, themselves huacas, were used as part of this astronomical system by marking the passage of the sun at key times in the year. The astronomy timed the ceremonial year which in turn was linked to the agricultural cycle.

Zuidema has traced an Inca pilgrimage route which commenced at Huanacauri, a sacred mountain which was one of the huacas in the ceque system. The pilgrimage took place in

June, and celebrated the birth of the sun (the June solstice is midwinter at this latitude):

> It was conducted over a complex 21-stop course ... This pilgrimage proceeded in a linear direction that followed the Vilcanota River upstream to a place known to the Spanish as La Raya, or 'dividing line' (also called the village of Vilcanota, after House [*nota*] of the sun [*villca*] in Aymara). What is also interesting about this straight line course is that it points in the general direction of SE, the region of the December solstice sunrise. One of its stopping points, Omotoyanacauri, may have been the place from which the Inka precisely observed the December solstice sunrise from a sun temple (Puquincancha) in Cuzco proper ... There is some evidence ... that this straight line emanating from Huanacauri may have continued well past Vilcanota, all the way to the Island of the Sun in Lake Titicaca ...[15]

Another, rather grim use of certain ceques was as routes for children to come or go to their original part of the empire for sacrifice at times of great crisis or exceptional ceremonial significance.

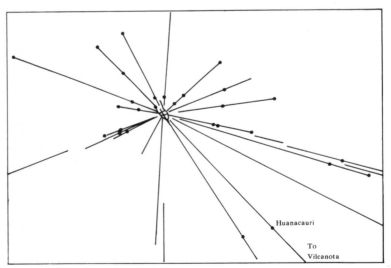

Huanacauri

To
Vilcanota

Figure 27. A plan of some ceques *(about half of the total number) radiating through the Cuzco valley from the old Inca capital. The black dots represent selected* huacas *or shrine sites. A straight-line pigrimage took place in Inca times along the* ceque *from Huanacauri to Vilcanota, and, possibly, much further beyond (see text). (Redrawn and simplified after T. Zuidema)*

Ceques are usually assumed to be conceptual, created just by site (huaca) alignment, but in fact sections of them have been photographed using infra-red techniques by Tony Morrison.[16] In these false-colour pictures, the ceques show up as straight, dark lines against the surrounding vegetation. So at least some ceques must have been old straight tracks.

The basic radial pattern of the ceque system, its complex, multiple functions and its associations with water are all factors Aveni took note of when he came to study the lines at Nazca in the 1980s.

Nazca

Nazca is situated a few hundred miles south of Lima, Peru ('Nazca' should be spelled with an 's', but through an error a century old, the accepted practice nowadays is to spell the *place* with a 'z' and the ancient Nasca *culture* with an 's'). Between the coast and the high Andes are desert tablelands, *pampas*, that are traversed at places by deep, lush gorges cut by rivers on their way from the Andes to the sea. The pampas between these rivers are arid, and littered with flattish rocks. The wind doesn't move these rocks, and precious little rain falls, so there is little to disturb the surface structure, except the actions of human beings. On some of the pampas, notably around Nazca but also at points far away, are concentrations of ground drawings or markings. Properly termed *geoglyphs*, they have been created by the removal of the dark, oxidised desert varnish to reveal a lighter-coloured and looser subsoil. The rocks cleared to create the geoglyphs were sometimes stacked in linear heaps or used as edgings. It has been shown that the construction of such geoglyphs can be accomplished relatively speedily.

The markings fall into distinct types. There are the figures — animals, plants, humans and supernatural figures ('biomorphs'), and patterns such as spirals or apparently abstract config-urations. These geoglyphs are *unicursal* — a single line (or path) traces them. Then there are the cleared geometric surfaces — often called 'trapezoids'. These, the largest of the Nazca

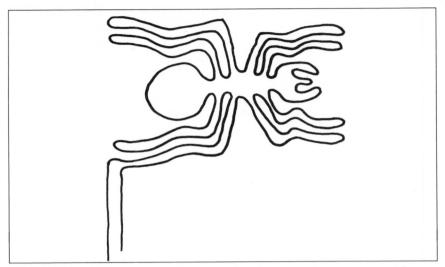

Figure 28. One of the unicursal 'biomorphs' drawn on the pampa near Nazca. This spider measures 150 feet (46 m) in length.

markings, range from being triangular to only slightly misshapen rectangles, and can be the focus of straight lines at one end. The straight lines are sometimes paralleled by one or more lines (reminiscent of Chaco) and can run for many kilometres. They sometimes pass straight over hills and ridges as if they did not exist — to use Andrew Fleming's term (Chapter 2), they are 'terrain oblivious'. Finally, there are small, ill-defined, areas of the pampa that have been cleared of stones and called *campos barridos*.

The most famous — because most frequently photographed, visited and studied — sets of geoglyphs are found on the pampa between the Nazca valley and that of the Ingenio River to the northwest, though there are also markings on surrounding pampas and even in the valleys immediately north of the area.

The lines were brought to modern academic attention by a Peruvian archaeologist, Toribio Mejia Xesspe, who noticed them by accident. He thought of them as ceremonial roads, associated with nearby ancient aqueducts and cemeteries, and used the term 'ceques' to refer to them. The lines came to more general attention in the 1930s, as airline routes began to regularly overfly the pampa, and the geoglyphs, particularly the trapezoids and lines, showed up clearly from the air. Hearing of Mejia Xesspe's findings, American historical geographer, Paul Kosok, visited the pampa in 1941, thinking the lines to be perhaps ancient irrigation systems, but he immediately appreciated that they were something else. Happening to witness a solstitial sunset over the end of one of the lines, he suggested that the Nazca complex could be 'the largest astronomy book in the world'. His enthusiasm was transmitted to Maria Reiche, a German mathematician, who went on to spend most of her life working on and guarding the lines. Now in her nineties, she is still there. Over the years, various other researchers have conducted studies of the lines. The features achieved greatest popular prominence in the 1960s, when bestselling 'ancient astronaut' author Erich von Daniken suggested they were the landing strips for alien

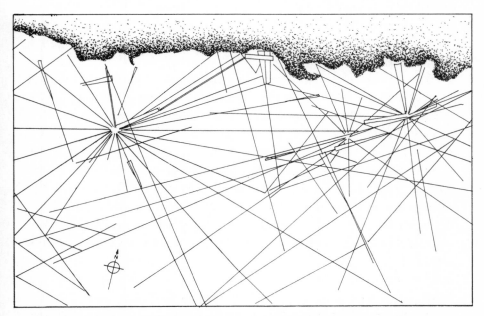

Figure 29. A detailed area of the northern edge of Nazca Pampa, overlooking the Ingenio Valley (top of plan). Apart from straight lines, trapezoids can be seen, and a 'ray centre' (in upper left). (Redrawn after Maria Reiche)

spacecraft in prehistory. This spurious nonsense still persists to some extent in the popular mind.

The greatest myth associated with the lines is that they were created for astronomical purposes, yet in the late 1960s, Gerald Hawkins, of the USA's Smithsonian Institution, carried out a survey of the lines, and was unable to find any really significant astronomical rationale for them.[17]

It has taken the relatively little-known, interdisciplinary research of Anthony F. Aveni and colleagues throughout the 1980s to bring about a deeper understanding of the geoglyphs. There is, unfortunately, space here to give only the briefest summary of some of their conclusions to date, and the interested reader is directed to the volume containing their detailed studies identified in the references.[18] They constructed no hypotheses regarding the lines outside what is known about ancient and current Andean culture. They examined the earlier theories and 'found them wanting', and were alarmed that the entire pampa surface had not previously been fully surveyed or properly checked for artefacts: 'That completeness and rigor had not emerged as underlying criteria for proposing explanations came as a surprise to us.'[19]

One of their fundamental findings was that there was a network pattern embedded in the mesh of straight lines. Maria Reiche had noted what she called 'star-like centres', which Aveni and his team came to distinguish with increasing ability. These 'ray centres' or 'line centres', as Aveni's team called them, consist of 'one or several natural hills or mounds often topped by one or more piles of boulders and from which several lines of various widths emanate'. Like the spokes from a wheel hub: here was the same element of *radiality* that had been noted at Cuzco. The researchers eventually identified over 60 of these nodes amongst the plethora of pampa lines. At least one line from such a centre would connect with another. Some lines, though, go out from and turn back towards the same centre.

The layout of the geoglyphs seemed in many cases to relate to water: crowding at the river valley edges of the pampa, clusters of triangular forms close to the ancient aqueducts

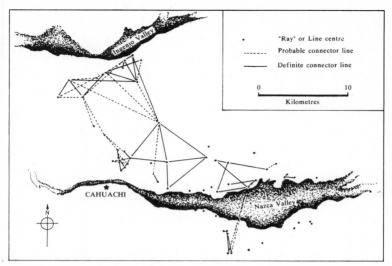

Figure 30. A very simplified plan of the 'ray centres' on the Nazca Pampa with some principle connecting lines. (Redrawn and simplified after A. F. Aveni)

(subterranean canals) that brought water down into the valleys, or running to or glancing along the numerous fossilised river beds (*quebradas*) on the pampa.

That the lines must have been designed to be seen from above remains a strong impression, but Aveni points out that 'anyone who sets foot on the pampa will realize immediately that whether astronomy or hydrology, or both, played a role in the design and layout of the Nazca lines, they surely were intended to be walked on'. Indeed, aspects of the lines are shared with Inca and pre-Inca roads (the Nazca lines are much older than the Inca culture): straightness, nodal patterns of radiality, and the way stones were used as edgings. Archaeologist Persis B. Clarkson, who has examined the Nazca geoglyphs closely, on foot, has noted that some lines 'have been preferred for an undefinable amount of time as footpaths, as evidenced by twisting trails that weave within the confines of the straight lines'.[20]

But no one is in any doubt that the Nazca markings are not mundane roads. People do sometimes need to cross the Nazca pampa, and perhaps some tracks within the lines can be accounted for in that way, but if walking has occured to a great extent on some of the lines, as it has, then we have to suspect *ritual walking* also took place. At Cuzco (above), we noted that there was indeed 'ritual walking along straight predetermined routes'[21] during the June pilgrimage. (Later we will note this type of practice in other cultures.) Also, the human sacrifice *(capac hucha)* was required to travel along certain ceques, as Zuidema notes:

> ... The third context [of ceques] is that of the *capac hucha*. Here the visual connection is expanded by the act of the *acclla* actually travelling as a *cachahui* ('messenger' ...) between two distant points ... in a straight line ...[22]

We have previously noted (see Chaco Canyon, above) the Hopi ritual practice of initiates running in a straight line to horizon points of solar calendar significance. So several ritual uses of walking or running the lines may have existed.

In the Nazca valley immediately south of the Nazca pampa and 13 miles (21 km) west of Nazca town, there are the remains of a major religious centre of the Nazca culture called Cahuachi (see Figure 30). The Nasca culture emerged in the last few centuries BC and flourished from about AD 1–750. At Cahuachi are six natural mounds that had been 'faced with tall wedge-shaped adobes'[23] to form pyramids. The tallest was some 65 feet (7 m) and overlooked a walled court over 4000 yards (3600 m) square. The pyramids and walls of the centre have been heavily eroded. Alongside was a structure that used massive timber pillars, but the roof of this presumed temple has long since disappeared, and the array of posts has also been badly robbed in recent decades.

Helaine Silverman has been conducting detailed research at this site. She describes Cahuachi as 'a site of natural *huacas*. . . an irruption of the sacred, an axis mundi . . .'.[24] Linear geoglyphs have been discovered on the Pampa de Atarco just to the south of Cahuachi, and Silverman has found that some of these point to certain of the Cahuachi mounds. Furthermore, she notes that 'from certain mounds at Cahuachi . . . there is a superb view of the Pampa de Nazca opposite . . . on which the majority of the lines and figures are found . . .'.[25] She feels that Cahuachi was a pilgrimage centre, which pilgrims approached ritually walking along some of the pampa lines. Furthermore, it seems that there are etymological associations between 'Cahuachi' and the Quechua word *qhawachi*, which means 'make them see, make them observe, note, look'; to make one look at something for you — by association, prediction. Silverman suspects that 'the Nasca priest–scientists observed the natural and supernatural world from Cahuachi and from the pampa'.[26] She also suspects, along with others, that the lines, during their period of use, were *ritually swept*. Not only was this a religious act, she points out, but it would also freshen, highlight, the line being prepared, by removing the desert varnish, which gradually darkens the exposed surfaces of the lines. Different lines would doubtlessly be the responsibility of various ayllus, as at Cuzco. This system of shared-labour responsibility was known as *mit'a*, and applied also to the upkeep of Inca roads, irrigation canals and so on. Anthropologist Gary Urton witnessed this system still being practised in a ritual context when he stayed at the Andean community of Pacariqtambo. The plaza in front of the church and town hall there is subtley divided into strips. Each ayllu of the community has the duty of caring for the strip assigned to it, and must prepare it for all festive occasions. These activities include the ritual sweeping of the plaza strips. The saint's image is carried around during the festival, so 'the churchyard and plaza are transformed into sacred spaces at the time of religious celebrations, and therefore they must be cleaned and made presentable for the saints.'[27] It is not a big leap from these plaza strips to the Nazca lines.

(This business of ritual sweeping is more important than it might seem at first glance. Later, we will see that the act relates directly to what I shall be suggesting is the fundamental factor underlying the straight, ceremonial landscape line.)

Strips somewhat similar to Urton's Pacariqtambo examples are marked by regular lines of small stones in the forecourt of the ancient burial chamber at Quebrada de la Vaca on the coast.

Aveni and Urton have found that the strips at both places are oriented approximately towards sunrise on the two days in the year when the sun passes overhead on its zenith path, and the complement of that, when it passes directly 'below' the location, on the other side of the Earth — the 'anti-zenith'. These same orientations were also noted around Cuzco, and Aveni has found that amongst the Nazca lines there is a slight excess of lines pointing in the direction of sunrise and sunset on the days of the passage of the sun across the zenith.[28] Apart from that, he and his team found no other astronomy markedly apparent in the arrangement of the Nazca geoglyphs, and consider it 'unreasonable on cultural grounds to hypothesise that the whole of the pampa would constitute a calendar.'

Numerous other artefacts are to be found on the Nazca pampa as well as the geoglyphs, and Clarkson has made a record of them. There are stone rings made of boulders, for instance. These, it seems likely, provided curbs for covers to protect people either building or using the lines from the occasional strong winds that can whip across the pampa. There are also cairns, which are highly visible to the ground observer, as well as stone piles which mark where a line suddenly narrows or widens. Clarkson found deposits of small stones, shells, and, above all, ceramics as she traversed the geoglyphs. The pottery was mainly in fragments, almost certainly deliberately smashed in most instances, though a few whole or nearly-complete pots have been reportedly found too. Some ceramics seem to have been simply water jars, but others were certainly ritual offerings. Such artefacts are concentrated at the line centres.

The pottery can be approximately dated by variations in style. It has long been noted that motifs on Nascan pottery are similar to the figurative geoglyphs on the pampa. For instance, there is the ground marking of a heron or cormorant which has a distinctive wriggly neck. Just such a motif occurs on a Nascan pot. (The wriggle is an accurate observation of the bird's neck action as it swallows food.) As a result of recording the types of ceramics she found at line centres and at the figurative geoglyphs, Clarkson has tentatively suggested that the biomorphs may belong to the Nasca period, but that the lines and trapezoids may have been made later — perhaps up to AD 1000 or even considerably after that. Certainly, there is no reason to suppose automatically the myriad markings of Nazca to have been contemporaneous. Some cross over one another suggesting superimposition over a long period of use. However, in her concern to preserve the lines, Maria Reiche swept some of the markings, and it seems this has made it difficult for today's researchers to determine which marking preceded which where overlaps accur. And, of course, such action has disturbed the important ceramic deposits. However, Helaine Silverman and David Browne have investigated pristine examples of geoglyphs in the valleys to the north of the Nazca pampa, and, on the basis of ceramic dating there, conclude that the lines date to the Nasca culture of around 100 BC–AD 500 ('Early Intermediate Period'), and that there is 'little evidence in our body of data for the temporal precedence of one form of geoglyph over another'.[29]

This whole body of work by these various investigators has produced a complex picture of the Nazca lines, as Aveni concedes; 'Water, walking, astronomy, kinship, division of labour and ceremonial responsibility, sweeping, radiality — what a strange set of explanatory bedfellows! Our inter-disciplinary studies suggest we must find a place for all of these actions and concepts in the story of the Nazca lines.'[30]

We can no longer think of one-shot explanations. The lines are the outcome of quite different worldviews to anything we have today. And there may be yet deeper and stranger associations that will have to be made, as we shall see.

Bolivia

South and west of Nazca, we come to the high plain, the *altiplano*, of western Bolivia, where old straight Indian tracks also can be found — some of them longer than anything at Nazca. Dead straight, they run over valley and ridge without deviation. They seem to have been first brought to Western attention by French anthropologist Alfred Métraux in the early 1930s. He found earthen shrines set out in straight rows from a small village on the altiplano. These rows stretched for several miles, and were placed along pathways that were 'absolutely straight, regardless of the irregularities in the ground'. The examples Métraux studied did not seem to have been used for a long time. The Indians either did not have information about the lines to impart to Métraux, or chose not to give it. A village priest would only say that they were used for 'superstitious' purposes.

More recently, Tony Morrison has given a good account of these lines and made pictures of them available.[31] It seems knowledge of the paths re-emerged in the 1960s during aerial photography for a new map of Bolivia. Morrison and colleagues investigated some of the lines on the ground, and found that the responsibility of tending to the lines is in some cases dying out with the older inhabitants of the altiplano communities. Consequently, many of the lines, which are formed merely by the clearing of bushes and stones, are disappearing by growing back into the landscape. However, he did also find fresh offerings at cairns on some of the lines.

Some of the holy places on the old straight paths have been Christianised. These usually are adobe shrines, but sometimes churches stand on the lines, as at Sajama. These old Indian tracks, of all the American lines, come closest to Watkins' image of a ley, including even this Christianisation of marker points. Lost in a South American limbo between paganism and Catholicism, some of the lines are still used. In 1985, anthropologist Johan Reinhard witnessed an Indian procession along one of the lines that went to a mountain top. With dancing and music, the Indians walked the line to and from the peak, where they made offerings to a local deity, appealing for water.[32]

Chile

Morrison has noted lines on the Atacama Desert in northern Chile, possibly an Inca road. We can be quite sure that there are numerous other examples of the old straight Indian track in the Andean reaches of South America still to come to light.

If we look at the Indian lines as a whole, it is surely impossible not to sense that we are dealing with what seems at base to be a *single phenomenon*. There are remarkable similarities between the Nazca and Chaco lines, for instance, yet there is no evidence that these cultures were in any sort of direct contact with one another. While it is right and proper for Aveni and colleagues to attempt to tease out the Nascan mindset in order to understand the pampa geoglyphs, there is also the risk that fundamentals of the Amerindian line phenomenon get lost in a plethora of cultural overlay. There need be no doubt that the lines, paths, or ceques produced by different Indian peoples are evolved features, and had specific attributes and functions peculiar to each culture. But to miss seeing the remarkable similarity of the features, ranging as they do from California to Chile — and probably more extensively than even that — is perhaps to miss an important observation. Why ancient Amerindians displayed this linear trait more or less throughout the Americas is a question we will touch on again later: it is enough for us to note it here, and to be aware that even in these formally simple, supremely ley-like lines we are still dealing with highly evolved features.

PART TWO

THE MYSTERY

CHAPTER 4

THE KING AND THE LAND

The original form of human spiritual expression was animism, in which nature was seen as sacred in itself. This took various forms. There was a diffuse 'sense of the sacred' in the land as a whole: the earth was alive. Topography could become anthropomorphised — here were hills that looked like breasts of the Earth Mother, there a rocky cragg that looked like the face of a god. The landscape became the stage for legendary events and beings, the creatures of mythic time. In a slightly more focused form of animism, selected places such as hilltops, rocks, trees, waterfalls and so on were seen as being inhabited by spirits — hence the idea of 'spirit of place', *genius loci*. The vague echo of this approach to nature has crossed the ages in beliefs in, and claimed perception of, fairies, nature spirits, elementals; we all, to greater or lesser degrees, have times when we 'sense' the numinous qualities of a place. Animism was a religious mentality associated particularly with nomadic, hunter-gatherer peoples — the sort of societies associated with the Palaeolithic (Old Stone Age) and Mesolithic (Middle Stone Age) eras.

Totemism was an evolved strand of animism. In this, a specific animal species was seen as related to a particular clan. Totemism, too, could take many forms, but, in simple terms, a given animal was seen to have a 'group soul' — sometimes identified as the 'Animal Master' spirit or deity — that related to the group soul of the clan. The fortunes of both were related; if an animal of the totem species was killed, or killed in a manner inappropriate to ritual rules, the death shortly afterwards of a clan member would be seen as a related incident. Therefore special treatment was meted out to the representatives of the totemic species: it might be taboo to kill a totem animal, or it could only be killed in certain ways, or its meat should be eaten only at certain times. Totemic societies would attribute a common ancestry to itself and its totemic animal species: 'An immemorial covenant', as Joseph Campbell described it.[1] Totemism is associated with tribal societies. Campbell observed that the bear-skull sanctuaries of the circumpolar Bear Cults of Palaeolithic times provide 'the earliest evidence anywhere on earth of the veneration of a divine being'.[2]

Out of the universal magico-spiritual background of animism and totemism emerged the catalytic religious phenomenon of shamanism. Neville Drury has defined shamanism as being 'applied animism, or animism in practice'.[3] The shaman was an intermediary between the spirit world of nature and the tribe. Through what Mircea Eliade called 'archaic techniques of ecstasy', some of which we shall discuss later, the shaman would enter trance, or altered states of consciousness, and travel to the spirit worlds in order to seek information required by the tribe, to reclaim the wandering or abducted souls of sick tribal members, to guide the soul of a dying person to the Otherworld, to engage the aid of spirit helpers, to ward off the attacks of shamans of other tribes, or perpetrate his own. The shaman could see back in time and was the repository of the tribal history; he or she could see ahead in time and predict forthcoming events (remember the probable meaning of Cahuachi at Nazca).

An important element in shamanism, as we shall discover, was the ability to apparently travel in mind through the environment and observe distant events; this was accomplished either by assuming the form of an animal or bird, or directly in what we would call an out-of-body experience. This 'magical flight' is, in fact, the essential meaning of 'ecstasy' — 'out of the senses'. It was one of the fundamentals of shamanism, and brought to its most sophisticated expression there.

The basic shamanic cosmology consisted of three worlds, the

'Middle Earth' of human reality, the upper world of spiritual beings, and the hellish underworld. (This basic model has had many variants around the world and through the ages, particularly involving schemes of seven or nine.) Access to these Otherworlds was by means of a conceptual axis that linked them: a World Tree, a Cosmic Mountain, or actual features that symbolised such an axis, such as a tent pole, smoke rising through a tent's smoke-hole, a beam of sunlight, a rope or a ladder. By symbolically travelling in trance states along this axis, in whatever form, the shaman could ascend to heaven or enter deeply into the body of the earth, the Underworld.

The shaman would also be a healer, a witchdoctor, and, in many ways, an actor, being able to present (and facilitate) healings by impressive displays of sleight of hand and the use of theatrical performance and ventriloquism, with great psychological effect on the patient and watching tribal members. A witchdoctor or healer was not necessarily a shaman, however.

Animals belonging to a shaman were spirit helpers, 'familiars' to use European witchcraft terminology, and he or she would often be accompanied by spirit helpers in animal forms visible only to the shaman.

A person who became a shaman would probably have had a childhood or early history of illness or other crisis in which the spirit world revealed itself. These altered states could initially produce conditions within the person akin to what we would call schizophrenia. The potential shaman might become reserved and effectively a social outcast. Androgeny, even transvestism, was also sometimes a characteristic. The person who survived shamanic initiation and apprenticeship learned how to control and integrate their altered states, and psychosocial realignment, and assume a major role in tribal life. It is that element of control which marks the shamanic ability, and differentiates it from some forms of mediumship. The shaman had the ability to survive death and rebirth. Shamans were active in the spirit world. They could come back with the knowledge of the Otherworlds, and use it for the good of the

Figure 31. A Tungus shaman's ritual costume, bearing a depiction of the World Tree.

tribe. Indeed, it is thought that the very name 'shaman' comes from the Tungus noun *saman*, deriving from the verb *sa*, 'to know'; 'he who knows'.

Joan Halifax writes that the way of the shaman is 'nearly as old as Human consciousness itself . . . Through the ages, the practice of shamanism has remained vital, adapting itself to the ways of all the world's cultures . . . The shaman lies at the very heart of some cultures, while living in the shadowy fringe of others . . . Shamanism's origins in the Palaeolithic period inevitably link it with the animal world of the hunt. The shaman became identified metaphysically with the untamed creatures which provided food, clothing, and even shelter.'[4] It seems that various species of deer, for instance, became particularly associated with shamanism in many parts of the world, from Siberia to southern Africa to the Americas. Hence a common

99

Figure 32. A Tungus shaman wearing antlers and beating his trance-inducing drum. (Detail from N. Witsen, 1705)

headgear for shamans in many times and places consisted of antlers. Halifax considers that this was because they were 'symbolic of regeneration and growth, because of the way they are renewed' and were 'often associated with the Sacred Tree and the mysteries of death and rebirth.'[5]

German ethnopsychologist Holger Kalweit describes shamans as 'technicians of the Sacred, the specialists of the Beyond. The shaman is the classic investigator of the realm of death . . .'[6] In similar vein, anthropologist Marlene Dobkin de Rios refers to shamans as 'technicians of the supernatural'.[7] American anthropologist Michael J. Harner defines a shaman as 'a man or woman who is in direct contact with the spirit world through a trance state and has one or more spirits at his command to carry out his bidding for good or evil.'[8] That great scholar of shamanism, Mircea Eliade, noted that 'Magic and magicians are to be found more or less all over the world, whereas shamanism exhibits a particular magical speciality . . .: "mastery over fire",

100

"magical flight", and so on ... the shaman specializes in a trance during which his soul is believed to leave his body and ascend to the sky or descend to the underworld.'[9] Eliade further appreciated that the basics of shamanism occured in many parts of the world; it was a primary experience of human consciousness, not a learned affectation. However, he considered that shamanism 'has had its most complete manifestation in North and Central Asia'.[10]

Shamanism was the precursor of some of the major religions of more structured societies, such as Buddhism, Taoism, Zoroastrianism and Tantricism. It could be said that these religions represented modified shamanism, and they in turn affected continuing if marginalised shamanic traditions in the cultures they dominated. Eliade remarked that even in the central Asian heartland of 'classic' shamanism, religions 'extend beyond shamanism in every direction, just as any religion extends beyond the mystical experience of its priviliged adherents.'[11]

The occurrence of shamanism varied amongst societies. In classic cases, the shaman was the 'holy man', the solitary religious focus, for the tribe. In other cultures, shamanism was more widespread, even amongst the ordinary members of the tribe; defined ceremonial sessions took place where everyone had direct experience of the supernatural realms. In yet other societies, there would be varying grades of shamans, lesser and greater ones.

In some cases where shamanism was performed by a single individual, the role of the priest was born. Anthropologist Gerald Weiss has observed that the shaman belongs to tribal cultures and the priest to state formations, so 'presumably, later in appearance, although the overlap between the two may occur'. The shaman was characterised by trance while the priest conducted 'routine propitiatory acts of adoration, prayer and offerings'. Leo Sternberg suggested a 'development from shaman to priest with a concomitant shift from possession to solicitation, from spirit to god, from hut to temple'. Weiss noted that in many cultures the shaman gave performances or seances 'while the assembled laymen remain passive observers'. It was perhaps only 'a slight shift' from this into a priestly ritual. This was perhaps the 'behavioural link between generalised shamans and specialised priests that could have permitted the transition from one to another.' He studied shamanic practice in the Campa Indians of Peru where he felt this transitional situation was perhaps actually occurring.[12]

In societies which became more structured or hierarchical, theocracies appeared: religious rule, in which priesthood and government were combined. In certain instances this evolved into the idea of the chief being divine, and celestial lineage was claimed: the Divine King. But even this evolution retained vestiges of shamanism. For example, Eliade refers to the first king of Tibet, Gna-k'ri-bstan-po who 'is said to have come down from heaven by a rope named *dmu-t'ag*. This mythical rope was also depicted on royal tombs, a sign that the sovereign ascended to heaven after death. Indeed, for kings, communications between heaven and earth were never altogether broken'.[13] (The shamanic-based tradition of Bonism of course flourished in Tibet prior to Buddhism, and, indeed, never really died out.) Sir James Frazier gave many examples of sacred kingships throughout the world in his famous *The Golden Bough* (1922). He concluded that the institution of kingship 'appears to have originated in the order of public magicians or medicine-men'. In 1919, Harold Bailey observed that even in the institution of the British monarchy the 'notion of Imperial divinity is not yet dead . . . though the spirit may now have fled, its traces still remain in our regal ceremonial'.[14]

Of course, such developments are not to be seen as some great, common chronological stream of evolution: they did not occur universally, and there were countless variations on these basic themes. Nevertheless, human societies have experienced these forms of spiritual persuasions, and the social structures associated with them. And to greater or lesser extents, we still find versions of them all in the world today. What I shall be developing in this second part of the book is the suggestion that *the motif of the ceremonial, straight landscape line originated in one of*

102

the central elements of the shamanic experience, and that the range of surviving linear features in ancient sacred landscapes itself reflects the kinds of evolution indicated above. We can follow one train of research here that provides at least a fleeting glimpse of this multifaceted situation, and which opens up the way to solving the linear enigma.

An Indo–European clue

The term 'Indo–European' does not refer to a racial group but to peoples sharing a *linguistic* ancestry stretching from India to western Europe. From about the first century AD, languages were being spoken across this vast area that can be traced back to a common ancestor that was spoken in Eurasia 6000 years ago. 'We call the people who spoke this ancestral language the Indo–Europeans or Proto-Indo–Europeans,' scholar J. P. Mallory informs. 'But although we can give them a name, they are unlike almost any other ancient people we are likely to encounter. As the linguistic ancestors of nearly half this planet's population they are one of the most important entities in the prehistoric record — and yet they are also one of the most elusive.'[15] Mallory points out that the Indo–Europeans 'did not burst into history; they straggled in over a period of 3500 years', leaving their linguistic mark in clay tablets in Greece, inscriptions on an Iranian cliff-face, a dedicatory inscription on a German helmet, and elsewhere. The evidence for Indo–European language traits is of course older in the east because of the earlier appearance of writing there.

The Indo–European linguistic influence came to extinguish almost all the indigenous non-Indo–European languages. The Indo–European language structure we call Celtic seems to have been associated with the Iron Age La Tène culture of western Europe, and this spread Indo–European linguistic influences widely. Although Latin was originally simply a regional Indo–European language, its eventual association with the expansion of the Roman Empire made it an important later influence in the Indo–European spread. But the nature of the initial expansion from the Proto-Indo–European ancestor language poses more difficult problems, and of course raises the spectre of where the original Indo–European homeland was situated. There were naturally many languages spread across prehistoric Europe and Eurasia, and the record is quite clear that Proto-Indo–European must have been one of them, roughly within the 4500–2500 BC time-frame. By tracing back through the known Indo–European languages, experts have been able to reconstruct some of the vocabulary of the proto-language, but the whereabouts of the homeland of the people speaking it is a problem scholars have not yet fully solved. Working from a wide range of clues, their best guess is a zone stretching west-east immediately to the north of the Black and Caspian seas, provisionally as far as the Ural River, the 'Pontic-Caspian' region. This zone is better attested by linguistic evidence than by archaeological matter, although there are interesting archaeological possibilities within the areas as well. Although different scholars have posited various locations, the Black Sea steppe area figures as a component in most suggestions.

The way this Proto-Indo–European influence was transmitted is similarly the subject of debate. There seems to have been an influx of 'kurgan' burials (the building of mounds over burial shafts characteristic of the Black Sea region) into the regions around the Pontic–Caspian zone at the right sort of period of prehistory that we would be looking at for the expansion of an Indo–European homeland. Archaeologist Marija Gimbutas has for decades argued that the expansion of the Kurgan people was the Indo–European revolution, conjuring a picture of the pastoral hordes from the steppes with their horses, chariots, marital proclivities and patriarchial society, swamping and overpowering the more peacable, matrifocal, agricultural-based non-Indo–European indigenous inhabitants of Europe. But unless we can identify the Proto-Indo–Europeans properly, we will not know quite what *their* disposition was, and might be reading too much into the evidence of intrusions into southeast Europe. Mallory warns 'there is no reason for assuming an inherently warlike character for the Indo–Europeans'.[16]

Archaeologist Colin Renfrew argues that the vehicle for the expansion of Indo–European influence was simply the Early Neolithic 'basic and widespread cultural and economic change' in Europe, transforming hunter-gatherer societies into agricultural ones.[17] Again, American anthropologist John Robb has suggested that the dominance of the Indo-European language structure could have arisen simply as a natural consequence of many minor interactions between adjacent language communities that gradually set up a sort of linguistic and social 'Brownian motion' (the frequent and random fluctuations of particles) that ultimately produced a meta-pattern that was Indo–European.[18]

Nevertheless, whatever the current difficulties of research, there was an expansion of an Indo–European language pattern from a Proto-Indo–European society. The linguistic detective work tells us that those people raised sheep and cattle, and probably had the yoke and plough — the evidence indicates the use of oxen for traction. The sickle is also an attested Proto-Indo–European word. We do not know the nature of their dwellings, but it seems likely that some sort of fortified settlement or refuge existed. They may have known about copper, and they knew of hemp (this may be a more interesting detail than it sounds, as we shall see in a later chapter). They also certainly had the wheel, and proto-words for axle and wagons have been strongly attested. They seem to have had oar-powered boats, too. Perhaps the most profound and distinctive Proto-Indo–European item, though, was the horse. The horse was a major factor in both the secular and religious life of the Proto-Indo–Europeans. Most experts agree that they had domesticated the horse.

Social organisation appears to have been male-dominated with patrilineal descent. There were clans, and apparently a warrior class or institution. The social arrangement seems to have been a threefold division into priests, warriors, herders/ cultivators, as in the Celtic society of the Gauls, for example, druides, equites and plebes. This tripartite nature is reflected in Indo–European mythology, and such an association between social order and mythological structure is a recurring feature of many traditional societies.

The horse not only figured large in the secular life of the Proto-Indo–Eurpeans, as deduced by main themes in known early Indo–European societies, but also in their religion and in mythology. This is shown in the image of the twins, a prime motif in Indo–European mythology, for instance. Perhaps the best-known to us are Castor and Pollux or Hengist and Horsa (literally stallion and horse), but there were many more, and they were all horsemen. Versions of horse sacrifice appear in Indian, Roman and medieval Irish ritual. The pulling of the king's chariot by the sacrificial horse figured in the Indic ritual, and in many versions the body of the sacrificed horse was divided into portions and used as offerings to different deities. The pagan Irish kings would even bathe in a soup made from the remains of the sacrificial horse! Jaan Puhvel has reconstructed a Proto-Indo–European myth and ritual 'which involved the mating of a figure from the royal class with a horse from which ultimately sprung the famous equine divine twins'.[19] It certainly seems there was some sort of horse-centred ritual in Proto-Indo–European times, and one moreover that involved ritual intoxication with a form of mead (Proto-Indo–European *medhu*. The asterisk denotes a presumed word, form of a word, or sense.).

That the domestication of the horse would have had an immense impact on a society is to be expected, but why the ritual insistence on the animal? An interesting coincidence may reveal a shamanic antecedent. At sites in the Black Sea, Pontic–Caspian region, and to a lesser extent in southeastern Europe, stone 'sceptres' carved into the form of horse heads have been unearthed by archaeologists. More than 30 have so far been found. 'It is widely accepted,' Mallory reports, 'that these are objects ultimately of steppe inspiration, where the horse played an integral role in both economy and ritual and where a tradition of manufacturing stone-carved animal figures extends back well into the Neolithic.'[20] But the horse also figured prominently in shamanism. The trance-inducing drum of the

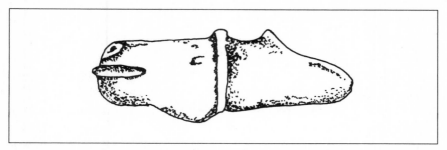

Figure 33. This stone 'sceptre' depicting a horse-head was found in a male burial at Suvorovo, Bulgaria. It is 17 cm long. (Redrawn after M. Gimbutas)

Buriat, Tungus and Yakut shamans of the Altaic language group of Central Asia, was called a 'horse', the steed which took the shaman to the Otherworlds. The Buriat shaman had a horse-headed stick, which was danced astride like a hobbyhorse (and similar to the broomstick of the medieval European witch, see Chapter 7). These ritual horse-head sceptres may have such origins of magical function and perhaps denote a shamanistic/ priest figure in the societies yielding these archaeological finds. One, at Suvororo (Figure 33) in Bulgaria, was found in a male burial, along with long flint knives and a pestle for grinding ochre. We can only wonder if the Proto-Indo–Europeans had contact with the Altaic shamanic cultures, either directly or through intermediary peoples. We do know from linguistic clues, however, that the Proto-Indo–Europeans were in contact with Finno–Ugric speakers, and this language group certainly included powerful northern Eurasian shamanic societies such as the Lapps, Komi, Voguls and Ostyaks. The Finno–Urgic languages formed one branch of the Uralic family of languages; the other was Samoyedic, which covered the shamanic groups of Northern Siberia.

Mircea Eliade remarked that 'we have very little certain knowledge concerning the religious prehistory and proto-history of the Indo–Europeans . . . The documents at our disposition bear witness to religions already elaborated, systemised, sometimes even fossilised.' Shamanism was not a dominant factor in Indo–European religious life, but 'techniques of ecstasy are attested'.[21] Eliade felt that the presence of tripartition (above) in Proto–Indo–European religious thinking 'certainly implied an inclusion of the shamanic ideology and experiences.'

Without doubt, shamanic elements are to be found in many Indo–European mythological texts. An example is the myth of Odin, which incorporates a World Tree (Yggdrasil); Odin's eight-hooved horse Sleipnir; the transformation of Odin's body into animal forms for magical travel and an eagle for magical flight, and spirit helpers in the form of his crows Huginn ('Thought') and Muninn ('Memory'). He also drank mead which turned him into animal forms, and we have already noted the associations of that drink. There are similar elements incorporated in the mytho-religious material of the ancient Greeks, Celts, Persians, Scythians, Caucasians and Indians.

Eliade noted that the vestiges of shamanic tradition in Indo–European religious life 'were principally grouped about the mythical figure of the terrifying Sovereign, whose archetype seems to be Varuna, The Master of magic, the great "Binder" '.[22] G. Dumézil has studied Indo–European king mythology closely, and deduced the nature of the Proto–Indo–European king from that. According to his findings, the priestly class embraced the function of sovereignty, combining both legal order and magico–religious roles. As one example he gives the fortunate survival of the record of the treaty of 1380 BC between the Mittani king, Matiwaza and a Hittite king. Matiwaza invoked the deities Mitra, Varuna and Indra amongst others. In the *Veda*, the first two gods are 'characteristically co-joined', as Mallory puts it, as Mitra–Varuna. Dumézil points out that Mitra relates to government and judicial aspects, and Varuna symbolises the magical and religious. This joint figure thus represents a double nature to Indic sovereignty.

This functional ambiguity of sovereignty relates to the kingship–shamanism complex, and brings us to a crucial word that existed in the Proto–Indo–European language: *reg-*. This ancient linguistic treasure brings the concept of straight lines into that complex, and brings us to the central core of our enquiry:

> The apex of Proto-Indo–European society, according to the standard handbooks of Indo–European culture, was ruled by a king whose title has usually been secured by the textbook series: Sanskrit *rai*, Latin *rex*, Gaulis *rix*, Old Irish *ri*, and possibly Thracian *Rhesos*. It has been assumed that this Proto-Indo–European **reg* which provides such meanings as stretch, draw out in a straight line, and straighten. Our English word right is a reflex of this root, and the same opposition which we employ between what is straight or right and what is bent or crooked, that is, dishonest or wrong, is encountered throughout the Indo–European languages . . . Jan Gonda and Emile Benveniste sought in the basic etymology of the word a hint of the original function of the Proto-Indo–European **reg-*. Gonda suggested that the word meant one who stretches or reaches out, a metaphor for the formal activities of a king . . . Benveniste argued that the fundamental meaning was 'one who determined what was right'. This suggested a leader who was more concerned with maintaining social and moral order than a secular sovereign . . . Indeed, Benveniste proposed that there may have been more overtly priestly functions associated with the Proto-Indo–European king in that the root meaning of 'stretching out' or 'straightening' might be associated with duties such as laying out limits, be they demarcations of sacred territory within a settlement, the settlement itself or the borders of national territories.[23]

Jim Kimmis was the first to bring ley hunters' attention to **reg-*.[24] He pointed out in *The Ley Hunter* that the physical, spatial linear associations of the word were extended in an abstract sense to become 'an analogue of honesty, justice, government and social order . . . Between the physical and abstract senses of this complex word stands a small group of cognates which signify "ruler" or "king" '.[25]

Kimmis referred to Eric Partridge's etymological dictionary *Origins*,[28] and, using that source, we list in Table 1 a selection of words from various Indo–European languages which relate to the Proto-Indo–European root **reg-*. They are placed under the headings representing the range of meanings and associations the word has inspired, as indicated by Kimmis.

A few moments studying Table 1 reveal how the meaning of physical straightness has leaked into the analogous terms. So

Table 1

SPATIAL

Latin:
regula (a straight piece of wood; a measuring bar); *regio/region* (a straight line, a boundary, a frontier); *regere* (to guide straight). The past participle of *regere* is *rectus* which gives the 'rect' element in some words of several languages. In Latin we have for exmple *rectum* (the straight part of the great intestine) and *rectitudo* (straightness, both spatially and figuratively).

French:
règle (ruler, straight edge); *réglage* (setting, adjusting lines [on paper]); *droit* (straight line; right [directional]). This word may seem unconnected with *reg-, but the key element is *roi*, which is dealt with below (under KINGSHIP). *Dresser* (to raise; hold erect; to erect; to direct; to arrange). This word comes via the Old French *drecier* (to direct, manage) from the Low Latin *directiare*.

German:
Rechteck (rectangle; right angle); *recht* (right [directional]). This last is also the same in Dutch.

English:
Right (directional); region; direction; erect.

KINGSHIP

Latin:
rex (king; Partridge feels this probably stands, due to 'vocalic change', for *regs); *regina* (queen); *regulus* (kinglet, prince). The feminine of this, *regula*, means a straight piece of wood (see above in SPATIAL), emphasising the conceptual link betwen kingship and spatial linearity.

French:
Roi (king): this derives from the Latin *regem*, the accusative case of *rex*, via Old French *rei*.

Spanish:
real (royal- see English 'royal' below for derivation).

German:
Reich (empire); derives from Middle High German *riche*, Old High German *rihhi* (realm) which itself came from Old Celtic *rig- (king).

English:
regal; regalia; regency; regent; regicide; reign; sovereignty; inter-regnum; royal (deriving from Old/Medieval French *roial*, the derivative of which, *roialté/royaulté*, gives the English royalty); realm.

Sanskrit:
raj (rule, reign); *raja* (king; prince); *rani* (queen; princess).

GOVERNMENT AND ORDER (SOCIAL, MORAL, MILITARY)

Latin:
regnum (power exercised by a king; his kingdom); *regentia* (office of ruler); *regimen* (governance);

French:
droit (right, not wrong; fair; just); *droits* (duty, customs, rights); *dressage* (training [of animals]), derived from the Latin *directus* by way of Old French *drecier* and later French *dresser* (to direct).

German:
Regel (rule, regulation); *regelrecht* (proper); *Regierung* (government); *regeln* (regulate, control).

English:
regime; regiment; regular; regulation; right (not wrong); rights (moral, legal, human); righteousness; direction (an order); correct; rectitude; rectify.

110

the French *roi* for instance can be seen in kingship terms as well as embedded in the word for right, *droit*, which itself can mean either a physical direction or one's human, moral or legal rights. *Tout droit* means 'straight ahead'. 'Right' in English has similar double meaning, of course, and a phrase such as 'keep right on' means 'keep straight on'. Similarly 'dead straight' means perfectly straight, or 'dead on' means accurate, on target, hence straight. (We will touch on the connection between death and straightness a number of times as we proceed.) The word 'direction' can have a spatial meaning or be a command. A perfect example of this blending of physical and abstract senses is the English word 'ruler', which means either a straightedge or a king/leader.

John Palmer has noted (personal communication): the Gaelic *ree*, 'to stretch on a deathbed, shroud as a corpse': the early Irish *regem*, 'I stretch'; the Welsh *reiat*, 'row'; and the Flemish *rei, rij*, 'row', *rek*, 'stretch', *reiziger*, 'traveller', and *reis*, 'journey'.

Straightness — linear order and movement — kingship — order, government. Why has such a set of connections developed? I believe it is because of a crucial evolution the notion of sacred straightness went through in some societies. The concept, and thus its physical expression, the straight ceremonial landscape line, went through such changes together; changes we must now identify.

Partridge gives a fascinating core meaning for the Proto-Indo–European **reg-*, the root of all the word derivations we see in Table 1: 'to set straight, to lead or guide straight, hence, as noun, a true guide, hence a powerful one, hence a chief, a king; perhaps the basic sense of **reg-* is "a straight line" or, better, "a movement straight from one point to another, hence a movement along a straight line" '.[26]

A movement along a straight line. We have seen earlier in this chapter how in some societies the king or chieftain figure evolved out of earlier priesthoods and theocratic institutions, themselves derived ultimately from the shaman, a chrono-logically remote entity in those cultures where such evolution

111

occurred. A residue of such a development was the belief that the king was either divine, or possessed a link with the Otherworld and had supernatural powers. So we can readily conjure the image of a Proto-Indo–European priest/king 'moving along a straight line'. But what was he doing? What was the nature of the movement? What was the meaning?

We have already noted in Chapter 3 the practice of ritual walking in the Andean region, notably the straight pilgrimage route used in Inca times along one of the *ceques*, and the footpaths found engraved within the boundaries of the straight Nazca lines. The Andean peoples were not the only ones with this kind of practice. In Ashkeit in the Sudan, for instance, there was a custom at certain times for the men to walk in a straight line from certain house to certain house through the community; these houses were community focal points. It took all day. When these people were resettled in Kashm el-Girba, they faced a problem: the new town layout did not easily accommodate such a straight ritual walk. Did the straightness matter, or would a more irregular form of walk do? After deep deliberation, the community elders decided that 'the straightness was the most important' aspect of the activity and built their new ritual on that basis.[27] I have given examples elsewhere of other straight walking practices, such as those recorded in folk tradition in Britain.[28] However bizarre such an activity may seem to us today, we must accept that some ancient peoples did do straight walking. Indeed, we may be sure that our concept of the ceremonial procession originates in such practice. It also seems that shamanic practice in some cultures involved straight walking — there are cave paintings in Ndedema Gorge, South Africa, for example, which show antelope-headed shamans marching in procession, and other ritual processional activities are noted elsewhere.

But what was our Proto-Indo–European priest/king *doing* walking in straight lines? Well, perhaps ceremonially reinforcing boundaries — probably sacred territory, a little like the modern folk survival of 'beating the bounds'. This would ultimately come to have connotations of sovereignty (a *reg-* word), a concept embracing both spiritual and territorial aspects. He might have been leading participants in ritual processions. But clearly, the emphasis on it in the language, and its involvement with the key office of state and its dispersal through other words relating to control and governing, indicate that this linear activity related to some deep-seated matter. I suggest that ritual walking was a ceremonial, public, and physical expression of a spiritual, or perhaps more accurately, a mental, non-material, reality — the reality that lay at the heart of what the straight line markings on ancient landscapes were about. *The physical movement symbolised another type of movement, a movement of the spirit.* We must now probe through another layer of evolution towards an understanding of what exactly that was.

King and country

In the Arthurian stories, the Grail is housed in a castle in a Waste Land inhabited by the Fisher King who is 'wounded through the thighs', a euphemism for genital injury. The recovery of the king and the concurrent restoration of the land to health and fertility depends on the right question being asked of the Grail (usually 'Who does the Grail serve?') and an answer being given. The king and the land are as one. This element in the Arthurian cycle surely encodes an archaic memory of the linking of the king and the land. In her *Arthur and the Sovereignty of Britain*, Caitlin Matthews perceptively observes that '. . . the subtextual energy of the Matter of Britain, is about sovereignty: who holds the land and by what right? It is only those kings and invaders who draw their empowering emblems and mystique from the deep, mythical framework of the land who are successful . . . Primarily the Goddess of Sovereignty is the *genius loci*, the spirit of the earth beneath us, who in many different countries assumes a localized appearance and a set of symbols appropriate to her cult'.[29] Matthews refers to the ancient Irish bardic tale called *Echach*

Muigmedoin in which the hero, Niall, along with his brothers, is unknowingly put through various trials to test for suitability for the future accession to the throne, what the Celtic Irish called *rigdamna* (note the **reg-* element), the right to rule. In one of these tests, Niall alone of his brothers accedes to a request from an ugly old crone guarding a well, to kiss her and sleep with her, whereupon she becomes a beautiful damsel and tells Niall: 'Lordship is mine; O King of Tara, I am Sovereignty . . . and your seed shall be over every clan.' Referring to the water that she gives Niall from the well, she says: 'smooth shall be thy draught from the royal horn, 'twill be mead, 'twill be honey, 'twill be strong ale.'

Alwyn and Brinley Rees note that the image of Sovereignty presenting herself as an old hag until transformed into fair maiden by the embrace of a destined king, recurs in English and French romances as well as other Irish legends.[30]

The various versions of the medieval Arthurian Romances embellished elements from earlier sources — such as the Welsh bardic text, *The Mabinogion* — which themselves came out of oral traditions of unknown ancestry, but certainly reaching back into Celtic Iron Age times. Indeed, there is a tantalising hint that there may be faint traces of much earlier elements, for the very name 'Arthur' has been claimed by some to derive not from the Welsh form of the Roman 'Artorius', but from the Welsh *Arth Fawr*, the Great Bear. John Michell notes that this was associated with the brilliant star Arcturus whose position in the night sky is indicated by two stars in the 'tail' of the Great Bear constellation (*Ursa Major*, 'The Plough' or 'Big Dipper'). The Great Bear was also known as Arthur's Wain or Wagon, 'being seen as the vehicle in which Arthur circled the pole.'[31] If these associations are valid, then it could be that there is a faint echo in the Arthurian tradition reaching even to the remote times of the Bear Cults at the end of the last Ice Age.

The underlying Arthurian theme in any case relates to the fact that throughout the world and from many former times the fate of the king and that of his realm have been viewed as interdependent, Frazer observed that 'the king's life or spirit . . .

114

(was) sympathetically bound up with the prosperity of the country'.[32] The king was responsible for the fertility of the land; if drought, pestilence or crop failure occurred, it was viewed as a fault of the king, because he had sinned or conducted an unjust reign. In some societies, the king paid for such disasters with his life.

The Celtic Irish spoke of the *banais rigi* (that *reg-* element again!), the wedding of kingship. The king was married to the land; he had union with the Earth Goddess, Sovereignty. Alwyn and Brinley Rees consider that Queen Medb of Connacht may have been an embodiment of Sovereignty. A daughter of a king of Tara, she married King Conchobar but left him. She was much courted by suitors seeking access to royal lineage. Irish tradition also tells of another Medb, a queen of Leinster, who was queen to nine kings, and they could not be kings until they married her. Interestingly, the name Medb is cognate with the Welsh *meddw*, 'drunk', and related to the English word 'mead'. Coomaraswamy and others have linked the Sovereignty of Ireland with the Indian goddess Sri-Lakshmi who is 'the spirit of Sovereignty', consort to Indra.[33] She brought the gift of Soma, the sacred drink — a subject we will return to.

The union between the goddess of the land and a king was also a key element in royal ritual in the Near East. Sacred prostitution emerged from that complex of ideas.

The mystical union between monarch and land was symbolised in numerous cultures by the king sitting or standing on a sacred stone during the crowning ceremony. (This is also acknowledged in the Arthurian tradition, when Arthur is the only one able to pull the sword Excalibur from a stone, or, in some versions, from an anvil placed on a stone.) Even today, the British monarch is crowned on a medieval wooden chair that holds a sacred stone, the Stone of Scone, in a compartment underneath the seat. This stone was a Scottish king-stone brought to Westminster to consolidate the English-based British monarchy, and was the focus of legends such as that it was the stone, the bethel, on which Jacob slept. Scotland

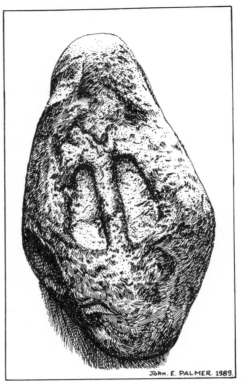

Figure 34. The St Magnus Stone. (John Palmer)

had several king-stones, such as the probable inauguration stone known as the St Magnus Stone on Orkney, which has two footprints carved into it. The king-stone of the Saxons can still be seen today, some miles up the Thames from Westminster, at Kingston-upon-Thames, now enclosed by iron railings, and, as might be expected, Ireland had several king-stones. At Castlereagh, the king-stone was fashioned into the shape of a seat; others had footprints carved in them in which the king placed his bare feet during the crowning — an example is the seven-foot-square stone of the Kings of O'Doherty in Derry (Londonderry). The most sacred kingly site in all Ireland, the Hill of Tara, which also contains a Neolithic chambered mound called The Mound of Hostages, is the location of the *Lis Fal*, a stone which was said to cry out when the correct king was crowned. At Tullahoge, in medieval times the capital of Tyrone,

116

a boulder was fashioned into a king-stone by having three stone slabs placed around it forming a throne. The Turoe Stone in Galway, covered with curvilinear designs that would seem to date it to around the third century BC, originally stood on a prehistoric earthwork. It is cylindrical with a domed top, and as Celtic scholar Anne Ross observes, there 'would seem to be no doubt that the stone is intentionally phalloid'.[34] There are no extant kingship traditions related to this particular stone, but it is very similar in shape to the omphalos stone at Delphi, for example. Omphalos, navel or umbilical stones marked the conceptual World Centre, the sacred, geomantic centre of a site, region or country, from where geodetic measure and division took place. The design on the Turoe Stone, interestingly, is so organised as to fall into four segments, probably indicating the Four Quarters of the world. A stone, a natural outcrop, at Uisneach, Ireland, was known as the Navel of Ireland. Like the human umbilicus, such stones represented the point of sustenance, but in a metaphysical sense. Again, they related to the idea of the maintenance of the health of the land and the spiritual life of the people. They typically marked places where traffic with the spirit world could occur, and are a version of the Cosmic Axis, which, as we have seen, is a major element in shamanistic traditions.

Evidence of stones linked with kingship and fertility occur throughout the ancient world. A phallic pillar was found at Pfalzfeld in Germany, with its glans placed downwards into the ground.[35] John Palmer remarks that 'at the royal stones, the Mora Stenar, near Uppsala, the Kings of Sweden were inaugurated and justice pronounced, and the Norse town of Konungahalla was connected with the Stone of the King, which served as a high seat in the *Thing* of Nidaros'.[36] Footprint stones have been found in Switzerland and rock chairs in France.

The king's power

In such mystical union with the land, with the goddess, the king infused the earth with his power, the divine power only the

117

kingly line possessed. In Oceanic societies, for instance, the king or chieftain was said to possess *mana*, a mysterious life force. In Polynesia:

> Mana could be contained in any person or thing; however, a man's potential capacity depended on his position in the whole hierarchy. Chiefs were the main vessels, acting as contact between god and man ... And, since mana flowed from high to low, an unguarded contact between chief and a commoner was therefore an evil thing: the chief suffered a loss of mana, which he should preserve for the good of the people, and the commoner, with his limited capacity for mana, might be blown out like a fuse.[37]

But what about our Proto-Indo–European priest/king? Recent research on **reg-* has thrown some fascinating light onto this 'kingly power' aspect, as J. P. Mallory reports:

> First, Andrew Sihler has argued that the underlying root is not 'to arrange in a straight line' but 'be efficacious, have mana'. Then Harmut Scharfe reviewed the Vedic evidence ... to discover that the word *rai* in the earliest Vedic texts was not the masculine noun meaning king but a feminine noun indicating 'strength, power'. If this is accepted, then we no longer have evidence for Proto-Indo–European kings ... Scharfe does observe that the correspondences between Sanskrit *raian-* and Greek *aregon* suggests a Proto-Indo–European word for 'protector' or 'person with power or charisma', but not 'king'.[38]

This only reinforces the curious secular/spiritual ambiguity we have seen connected with the **regs* figure. The king in later Celtic and Italic Indo–European societies simply fossilised this early, enigmatic secular/sacred role in a more structured form. It also suggests that the linear association evident in connection with **reg-* could have had a conceptual correlate to physical straight-line movement, something akin to 'mystical rule' — the broadcasting of the king's power or spirit through the realm. *Ruling the land* with the king's supernatural power. Frazer made a similar observation:

> To some extent it appears to be assumed that the king's power over nature, like that over his subjects and slaves, is exerted through an act of will ... His person is considered, if we may express it so, as the dynamical centre of the universe, *from which lines of force radiate to all quarters of heaven* ... [39] (My emphasis.)

118

Although Frazer tends to be viewed with some condescension by scholars nowadays, it is worth noting that he predated researchers like Sihler by a great many years when he wrote:

> The belief that kings possess magical or supernatural powers by virtue of which they can fertilise the earth and confer other benefits on their subjects would seem to have been shared by the ancestors of all the Aryan [Indo–European] races from India to Ireland . . . [40]

Vestiges of belief in this kingly supernatural power were still present in Britain until relatively recent centuries. It was believed that the touch of a monarch's hand could heal. Edward the Confessor, especially, was associated with healing power. The belief lingered particularly with regard to scrofula, which was known as the King's Evil. Queen Elizabeth I was known to exercise the healing touch, and on Midsummer's Day in 1633, Charles I cured a hundred patients at the chapel royal at Holyrood. It is said that Charles II applied his healing touch to almost 100 000 people during his reign. The tradition survived at least to the time of Queen Anne.

The association of lines and kingship do not only occur in Proto-Indo–European linguistic puzzles relating to kings or charismatic protectors. We see it in various forms in many cultures and societies. At Cuzco — a term which means 'navel' in Quechua, incidentally — the Inca, the Son of the Sun, ruled from the Coricancha, at the focus of the 41 straight lines or *ceques* (Chapter 3). We have seen that these lines had multiple functions. Could one conceptualised function of the lines have been the transmission of the Inca's spiritual power? Again, another divine leader, the emperor of ancient China, would sit on the Golden Throne, the throne of state, in the Forbidden City at Beijing. While the populace, through the ministrations of the Feng shui geomants (Chapters 1 and 5), had to avoid straight lines, the emperor sat on the straight, marbled meridian that was the cosmic axis of the Forbidden City, and at the focus of alignments of gateways: a set of lines radiating out towards all corners of the empire. The *Ard ri*, High King, of pagan Celtic Ireland, was inaugurated on the Hill of Tara, from which five roads radiated.

The sense of ruling literally with lines has passed on into relatively recent times, as an unconscious impulse of this old concept. Louis XIV of seventeenth-century France, also a 'sun king' and also a healing monarch, had an array of straight pathways radiating out from his palace at Versailles. We see this also in country houses laid out with radiating lines cutting through their surrounding estates, and Buckingham Palace of course, has the straight, ceremonial way of the Mall running out from it.

So it seems possible that ritual and ceremonial straightness, marked by processions, ritual walking, boundary setting, straight ceremonial ways and landscape lines may in a few societies have been outward signs of an invisible, linear kingly force; symbolic of mystical rule. This image certainly accommodates the ambiguities in *reg-*.

But why did the idea of the king's power as radiating out through metaphysical lines to all parts of the kingdom arise? I suspect we can understand it only by considering it as *spirit*, which means we have to reach back further into the evolutionary complex that has developed around concepts relating to the sanctity of the straight.

CHAPTER 5

SPIRIT LINES

In Chapter 2 we discussed the British Neolithic linear earthworks called cursuses and learned how they related to the long barrows, mounds whose function was at least partly related to rituals of the dead (though burials in them do not seem to have been universal). When commenting on the Dorset Cursus, R.J.C. Atkinson remarked that this association with long barrows 'can hardly be fortuitous' and suggested that the cursus must in some way have been connected 'with practices intended to ensure that the benign influence of the dead was transmitted... to the living users of the cursus'.[1] Richard Bradley observed that the 'deliberate alignments' of the Dorset Cursus 'emphasise *monuments*' and that the line of the cursus 'reinforces the distribution of long barrows' which clearly held 'extraordinary importance' for the cursus builders. The nature of the relationship convinced Bradley that the cursus has 'funerary symbolism', that it was 'a British Avenue of the Dead'. The deliberate alignments of the cursus were onto the mounds — 'it is the alignment that matters... and that alignment was meant to connect a whole series of monuments to the dead', Bradley has written.[2]

We will note this association of linearity and death recurring in many of the other examples given below. We are looking at a *spatial expression of a relationship with the dead — and, more precisely, with the ancestors*. That expression must have been based on some concept to do with the *spirits* of the dead, a concept, I suggest, that for some reason involves linking spirits with straightness. Dead straight.

We find the connection again at a ritual complex just outside

Godmanchester, near Cambridge, England. Archaeologists conducting rescue work at a site threatened with gravel extraction uncovered a trapezoid earthwork covering seven hectares and containing the holes for 24 wooden posts. Analysis has revealed startling astronomical alignments in this arrangement. The earthwork as a whole is astride the equinox line, and it opens to what the Celts would have called the Beltaine/Lughnassadh sunrise direction, the key agricultural festivals of early May and August. These orientations, together with alignments between certain of the poles, encompass all twelve major events in the solar and lunar cycles. The site, dated to around 3000 BC, is considered to be the most elaborate astronomical temple in western Europe, considerably more sophisticated than Stonehenge. But it was not simply some early observatory: ancient astronomy was never used in a scientific way in the manner we would think of: it was part of ceremonial life and a cosmological worldview. The Godmanchester site was certainly a temple: on either side of the entrance were buried the skull and jaw bones of an ox; ox-bones were found under one of the wooden posts, and a deer's antler was under another. Just outside the western corner of the complex was a dismembered human skeleton, apparently contemporaneous with the site's use. Some of the posts were more massive than others, and not all were involved with astronomical sightlines. The most massive post was on the western end of the sacred enclosure, and was the site's focal point. A line from it to another thick post in the centre of the entrance gave the Beltane/Lughnassadh sunrise alignment.

The site seems to have been deliberately destroyed after decades of use: the earthen banks were levelled and the posts individually burnt, except the focal pillar which remained. Then something very interesting happened, as David Keys explains:

> Very soon after the Godmanchester site had been ritually decommissioned, its destroyers appear to have built a great religious monument — an avenue, 90 metres wide, flanked by a bank and ditches on either side. This avenue, perhaps a sort of processional way, was up to 3 kilometres long and may have been

funerary in function. There are a number of graves exactly midway between the sides of the avenue, and similar avenues in other parts of Britain are thought to have been used for funeral rituals.[3]

The southern flank of the avenue, a cursus, was aligned to the focal point pillar and also marked the Beltane/Lughnassadh sunrise alignment. Like the temple complex, the cursus was ritually destroyed after a time. The massive post seems to have survived this too, and the site was used by the later Bronze Age societies and seems to have been respected even until Romano-British times.

A relationship with the ancestors may have been indicated at the Hill of Tara, the Irish kingship site referred to in the previous chapter, where archaeologists have found a cursus-like earthwork: 'a long sunken area resembling a Greek stadium in shape — seems to be a ritual roadway leading directly to the passage-tomb there known as the Mound of the Hostages'.[4]

As clear an association with straight lines and the dead as one could expect to find has been researched by John Palmer and presented in a series of papers in *The Ley Hunter*. He brought to general attention the existence of medieval 'deathroads' *(Doodwegen)* in Holland. These old roads had a prescribed width, and were inspected annually by surveyors and travelling magistrates. Dead straight, they converged on cemeteries. Examples of old *doodwegen* occur on Westerheide (heath) between Laren and Hilversum, North Holland. Palmer writes:

> These are absolutely straight roads... The heath is riddled with Neolithic and Bronze Age barrows, where is located the old Postroad, and three 'doodwegen'... Regularly spaced, these roads, thought to date from medieval times or earlier (their exact age is unknown) form a triangle which converges at the isolated St Janskerhof (St John's cemetery) precisely at the point where is the chapel.
> The burial area is located upon raised ground. The present chapel is not of ancient date but this may have replaced an earlier one (not checked) and the cemetery is still in use.[5]

Palmer found that the deathroads were also called *Iykwegen*, 'corpse road', or *spokenwegen*, 'ghost road'. As he observes,

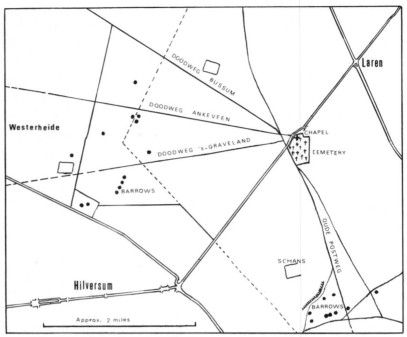

Figure 35. Straight 'deathroads' (doodwegen) near Hilversum. (John Palmer)

spokenwegen 'would tie in well with the "spirit path" idea for leys'.[6] Further, Palmer discovered that there had been a Dutch law which forbade the carriage of corpses to burial by other than the straight doodwegen. A formal undertaking by community leaders that the deathroads would be upkept was known as the Oath Formula, and this stressed the straight carriage of the dead.[7]

A Dutch landscape association between straightness, death and kingship has also been noted by Palmer. A *Koninsweg*, 'Royal Route', passes near a ruined dolmen on the Noordse Velde, which is studded with prehistoric barrows (mounds). Only a fragment is now visible in aerial photographs, but it relates to early archaeological investigations of a straight track across the heath, and it is known that Koninswegen were originally straight.

Ancestors, the dead, also figure in Amerindian straight lines, we noted in Chapter 3: the Cuzco *ceques* were multifunctional,

124

but one of the key elements was that they related to water locations, because the Inca people 'receive, by right of birth, the underground water directly from their ancestors who are believed to reside within the earth'.[8]

No one knows for sure the intended functions of the Nazca lines, but we noted that researchers suspected that they were probably closely related to those of the *ceques*, as similar themes appear to have run through the whole mentality of pan-Andean peoples. Certainly some of the Nazca lines seemed associated with water, and so possibly with some similar kinship-ancestor association. It is also the case that at least one line centre was built alongside an ancient cemetery (Pacheco) on the Nazca pampa, and isolated trapezoidal markings on the desert near Cerro Soldado in the Ica valley have their north ends terminating at a cemetery. This is not a recurring pattern, but it is difficult to obtain such clear-cut repetitive evidence when dealing with complex, multi-function features like these lines.

The lines of the Bolivian altiplano occur in the country of the Aymara Indians, and the possible vestige of a link between paths and spirits survives in one of their folk-healing traditions, as can be seen in this description by anthropologist Weston La Barre: 'Aymara Indians project disease spirits into objects they leave at a path crossing, there to be caught and carried out of the vicinity by the next passer-by'.[9] (It is perhaps worth noting the vaguely reminiscent tradition in the Celtic world that the meeting or parting of ways were supposed to have special supernatural properties, where access to the spirit world could be more readily achieved than at most other places.)

That spirit is associated specifically with straight lines in the northern Amerindian mind, at least, seems to be indicated by the layout of the sweat lodge. The lodge itself is supposed to house the spirits of all living things; a hollow scooped out of the ground in the centre of the lodge floor, designed to accommodate the hot stones, represents 'the centre of the world' (the world navel or omphalos concept again). During the sweat ceremony, the Great Spirit will inhabit the pit which will also accommodate the spirit of a beloved, dead relative who has returned to earth. The soil taken from the hole is formed into a straight ridge 'a path for the spirits' on the ground outside the lodge.[10] A mound is built at the end of the earthen line, and, a little further out from the sweat lodge but on the line of the spirit path, the ritual fire for heating the stones is made. Clearly, all the spirit/line elements are there in this miniature ceremonial arrangement. This consciousness is also detectable in the ceremonial layout within tipis used for the ritual ingestion of the hallucinogenic cactus, peyote. In the standard Kiowa layout, for instance, an alignment of bowls containing meat, fruit, corn and water lead from the doorway to the central fire, behind which are earthen crescents and an altar cloth all centred on the axial line through the tipi.[11] A similar vestige survived in a straight 'Peyote Road', representing Christ's ascent from His grave to the Moon, which provided the key axis in various peyote altar layouts associated with the Ghost Dance, a Native American eschatological movement of the latter decades of the nineteenth century.[12]

There is some evidence, such as the current use of the old straight Bolivian lines by altiplano Indians as observed by Johan Reinhard,[13] that lines can be addressed to locations in the landscape, such as mountain peaks, where a spirit or local deity dwells (again, this is also often associated with water). So some Amerindian lines may relate to nature spirits in addition to other functions.

Back in the Old World, in the parish of Laassa, Uppland, in Sweden, to be exact, archaeologists uncovered a straight, ceremonial Viking road.[14] It runs virtually due south to a glacial esker 200 feet (60 metres) high which has Bronze Age cairns on its summit. This site is known as 'Rösaring' from the earlier 'Röraring', meaning cairn ring. Examination of this three- to four-feet-wide (3.5m) 'cult road' shows it to have been edged by pebbles with its surface formed by smoothed clay brought from elsewhere. Small pits line the eastern edge of the road. A small mound at the northern end of the road revealed a rectangular setting of stones containing two postholes, an arrangement which was interpreted as the remains of a 'death

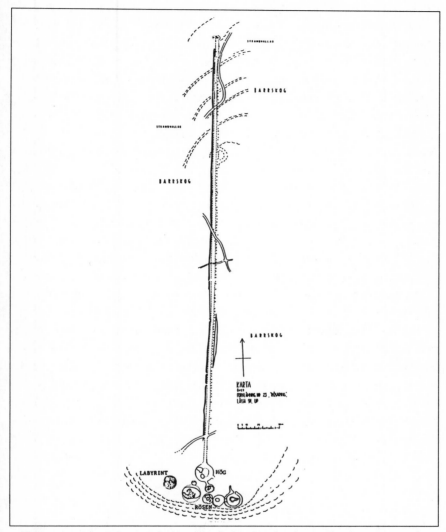

Figure 36. The Rösaring 'cult road'. (John Kraft after L. Löthman and G. Winberg. Courtesy Caerdroia magazine)

house'. Radiocarbon dating of road surface samples gave a date in the ninth century AD, and phosphate analysis indicated that dung had been dropped at various points along the road, perhaps by an animal pulling a cart. The investigators reconstructed a scene in which the chieftain's body was deposited in the 'death house' (possibly a form of ancient Scandinavian shrine called a *Horgr*, or the Celtic sacred enclosure, *Wih*) while a funerary ritual took place prior to it being drawn by a ceremonial wagon along the road to the large mound, and there interred. Elements of this procedure survived into medieval funerary practices in Sweden, in fact, and several ceremonial wagons have been found in archaeological digs in the Indo–European world.

At Rösaring, we again see the link between straightness and death, which, as I am suggesting, is essentially to do with concepts relating to the spirit(s) of the deceased. (For confirmation see Additional Notes, pp230-1.) This shows up here not only with the ritual procession and death road for the dead Viking chieftain, but also with the presence of burial mounds from the much earlier Bronze Age, once more possibly indicating a link with the spirits of the long-dead ancestors.

An interesting special feature at Rösaring is the presence of a stone labyrinth design built amongst the Bronze Age cairns. This has not been dated, and one can only wonder at its relationship with the overall arrangement of the site. Perhaps the labyrinthine coils could have acted, in clear distinction to the straight cult road, as a sort of *binding device* to prevent the spirits of the interred bodies from leaving? There are, in fact, strong hints that this was so. Hundreds of stone labyrinths exist around the shores of the Baltic, dating variously from perhaps

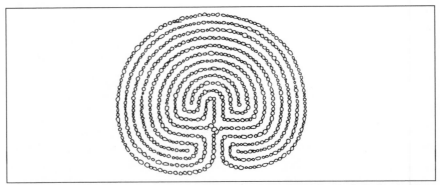

Figure 37. The stone labyrinth at Visby, on the Baltic island of Gotland. (S. Granlund)

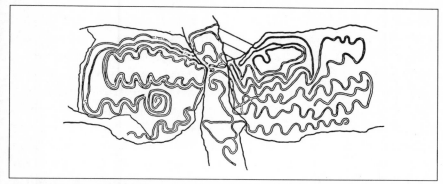

Figure 38. The labyrinthine meander pattern incised on a standing stone at the Neolithic site of Bryn Celli Ddu, Anglesey. (W. J. Hemp)

as early as the Bronze Age up to medieval times. One piece of folklore associated with these features was that before a fisherman set out to sea he would enter a labyrinth so that any trolls or bothersome sprites would follow him in and find themselves ensnared and thus unable to escape in time to board the fisherman's boat! This basic idea may go back a very long way. At the Neolithic chambered cairn of Bryn Celli Ddu on Anglesey, Wales, a meander pattern (morphically associated with the labyrinth design) was engraved on a standing stone. W.F.J. Knight argued that this pattern may have been to provide ritual protection for the sacred dead at the site, and also to prevent their spirits wandering: 'the dead were to rest, and . . . they were to let the living rest, also . . . the maze form habitually implies correlative notions of exclusion and conditional penetration. Deduction then offers us the inference that the same notions, however inchoate and confused, actuated megalithic man'. Knight remarked on the labyrinthine ritual dance of horsemen, sometimes conducted around tombs during funerals in ancient Greece. In studying the ancient Greek names of a similar horse dance, the Troia, common in ancient Italy, Knight discovered that the horse was important to its function, and also 'that it was connected with some supernatural relevance . . . something which would be expressed today by reference to the possession of *mana* . . .'.[15]

This idea of convoluted lines hampering spirit travel, the antithesis of the straight line facilitating it, is deeply embedded in northern European lore. Nigel Pennick describes a number of 'spirit traps' and 'witch bottles' of ancient country lore in his *Practical Magic in the Northern Tradition* (1989). Spirit traps were made with red thread. One design involved the fitting of a copper loop to a blackthorn stave. Red thread was twined around the copper circle in a radial pattern, except for a gap where a metal, preferably silver, *Dag* rune was fitted. 'Once made, the spirit trap is set up... on the pathway or spirit track... which the sprites will take to cause their disruption, for example, between a cemetery and a house....'.[16] Some witch bottles used the same basic principle, being filled with a tangle of lengths of thread to hold fast any intrusive sprite. It was also a tradition sometimes to place a kind of 'cat's cradle' of red thread on the chest of a recently-deceased person to stop the soul from wandering (Nigel Pennick, personal communication). There was, in fact, a great deal of lore relating to the use of knots to protect against spirits. In *The Golden Bough* Frazier records a tradition in Russia in which a fishing net was thrown over a bride dressing for her wedding to prevent any harmful influences from malevolent sorcery. 'But often,' Frazier wrote, 'a Russian amulet is merely a knotted thread.' A woman taken for burning as a witch in St Andrews, Scotland, in 1572, wore many strings and knots as a collar piece, and was greatly distressed when it was removed. She had felt that she could not die, *that is, her spirit could not leave her body*, as long as she wore it.

The Rösaring situation curiously echoes much more elaborate arrangements at the Imperial tombs near Beijing in China. These mounded tombs (*ling*) are situated in the valley of Shisan ling, selected for its purpose in 1409 AD. A necropolis some five by three kilometres in area, bounded by mountains to the north, contains mounds, walls, roads, triumphal arches and subterranean burial chambers of the emperors and their wives. The tombs occur in individual complexes through the valley. Each is comprised of the actual tomb — elaborate stone chambers covered by an earthen mound — situated at the end of a series of courts and pavilions, all arranged along a straight central axis. Entrance to the valley as a whole is marked by the Pailou, a massive stone triumphal arch. A straight road a kilometre long extends from that to the Great Red Gate, set into the surrounding wall of the necropolis. Here even the reigning emperor was obliged to dismount and walk. The straight road continues to the Great Stele Pavilion, which marks the commencement of the Spirit Way:

> Here, stone sculptures of guardian animals — mythical and real — civil and military officials and beacons flank the roadway for 1100 metres, guiding the spirit to its resting place. At this point, the Dragon and Phoenix Gate stands full square across the road, in order to deflect malevolent spirits which can only fly in straight lines. The first tomb is another four kilometres away.[17]

The key elements in the Imperial tomb architecture, including spirit ways, are to be found in the much earlier tombs of the Han period (206 BC – AD 221). There is also no doubt that the early Chinese religious traditions, such as Taoism, had shamanic antecedents.

Feng shui geomancy was certainly involved with the laying out of the Imperial tombs, only here we can see not only the obligatory spirit baffle of the Dragon and Phoenix gate, and an almost imperceptible curve put in the Spirit Way, but also a use of straight roads to guide the dead emperor's spirit to the necropolis. This links to the observation made in the previous chapter that the emperor sat on the Golden Throne for matters of state, itself on or at the focus of straight lines within the Forbidden City. Clearly, the emperors could use straight lines, while the general populace were told to avoid them. There is a hidden element here that has not been fully addressed by those researching Chinese geomancy.

Feng shui also relates to the dead and spirits. As one of the earliest commentators on Feng shui, the Reverend E.J. Eitel, commented: 'The leading principles of Feng-shui have their roots in remote antiquity, and it would not be an exaggeration to say that, though indeed modern Feng-shui was not a distinct branch of study or a separate profession before the Sung dynasty (AD 960–1126), yet the history . . . of Feng-shui is the history of Chinese philosophy. The deepest root of the Feng-shui system grew out of . . . veneration of the spirits of the ancestors . . .'.[18]

The matter of straight lines in Feng shui seems somewhat confused the more one studies the various interpretations and commentaries on the system. The idea of *ch'i*, the cosmic breath, has been turned into energy concepts by modern interpreters, a process that began with the Victorian commentators. For example, W.E. Geil thought of the 'dragon pulse' as 'meaning the magnetic currents' and E.J. Eitel referred to the Feng shui perception of terrestrial *ch'i* thus: 'there are in the earth's crust two different, *shall I say* magnetic, currents . . .'. (My emphasis.) These kinds of Victorian analogies have been very influential, as noted in Chapter 1, having been picked up on, quoted and embellished time and again by today's Earth Mysteries writers and 'energy dowsers', and have helped fuel the current juggernaut of 'energy leys' fallacies. In fact, the *ch'i* energies of the earth were regarded by the ancient Chinese as anything but straight. However, according to the system, certain topographical, meteorological and astrological factors could produce a bad form of cosmic breath, *sha ch'i*, and it was this that was thought to flow along anything straight in the landscape. Straight line features could also drain off positive *ch'i* if it ran across the frontage of a site. So a tomb or house affected by a straight line (a road, fence, ridge, row of trees, etc.) was likely to receive unfortunate influences. But did the root of this belief lie in concepts to do with 'energy' or with spirits?

The whole matter is ambiguous, as this quote from geomantic scholar Stephen Skinner demonstrates: 'Sharp bends, like straight lines, are unfavourable, as they act like "secret arrows" directing demons to the site *or* destroying or removing ch'i accumulations'.[19] (My emphasis.) The spirit interpretation is further strengthened by the surrounding context of Feng shui history and practice. Evelyn Lip recounts how a legendary giant blossom tree was haunted by evil spirits

132

who were conquered by the good spirits Shen Shu and Yu Lei. 'Since then,' Lip reports, 'people have painted the portraits of these good spirits on their main doors to ward off evil influences . . .'.[20] Such 'door gods', special mirrors, charms and other devices become regular tools to *frighten off the spirits* brought to the door by straight lines. Similarly, Indonesian temples have low walls inside their main entrances to bar the way to straight-line spirits which might otherwise penetrate into the holy of holies. This kind of standard Feng shui practice surely reveals an understanding that the cargo of the 'secret arrows' was of a spirit nature rather than 'energy' as such. Furthermore, we must always remember that Feng shui originates in ancestor worship, and, somewhat like the Inca system, with kinship too. *Feng shui was always to do with spirits*: the sinuous, indeed randomised, energies of the earth were studied in order to find auspicious spots for the tombs of dead relatives — ancestors — so that they might look with favour on their descendents. We must also be aware that tremendous socio-cultural accretions have built up in the Feng shui system over the centuries, and much of what is taken naively now as essential geomantic truth relates, in fact, to such mundane matters as taxation systems in medieval China![21] Furthermore, Taoism informed the early principles of Feng shui, and as Taoism evolved out of archaic shamanism, this undoubtedly provided a route for shamanic concepts to enter Feng shui practice. (The importance of the shamanic connection will become more obvious as we proceed.)

Feng shui lines are surviving conceptual lines rather than physical ones. Another type of conceptual line was the Irish 'fairy path', and this still survives to a limited extent. The tradition was that the fairies travelled along invisible straight paths between 'raths', prehistoric earthworks considered to be 'fairy castles'. It was thought unwise to build anything on the course of such a path. Dermot Mac Manus gives a well-known case of one man, a Paddy Baine, who carelessly built his croft on a fairy path. He suffered bad luck and experienced poltergeists. The local wise-woman, who could 'see' fairies, told Paddy that the corner of his dwelling was obstructing a fairy path and that he had better do something about it if he wanted peace and quiet. With unarguable Irish logic he did — he chopped off the corner of his cottage, and Mac Manus presents a photograph of the place after its alteration![22]

Fairy paths are invisible spirit paths, and W. Evans Wentz showed how 'ancestral spirits play a leading part in the fairy-belief',[23] revealing that deep-seated link with the dead yet again.

Another connection between paths and nature spirits occurred in Siberia. When reindeer-herder groups like the Chukchee took the hallucinogenic Fly Agaric mushroom (*Amanita muscaria* — see next chapter) they saw the mushroom spirits in their visions. These 'mushroom men' followed special paths and particularly liked to visit places where the dead were — the dead-line link again. The Yurk Samoyed peoples also saw the mushroom spirits during Fly Agaric intoxication. These creatures 'ran away along the path which the sun travels after it has set in the evening'.[24]

Finally, there is a curious example of linkage between spirit and lines in Australian Aboriginal native healing tradition, and which again involves a thread as a 'line'. Marlene Dobkin de Rios cites the case of an anthropologist's aboriginal informant who used the word 'trance':

> ...to refer to the filaments secreted by an insect which are joined to the native healer to form a long string which is attached to the patient, and then to a nearby tree. This provides a track over which the patient's departed spirit can return.[25]

This strangely echoes an element in the seance of the Siberian Tungus shaman, where poles were brought into the ritual *wigwan* and poked through the smoke hole. A long cord connected these poles with ceremonial objects displayed outside the tent. This cord was 'the "road" for the spirits'.[26] The Tungus of Manchuria similarly used cords during shamanic initiation. Red cords made from silk or even animal sinew were attached to three special trees and brought to where the shamanic candidate sat during the three-day ordeal. The cords were to provide 'roads', Eliade tells us, for spirits to come down from the trees to the initiate so they could whisper their secrets in his ear.

Enough has been presented in this chapter, hopefully, to enable us to discern that the underlying theme of ancient lines, whether physically surviving as landscape markings in symbolic landscapes, as threads or cords in ceremonial and healing arrangements, or conceptually present in the archaic mental landscapes of folklore and cultural traditions, is that of *spirit* in one form or another: the king's spirit, power or *mana*; spirits of the sick or the dead; spirits of the ancestors, or nature spirits. The old lines, leys, paths, alignments, ways and tracks are surely *spirit lines* — but the problem still remains as to why straightness and spirit(s) should be associated. To understand that, we have to peel away one last layer of the onion, so to speak; our journey back through the multifarious evolutions of the ceremonial, ritual straight line is not yet complete. Underlying the concept of spirit and straightness, the curious two-fold concept enshrined in the Proto-Indo–European *reg-*, is a deep, universal experience yielded by the human central nervous system, and lodged equally deeply in the past in the form of shamanic and related practices which left their mark on the land.

CHAPTER 6

TRANCE, DANCE AND MAGIC PLANTS

It is difficult for us, in our secularised culture, to appreciate the strong drive felt by most archaic and traditional peoples to access supernatural realms, to experience altered states of consciousness. So, bound by the perspectives of our peculiar Western lifeway, we have to make a special effort to try to understand the need for *trance*, particularly shamanic trance, in other kinds of societies, present and past.

Techniques of ecstasy

The word 'trance' derives from the Latin *transistus*, 'a passage', itself from *transire*, 'to pass over'. Trance is thus literally an *entrance* — to another world. Traditional techniques devised to produce trance have been legion: painful or fearful initiations or self-mutilations inducing psychological stress and physiological chemical changes in the body; drumming; singing and chanting; dancing; sensory and social deprivation; lack of sleep and general fatigue; lack of food; modification of breathing; drugs; exposure to extremes of heat or cold; single-point concentration; meditation; shock; the use of ritual sex, and doubtlessly many more approaches. A brief survey of some of these archaic techniques will suffice to show the variety of methods and the universal need that was felt (and still is in some cases) to access the Otherworlds in older cultures than our own.

The shamanic initiate of Australian aboriginal traditions could have a tough time. He might be rolled in the embers of a fire, have a tooth knocked out, or have quartz crystals pressed into a flesh wound or beneath his fingernails. In some initiation rituals candidates were laid out in the heat of the sun for long periods and had stinging insects sprinkled over them for good measure. An old anthropological photograph of one of these initiations shows about half of a group of approximately twenty candidates with a white stick by their heads, denoting that they had died.

Things could be just as rough in the Eskimo's (Innuit's) world, too. For example, the Caribou Eskimo woman shaman, Kinalik, was tied to a post out in the bitter Arctic weather for five days. At the end of that time she was shot! The gun was loaded with a small pebble rather than a bullet, however, and she was 'only' knocked unconscious. She experienced a death–rebirth experience and acquired her shamanic powers. In a more generalised way, the habitat of the Eskimo can encourage the altered state of consciousness known as 'Arctic hysteria' or *kayakangst*. When hunting or out on a *vision quest*, the Eskimo alone in his kayak for extended periods in a featureless sea can begin to hallucinate, especially experiencing apparent changes in body image (getting larger or smaller, disappearing, etc.). Disorientation and perhaps a meeting with a supernatural entity can also be experienced.

The vision quest is a common theme of shamanic initiatory ordeal, and its main themes are social deprivation, lack of food and sleep and psychological stress. In Tibetan *chöd*, the candidate has to go to a remote, wild place — preferably to a location where violent death has occurred. The vision quest, as described here by anthropologist Weston La Barre, is a major plank of Amerindian and Siberian shamanism:

> Usually about the time of puberty, the individual goes alone to some remote place where he fasts and struggles to stay awake for four days and four nights. During this time he may receive an hallucinatory 'vision' that gives him great medicine-power, embodied in his medicine bundle, collected on the same vigil. So important is this vision that it may give direction, normal or pathological, for the rest of his life. The shamanic vision quest is so

ubiquitous and ancient in Eurasia and the Americas that it is evidently of at least Mesolithic cultural horizons.[1]

Drumming is a key technique in promoting trance, particularly in Amerindian and Eurasian shamanism. The shaman's drum was a specialised instrument. Typically, it was oval in shape, covered by reindeer, horse or other animal hide; its wooden frame was, traditionally, formed from a branch of the World Tree. Marked with magical and protective symbols, the instrument was the shaman's vehicle or steed which took him to the World Axis where he could cross the threshold into the Otherworlds. Michael Harner cites research which indicates that certain drum rhythms can affect brainwave patterns in the listener, possibly helping promote altered states of consciousness.[2] When the shaman collapsed in trance, he would have his drum placed on his back by a helper as a sign that he must not be disturbed (which could be dangerous) during his 'journey' to the spirit worlds. The Tungus shaman drummed himself into ecstasy then collapsed onto a reindeer skin: 'he has descended into the Kingdom of Shadows "through the drum as through a lake".'[3] In certain Eurasian tribes, the drum was called the 'canoe' and 'a shaman in trance is said to sink'.[4]

Along with the drumming, singing and chanting is a powerful mind-altering tool:

> Dark night, with a flickering fire, is the best time for ritual. The long ecstatic drumming and singing of the ecstatic Siberian shaman, his uncanny replication of the bird calls of his attendant spirits, ventriloquism of voice against the reverberant taut cone of the skin tent, magic shaking of the tent itself, loss of sleep, shamanic calls, and repetitive response by participants — all these induce an empathic half-hypnosis of the whole group. It has been suggested that music itself began in the singing of shamans, who wanted a special language other than speech with which to address the supernaturals. Music is the *sine qua non* of ritual... Pronounced rhythm in song and dance, especially in crowd situations, may constitute sensory overload, hence induce an altered state of consciousness.[5]

The flicker of a fire can also promote particular brainwave rhythms, conducive to the onset of trance states. Certain

138

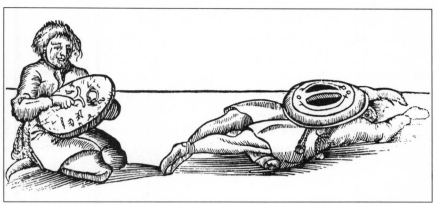

Figure 39. Two Lapp shamans. The one with his drum on his back is 'journeying' in the spirit world. (J. Schefferus, 1673)

hallucinogens (see below) seem to produce specific responses to sounds like shamanic drumming and singing.[6] Chanting and singing, apart from the sound component, also, of course, affect breathing rhythms.

Trance dancing is another major technique. Long, repetitive movement is a powerful promoter of altered states of mind, especially when coupled with rhythmic sound, light flicker, fatigue, chanting, and, perhaps, the ingestion of hallucinogens. In Bali, trance dancing is presented as a stylised drama, in which myths are acted out. The *balian* or shaman of the Batak pygmies of Malaysia uses dance as the chief means of entering trance. The old emperors of China knew dance steps that related to 'the dances that induce trance in the sorcerers . . . The ecstatic dance forms part of the procedures for acquiring a power of command over men and nature.'[7] The Buryat shamans of Asia conducted their trance dances astride a horse-headed stick — another example of the steed image. The Tungus shamans of Manchuria carried out their trance dances in a tight space amidst many onlookers, wearing costumes carrying more than 30 pounds of iron ornaments. The nineteenth-century Amerindian Ghost Dance movement had a ritual which involved dancing continuously for five or six days in rings around a fire, but there was no drumming. The dancers went into trance through such activity, and spoke with the dead ancestors who promised them the salvation of the Amerindian peoples. Although a religion doomed to fail in its prophetic purpose, the Ghost Dance nevertheless did produce some authentic examples of shamanism.

Dancing was of course an important element in trance-producing rituals for many peoples, but perhaps the best preserved and studied case where it is the key factor in trance induction is that of the hunting–gathering !Kung (the exclamation mark denotes a glottal, click sound) of the Kalahari region of southern Africa. They have three main ritual dances — Giraffe Dance, Drum Dance and Trees Dance. The aim of the dances is to produce *kia*, an altered state of consciousness dependent on the welling up of *num*, a primordial life energy within the body and perceived as infusing all things in varying degrees. When awakened during the trance dance, the num rises up the spinal column, generating great heat. In this state the dancer can feel an overpowering urge to leap on a fire, or handle and walk on glowing embers. (The rising of num is, of course, remarkably similar to Indian concepts of *kundalini* energy rising up the spine.) Num resides at the base of the spine (also like kundalini) and in the pit of the stomach when not awakened. When num 'boils' and reaches the base of the skull, kia, trance, occurs.

One of the several supernormal abilities the dancer acquires during kia is the perception of disease. The dancer is healer and can see with X-ray vision into the bodies of ill people, perceive the disease (often in the form of spirits) and 'pull' it by sucking it out. This facility of X-ray vision during trance is often represented in shamanic art around the world, and is a characteristic effect of mind change. (I recall studying a flower during a highly altered state of consciousness, for example, and suddenly being able to 'see into' the plant, observing miniscule drops of water circulating through it.)

A large proportion of the !Kung population seek num, but there are naturally varied abilities — some exceptionally gifted healers rise far above the average. The main healing dance is the Giraffe Dance, at which both women and men help in the generation of num, but it is mainly the men who experience kia. In the Drum Dance, kia is mainly attained by women, but this dance is less frequent and the kia is not used for healing purposes.

In the Giraffe Dance, the women sit around a fire singing and clapping while the men circle around them, stomping in energetic motion. No special clothing is worn, but rattles are often attached to the men's calves to help add to the rhythmic sounds of the dance. A walking stick may be used to emphasise dance motions or to provide support as the dance wears on and fatigue sets in, for the dance goes on for many hours, usually at night. One old !Kung healer, Kinachau, explained the experience of num to anthropologist Richard Katz:

> You dance, dance, dance, dance. Then num lifts you up in your belly and lifts you in your back, and you start to shiver. Num makes you tremble; it's hot... when you get into kia, you're looking around because you see everything... Rapid shallow breathing draws num up. What I do in my upper body with my breathing, I also do in my legs with the dancing. You don't stomp harder, you just keep steady. Then num enters every part of your body, right to the tip of your feet and even your hair...
> ...When we enter kia, we are different from when our num is not boiling and small. We can do different things.[8]

The process of generating num is not entered into lightly, and fear of the rush of num is felt by all participants. As another healer, Kau Dwa, put it: 'As we enter kia, we fear death. We fear we may die and not come back!'

In the course of a dance, only a few men will enter kia, and at different times. The dancer's arms and legs will shake and tremble; the dancer may collapse or rush towards the fire. The whole process is well managed, with people on hand to support and look after the person entering kia. Experienced healers are able to stabilise their condition to some extent, and may conduct healing.

The !Kung speak of *num k'au* — 'owner of num'. The trance dancer, the shaman, activates his num. We may have here a version of the idea lodged within the *regs* complex we noted in proto-Indo–European society — the shamanic chieftain who led in straight lines, the charismatic leader, the king with *mana*.

Location

So we can see that a huge variety of techniques have been employed by people throughout time to alter their consciousness or 'enter the spirit world'. Yet one candidate never seems to be given much consideration by modern scholars of such matters — *geophysical*, environmental conditions. So active has human psychospiritual opportunism been in making use of any trance-inducing agent or action in any given environment, that it is difficult to believe that such possibilities were ignored. Harner comments that the Jivaro Indians of South America might retire to 'a cave, the top of a mountain, or a tall waterfall' in their quest for a guardian spirit.[9] Eliade records how the Aranda shamanic initiate of Central Australia goes to sleep in the mouth of a remote cave. The spirits come and carry him into the cavern's interior, where the Aranda's paradisical land is situated. The Greek legend of Epimenides recounts how he 'slept' and fasted for a long time in the cave of Zeus on Mount Ida in Crete. He emerged as a master of 'enthusiastic wisdom', or, as Eliade puts it, as a master of 'the technique of ecstasy'.[10] The point is, *location is not neutral to the undertakings of initiation*. Caves, mountain peaks and waterfalls are all places where natural ionisation occurs, and ionised air is known to have an effect on certain hormone levels in mammals, and hormones in turn can have noticeable effects on brain function and hence consciousness. Cave mouths tend to attract lightning owing to ionisation, and mountain peaks (for example in the Andes) can sometimes be seen with ionised glows around them — light phenomena have even been seen around the apex of the Great Pyramid.

Cave environments can also contain heightened levels of radon. During its work investigating the geophysical charac-

142

teristics of prehistoric sacred sites, the Dragon Project Trust has noted that areas of enhanced natural radioactivity seem able to trigger spontaneous or transient mind-change effects in certain people.[11] The project has also identified stone circles containing granite megaliths that have particularly active spots on them that emit constant streams of gamma radiation. Alberto Villoldo reports that the contemporary Peruvian shaman, Don Eduardo Calderon, teaches his students to place their spine or foreheads against certain ceremonial stones at Machu Picchu. This site is on geological faulting and the stones are granitic.[12] (Many other sacred places around the world are on or close to geological faulting, areas of the earth's crust where geomagnetic and other energy anomalies tend to exist.)

Magnetic anomalies, too, have been found at sacred sites. I have found that a claimed Indian 'power point' on Mount Tamalpais, San Francisco, has rocks that will dramatically disturb a compass needle. Stones in cardinal positions in British stone circles, or acting as outliers indicating astronomical alignments, have also been found to harbour magnetic material detectable by compass needle disturbance, while other stones have exhibited curious pulses of low-level magnetic change measurable by magnetometer.[13] A particularly interesting site that came to the attention of the Dragon Project is Carn Ingli, the Peak of Angels, in the Preseli hills of southwest Wales, where the bluestones of Stonehenge are said to have originated. This rugged summit has prehistoric stonework laced around it, and was used by the sixth-century Celtic anchorite and healer, St Brynach, as a place of meditation and fasting. He is said to have had visions of angels there. In 1986, a woman passing by the peak felt profound physiological discomfort which she identified with its proximity. Subsequent investigations revealed that at points on Carn Ingli compass needles can be reversed to point south instead of north. Magnetic fields are known to be able to affect parts of the brain such as the temporal lobes, which handle dream and memory functions. It is therefore possible that St Brynach's fasting and meditations were augmented by his geophysical environment.

143

This site also attracts odd light phenomena. Aurora-like ionised glows have been seen around the peak at night, and in the early years of this century, W. Evans Wentz collected reports of 'greenish' lightballs at the tiny village of Nevern, near the foot of Carn Ingli and where St Brynach had his cell. These were considered to be 'death candles' in local lore.[14] In March 1991, inhabitants of Nevern reported being plagued by half-metre-wide balls of light that seemed to take an inquisitive interest in them!

Such 'earth lights' are recorded by many traditional peoples. Sorte mountain in Venezuela, for instance, can produce lights near its peak at sunset. They are thought by contemporary shamans to be spirits, and to see them is a good sign that healing there will be effective.[15] To the Lapps, such strange lightforms were shamans having fights, while *min min* lights to some Aborigines and *eskuda'hit*, 'fire creatures', to the Penobscot Indians of Maine were shamans in flight. Hawaiian Islanders saw their *akualele* lights as spirits, and people in the Himalayan foothills were warned not to approach the lanterns of the *chota admis*, 'little men'. These kinds of strange light phenomena have been noted by peoples throughout the world from the remotest times. There are even ethnological records of shamans deriving their powers from encounters with such lights.[16] Modern research associates the lights with fault zones, areas of mineral deposits and geological stress, but their exotic nature and essential mystery remain.[17] There is also a suspicion that because of energy fields surrounding them or occurring in association with them, close encounters with such lights can cause altered states of consciousness and periods of amnesia.[18]

It may thus have been that such lightforms were yet another environmental factor sought for trance-induction. Certainly, as I catalogue in *Places of Power* and *Earth Lights Revelation*, reports of lights playing lazily around old sacred places are well documented. In India and China, at least, temples have been purposefully constructed at locations where earth lights are regularly seen.

Hallucinogens

Physiology, meteorology, geology, geophysics — anything and everything was pressed into the service of trance-induction. And nothing more so than botany. It seems that in their long probing for ways into the Otherworld, human beings have identified every plant, fungus, leaf, bark, vine and root that can produce trance states.

It is difficult nowadays to discuss sensibly the enlightening use of drugs. Our culture so immediately associates the word with dangerous practice, degradation and anti-social behaviour that it is almost impossible for us to comprehend that earlier and traditional societies used (and use) certain types of plant-derived drugs as sacraments in rituals which helped to reinforce the psychological wholeness of their people. We have to try to put aside our prejudices if we are to see the undoubtedly positive effects hallucinogenic plants have had on earlier societies, and on the development of art and language as a whole. It is a role that is only just now beginning to dawn fully on anthropologists. As Marlene Dobkin de Rios says:

> Recent re-evaluations of the roles of mind-altering plants in non-Western society have shown that their impact was much greater than has been generally imagined...

A Czech scholar, Pokorny, has argued that plant hallucinogens are the key to understanding the stylizations and ornaments in palaeolithic art from Prodmosti, Avjejeve and Mozin in Czechoslovakia...

Plant hallucinogens may even have played an important role in the evolution of *Homo sapiens* as a species. Some of the psychotropic plants that were experimented with from early times might have stimulated language and communications about the unusual perceptions of reality that followed their ingestion. Hunters and gatherers, rather than farmers, were probably the first to learn about hallucinogenic plants.[19]

Experiments have shown that animals will seek repeated contact with hallucinogens in their environment, so we might suppose that human beings were no less responsive. In fact, it may have been the behaviour of animals that showed ancient hunter-gatherers the properties of hallucinogenic plants. (This may even have provided a formative influence in ideas like totemism and a shaman's animal familiars.) Although we can conduct only a lightning, sample survey in these pages, it will be enough to show how widespread, ancient and deep-rooted the use of hallucinogens has been in the world and their great significance to even our own cultural history.

If we first come 'out of Africa', we can visit the !Kung once more. Although the trance dance is their key form of trance induction, Katz was informed that they also sometimes used marijuana (cannabis) 'if a fellow fails to find kia'. However, one can only kia on it if one has experienced kia before, otherwise the drug would simply 'make his thoughts whirl like being drunk'. The marijuana would be smoked in conjunction with dance. Certain herbs, 'strong in num', are often imbibed during trance dancing. Katz was also told about a root which the !Kung call *gaise noru noru*. Knowledge of its preparation was known in the 'old days', but the !Kung were rather ambiguous about whether its proper usage was known now. The root was for teaching about kia rather than as substitute for the trance dance.[20] La Barre claims the Bushmen also used *kwashi* bulbs as an hallucinogen.[21]

The euphoriant and hallucinogen *kanna* was chewed or smoked by the Hottentot; and there seems to have been ancient usage of a psychotropic plant throughout eastern and north-eastern Africa which has come down to us through ancient Egyptian records as *khat*, 'the shrub' or 'the tree'. 'Indeed, the fame of *khat* passes straight across Africa to Angola where, in the Lunyaneka language, it is known as *otyibota*', writes Charles Musès.[22] In Zaire, the Fang use the hallucinogenic plant *Tabernathe iboga*. It used to be taken to ease fatigue and to sharpen senses as an aid in hunting, but is now used in the context of the Bwiti religion.[23] The Bantu also used this plant. Cannabis, as *dagga*, was used for magico-religious purposes in sub-Sahara Africa, and as *kif* it is used in Morocco.

Cannabis is hemp ('cannabis' gives us 'canvas') and was known as an intoxicant in addition to its uses for making fabric and ropes throughout the Indo–European world. La Barre has traced equivalents of the word cannabis in all Indo–European languages, from the *konoplya* of the Balkans and the *kannabis* of the Greeks to the *canaib* of the Irish.[24] The ancient Indo–European text, the *Atharva Veda*, refers to cannabis as the 'liberator from sin' and 'heavenly guide'. Herodotus tells us that after funeral rites the ancient Scythians, who lived on the northern side of the Black Sea (and thus within the scope of the supposed Indo–European heartland — see Chapter 4), threw hemp onto heated stones and inhaled the vapour. Eliade has noted that this practice coincided with Turko–Tartar shamanistic procedures. Cannibinol-containing parts of the hemp plant were found in a fifth-century BC (Iron Age) funerary urn at Wilmersdorf, suggesting the long narcotic use of cannabis.[25]

Poppy capsules have been found in Stone Age camps and lake dwellings in Switzerland, and the use of opium is mentioned in texts going back two millenia BC. A terracotta head from Knossos depicts a headdress made from poppy capsules, and the drug was known to the Mycenaeans also.

Possibly one of the most important Eurasian hallucinogens was the white-spotted, red-capped *Amanita muscaria* or Fly Agaric mushroom. The first written accounts of the use of this fungus were made in the seventeenth century, and the Chukchee, Koryak, Kamchadal and Yukagir Siberian tribes have been best documented. It is known that Siberian shamans often took the mushroom prior to entering their trance, but it was also used by ordinary members of a tribe for dream interpretation, divination and so on.[26] The taking of Fly Agaric could cause vomiting, and it was found by the reindeer herders that the urine of a person who had eaten one was also psychoactive and could be re-used without the unwanted side-effect. It seems that there could be four or five cycles of the urine before it lost its potency. 'Every Koryak man carries a vessel made of seal skin, which he suspends from his belt as a container to catch his own urine,' Dobkin de Rios informs.[27]

The reindeer-herders also made the bizarre discovery that runaway reindeer acquired a special longing for human urine when they ate lichens, and could be enticed back by pouring urine on soft snow! Reindeer under Fly Agaric intoxication stagger as if drunk — perhaps that was why Rudolph had a red nose...

The distinguished amateur mycologists (students of mushrooms), the late R. Gordon Wasson and his wife, considered that the use of *Amanita muscaria* went back perhaps 10000 years. The Wassons also seem to have solved the riddle of the ancient hallucinogenic drink, *soma*. La Barre writes:

> ...the long mysterious 'soma' of the *Rig Veda* was without question the major religious hallucinogen of ancient Eurasia and one, moreover, that has exerted an incalculable influence on later religions... once the Aryans entered India around 1500 BC, the identity of the plant, which does not grow south of the Himalayas, was lost and never rediscovered in Hinduism... In the *Rig Veda* only priests drank the ritually prepared soma, which conferred divinity on the Brahmanic 'living gods' much as in Greek legend the gods, originally shamans too, obtained immortality by imbibing odorous 'ambrosia' with 'nectar' (the latter probably pan-Indo–European mead, traces of whose use reach even as far back as mesolithic wall engravings).[28]

The word 'soma' is Indo–Iranian, but most scholars think that 'ambrosia', cognate with the Sanskrit 'amrita', is another term for the ancient soma. Wasson traced all the clues relating to the soma–ambrosia complex back to the Indo–European heartland, and found a curious linguistic link with Agni, the god of fire. Through a jungle of interconnections that cannot be addressed here, a development appeared, as La Barre explains: '...fire emerges from the mysterious striking of Promethean sparks from "thunderstones" (flints) into punk tinder; and a very old European tinder was *Fomes fomentarius*, a punk fungus discovered in quantities in the Mesolithic (Maglemosian) camp at Starr Carr in Yorkshire, where many objects of hunting magic were manufactured.'[29] The image of fire linked with light-giving celestial bodies, particularly the moon and sun, which in turn linked to the original high god of the Indo–Europeans, **diw*, 'the shining one', from which comes *deus*, *Zeus* and so on.

148

The thunderbolt from the sky god in European lore was equated with flint hand axes and arrow heads (of Palaeolithic origin) which were assumed to have been hurled from the sky. A related pattern in European lore was that toadstools are created by lightning bolts (both toads and fungi often appear after rain, and some toadskins are hallucinogenic). The Greeks referred to mushrooms as 'the food of the gods', and in early times they used the common European word for mushroom, *sp(h)ongos*. The Indo–European root for the fungus–punk–*sp(h)ongos* group of words is the exceptionally ancient **panx*, which in Siberia was used in words associated specifically with Fly Agaric, the fiery-red mushroom.

Further, the metaphors for soma in the *Rig Veda* have been found to match closely the botanical features of Fly Agaric.

We can also, perhaps, see another link between soma and the Fly Agaric mushroom. We noted in Chapter 4 that the Irish goddess of Sovereignty was equated with the Indian goddess Sri-Lakshmi, consort to Indra (a thunderbolt-wielding sky god), who 'verily drank the soma' from Sri-Lakshmi's lips. We saw that names of Irish queens associated with Sovereignty were 'Medb', etymologically linked to 'mead', and mead was ritually drunk during a king's inauguration or marriage to the land, to Sovereignty. Now, the Icelandic name for *Amanita muscaria*, Fly Agaric, is *berserkjasveppur*, reflecting its believed association with the Berserkers, the fierce Viking warriors who seem to have been martial shamans.[30] These wild men were the 'warriors of Odin', another sky god and 'the Terrible Sovereign and Great Magician'.[31] Odin, we have already noted, is the archetypal shaman: he rides his eight-legged horse Sliepnir, he hangs on the World Tree, he *drinks mead* and changes his form into animals and birds, he has spirit familiars, and can fly. The implication is that the Indo–European ritual mead was indeed ambrosia/nectar, was indeed soma, which involved Fly Agaric in its preparation. The marriage of kingship was indeed a resonant echo of archaic shamanism in Europe.

There has been speculation that the sacramental drink at the Mysteries of Eleusis in Greece, in which notaries like Plato took part, was prepared from ergot, an LSD-like parasite of rye.

Whatever, La Barre does not flinch from claiming that 'the whole thrust of Indo–European religion may well be (among religions at large) the rather specialized goal of obtaining immortality — through eating and drinking substances, some of which are undoubtedly ancient hallucinogens.'[32]

Although Christianity has pulled a veil across the ancient shamanic practices of Europe, and repressed much of the knowledge we might otherwise possess, the Old Religion still survived in rural contexts: paganism was never far beneath the surface. Ironically, it was the documentation produced during the Church's witch persecutions of the Middle Ages that threw a brief light on the hallucinogenic survivals present in European witchcraft of the time, Harner informs:

> Probably the single most important group of plants used by mankind to contact the supernatural belongs to the order Solanaceae (the potato family). Hallucinogenic members of this group are widespread in both the Old and New Worlds. Besides the potato, tomato, chile pepper, and tobacco, the family includes a great number of the species of the genus *Datura*, which are called by a variety of names, such as Jimson weed, devil's apple, thorn apple, mad apple, the devil's weed, Gabriel's trumpet, and angel's trumpet, and are all hallucinogenic. *Datura* has been used widely and apparently from ancient times in shamanism, witchcraft...
> Other hallucinogens in the potato family closely resembling *Datura* in their effects includes mandrake (*Mandragora*), henbane (*Hyoscyamus*), and belladonna, or deadly nightshade... Each of these plants contains varying quantities of atropine and the other closely related tropane alkaloids hyoscyamine and scopolamine, all of which have hallucinogenic effects. These alkaloids can be extremely dangerous...
> One outstanding feature of atropine is that it is absorbable even by the intact skin...[33]

Because of this characteristic, European witches were able to make hallucinogenic ointments, prepared from plants such as belladonna, mandrake and henbane, which they smeared on their bodies or applied with a feather or a broomstick (see next chapter) while intoning incantations. The Church chroniclers described such 'witches salves' or 'flying ointments' as greenish in colour. (The dangerous nature of these preparations is

150

exemplified by the case of the occult historian Karl Kiesewetter, who died while experimenting with witches salves.) Some witches travelled by flying basket, and smeared a basket as well as their bodies before getting in it.

The feeling in some trance states that one is turning into an animal, an experience shaped by whatever the belief system was that prevailed, may have contributed to the idea of lycanthropy, the belief that a human can turn into a wolf or other animal. (However, there may be other, more physical aspects to this belief as well.) This sensation was well described by the great psychologist William James in an account of a vision had by a friend who took cannabis. The person was lying on a sofa, watching a cascade of hallucinatory objects, when he happened to think of a fox:

> ... and instantly I was transformed into that animal. I would distinctly feel myself a fox, could see my long ears and bushy tail, and by a sort of introversion felt that my complete anatomy was that of a fox.

In one medieval report, seven (male and female) witches confessed to rubbing ointment on their bodies, then putting on wolfskins and going 'on all fours' and running 'about the country'.[34] Harner has pointed out that there were two types of witches' gatherings, the Sabbat and the Esbat. The latter was a physical, 'business' meeting, but the Sabbat, he suggests, was a magical, hallucinated gathering. The ritual and trance aspects had to be separated because solanaceous hallucinogens tend to be so strong one cannot function in the outside world while under their influence.[35] South American Indians have found the same problems, and use non-solanaceous hallucinogens for shamanic purposes.

Another common and powerful hallucinogen, various species of which grow in Europe as in many parts of the world, is the psilocybin mushroom; the 'Liberty Cap' being the best known. It is this type of mushroom that is commonly referred to as 'magic mushroom' today.

La Barre makes the interesting suggestion that Christian Europe's unusual hostility towards the consumption of hallucinogens could be because of 'the survival of the practice of using a number of the most powerful ones... from pagan times into European witchcraft'. At one time, Eliade considered the use of hallucinogens to be a sign of the degeneration of shamanic practice, but in 1973 moderated this view.[36]

The use of hallucinogens was a major factor in the lives of most Amerindian peoples, a characteristic that still survives to some extent, especially in South America. Harner points out that one reason for this is that 'the New World is unusually rich in hallucinogenic plants, a factor which undoubtedly facilitated their use by North American Indians, but especially by Middle and South American Indians.'[37] Both Harner and La Barre also point out that shamanism played a particularly important part in Amerindian societies: 'given their ancient vision quest and universal shamanism, perhaps Indians are *culturally programmed* to value, seek for, remember, and use any psychotropic plants, since these provided a manifest experience of the supernatural world'.[38] The prevalence of shamanism in the Americas gives the clue that the 'New World' may, in fact, harbour the best-surviving strands of the oldest form of religious experience. It seems to me that it is no accident that in the Americas we have the best examples of *relatively well-preserved surviving shamanic* practices and relatively well-preserved surviving straight *landscape lines* (Chapter 3). Safe for so long from the attentions of Christian Europe, the Americas kept intact archaic shamanic practices and *shamanic landscapes* for longer than anywhere else. This is the jewel of the Amerindian legacy.

This of course raises the question as to the origins of the Amerindian, a thorny topic but which seems to boil down, in some form or other, to the fact that the Amerindian came from Palaeolithic central Asia, home of 'classic' shamanism, crossing into the Americas by a former land bridge across the Bering Strait (though in South America there is controversial evidence of entry from the Pacific). Joseph Campbell had no doubts:

> As the glaciers retreated and forests from the south overgrew in Europe what had formerly been tundra, then grassland, the great

herds moved gradually northward and eastward, followed by their Palaeolithic hunters. The way of this dispersal is marked by four unmistakable trace-elements: (1) ceremonials associated with worship of the bear; (2) shamanic practices; (3) an art style, associated with shamanism, in which skeletal and other internal features appear, as if by X-ray; and (4) the Great Hunt with spear and spear-thrower (the atlatl). All four of these items can be followed into the Americas...

... In Central Asia, subsequently, there were important developments that never crossed the Bering Strait; likewise, in the Americas, local developments occurred that were never carried back to Asia; so that there has been through time and space a history of shamanic forms. Yet, in all essentials, the complex remains constant from Norway to Alaska and south to Tierra del Fuego.[39]

La Barre considers that the Amerindian use of hallucinogenics amounted to a 'New World narcotic complex', so rich is the range of such substances in the Americas. Ethnobotanists have estimated, indeed, that the New World has 80–100 botanical psychotropics and hallucinogens.

The use of hallucinogens probably goes back as long as there have been peoples in the Americas, but the archaeological evidence of hallucinogens in North America is currently to be found in southern Texas and northern Mexico. Frightful Cave, which shows human activity back to the eighth millenium BC, has yielded the highly hallucinogenic mescal bean (or 'red bean'), as has Fat Burro Cave which harboured humans at least as far back as 3000 BC.[40] (The mescal bean was valued by North American shamans right up to the nineteenth century.)

Evidence of another kind of early use of hallucinogens comes from the 1800-year-old Hopewell culture (Chapter 3), known for its geometric earthworks. This seems to have been a religious sphere of influence. Centred in the Ohio area, its impact and interactions extended widely. It was certainly a shamanic culture. At the Hopewellian necropolis known as the Mound City group at Chillicothe, Ohio, for instance, finds have included shapes cut out of mica and copper sheets that depict features like eagle claws and bird forms which were once attached to shamans' robes; a mask to slip over a shaman's head; many anthropomorphic and zoomorphic pipes, and a

Figure 40. This wooden effigy of a 'magic' mushroom, over a foot long, was found with the central burial in a mound at 'Mound City', Chillicothe, Ohio. The burial was covered with mica pieces, and was almost certainly that of a shaman.

copper-covered wooden effigy of a 'magic' mushroom over a foot long.

In the main, however, distribution of specific hallucinogens amongst Amerindians can only now be deduced by what documentation we have of the Indians who were found in the Americas from the time of the European settlers. (The first such piece of documentary evidence was by Columbus himself, in fact, who referred to a narcotic snuff used for spirit communication in the Caribbean area.)

The Plains Indians, ranging between the Rockies and the eastern woodlands, and south towards Mexico, used mescal bean (obtained by trade with western neighbours), Jimson weed (of the *Datura* genus, see above), known to some Indian groups as 'wysoccan', and highly concentrated forms of tobacco. *Datura* hallucinogens were also widely used by Indians in the American southwest and in California. Shamans of the Chumash of southern California, for instance, would take Jimson weed at midwinter, retire to a special cave and witness the entry of the rising sun's beams into the dark interior. Such Chumash caves were decorated with paintings of patterns and figures, which are taking on a new research significance as we

154

shall see in the next section. The Chumash also used mugwort, a hallucinogen used likewise in European witchcraft. The Miwok Indians of the California sierras used *Datura*, and they also laid the long, dead straight tracks mentioned in Chapter 3. The Hopi, Zuni and other Pueblo peoples, amongst many others, also used these hallucinogens. The lost Anasazi people who built the remarkable, straight 'Chaco roads' dissolved into these Pueblo tribes long before the arrival of white settlers.

The use of the mescaline-based hallucinogenic cactus *peyote* influenced Indians in the US southwest in historic times, but its origin lies with the pre-Hispanic Mexican Amerindians, notable amongst them the Huichol. (Pre-Hispanic landscapes also bear the straight-line marks of shamanism.) La Barre makes the point that 'peyote is historically associated with shamanism'.[41] The fierce, warlike ancient Aztecs also used peyote, along with hallucinogenic mushrooms (*teonanacatl*, 'god's flesh'), *Datura* species, and the LSD-like Morning Glory seeds (*ololiuqui*). Joan Halifax maintains that 'use of the sacred mushroom, fly agaric. . . was brought to the Americas by Siberian peoples long ago.'[42] She cites the example of a clay effigy dating to around AD 100 found at Nayarit, Mexico: it depicts a distinctly *Amanita*-type mushroom with a figure seated beneath it. The arrangement, as Halifax notes, suggests a mycological representation of the World Tree.

One of the great hallucinogens of southern Mesoamerica is the range of about twenty species of mind-altering psilocybe and other mushrooms. Over a hundred 'mushroom stones' thought to go back to the first or even second millenium BC have been found in the highlands of Guatemala and the Pacific Coast plains, indicating the antiquity of the use of such substances. These artefacts are usually around a foot high, made from ceramics as well as stone, and sometimes show a human face emerging from the stipe, as in Figure 41. The ancient Maya certainly employed this hallucinogen, and it was they, we noted in Chapter 3, who built the ceremonial, straight *sacbeob*. (It is also thought likely that the Maya used a hallucinogenic toad.)

Figure 41. A 'mushroom stone' from the highlands of Guatemala. The girl or goddess emerging from the stipe holds a grinding stone of the type used even today for the preparation of sacred mushrooms. (Author)

In South America, coca is the all-pervading narcotic, used as an aid in coping with the high Andean altitudes and rigours of native mountain life as well as ritually. The Inca used it to create trance states and to them the fields where coca was cultivated were considered to be sanctuaries. The key hallucinogen of South America, however, is *Banisteriopsis*, as Michael Harner explains:

> The drink commonly called *yagé* or *yajé* in Colombia, *ayahuasca* (Quechua: 'vine of the dead') in Ecuador and Peru, and *caapi* in

Brazil, appears to be prepared, in part at least, always from one of the several known species of *Banisteriopsis*...

The distribution of the native use of *Banisteriopsis* is at present known to be from northwestern Colombia in the north to lowland Bolivia in the south, occurring both east and west of the Andes and extending eastward to the upper Orinoco area... *Banisteriopsis* species exist throughout Central America and Mexico, including the Yucatan Peninsula...[43]

If the reader cares to glance back through Chapter 3, it will be seen that these areas are the very ones where evidence of straight landscape lines still exists. Harner goes on to tell us that:

Typically, *Banisteriopsis* is taken by South American Indian shamans of the tropical forest in order to perceive the supernatural world and to contact and to affect the behaviour of particular supernatural entities... In many tribes, non-shamans, most commonly males, also take *ayahuasca* for such reasons as to obtain information with the help of the spirit world, to obtain visions, to achieve supernatural power, or to accompany a shaman in a curing or other ritual. Depending on the culture and the purpose, the person taking *Banisteriopsis* may drink the mixture alone or as a member of a group. Thus the individualistic and feuding Jivaro prefer to take the drug individually and to use it to cope supernaturally with enemies. The more gregarious Cashinahua and Sharanhua, on the other hand, tend to participate together in the hallucinogenic experience... The Campa also join together for *Banisteriopsis* sessions, but their shaman plays a directorial role... All four groups... shed light on the shamanistic function of hallucinogens in societies which have not yet been significantly altered by Westernization.[44]

In Peru, home of several locations of straight landscape lines, including the famed Nazca lines, there seems to have been an additional powerful hallucinogen in ritual use — the mescaline-containing 'San Pedro' or *cimora* cactus. Still used by modern shamans, the antiquity of this hallucinogen is indicated by the fact that its depiction occurs commonly on ancient Nasca pottery, and a carved stone relief at Chavin de Huántar, a temple complex in central Peru belonging to a culture dating back to at least 1000 BC, shows a god, demon or masked shaman holding a San Pedro cactus.

There are, of course, many other hallucinogens that were used in the Americas — even hallucinogenic fish! — but

Figure 42. A stone relief from Chavin de Huántar depicting the San Pedro hallucinogenic cactus.

enough has been presented to demonstrate the deep-rooted involvement with hallucinogens by the Amerindian peoples. This factor, along with shamanic practice in general, has great bearing on the meaning of the straight landscape line, as we shall see. But we have to pick up a few more items of information before we can address that.

Rock art

During the 1980s, new archaeological developments in the study of archaic rock paintings and carvings have brought the ubiquitous fascination with trance in the ancient world into sharp focus. It has also made bridges with new understandings in neurophysiology to do with imagery and inner sensations produced universally by the human central nervous system, however they may be culturally perceived.

To grasp the gist of the new work here, it is best to start with the neurophysiological elements. The Club des Haschichins, which had members such as Baudelaire, Balzac and Victor

158

Hugo, was formed in the nineteenth century to study the effect of cannabis. Their reports repeatedly refer to colourful, vivid images comprised of wheels, whirlpools, spirals and rainbows at certain stages of trance. In 1888, P. Max Simon studied the imagery of schizophrenic hallucinations and discovered repeated emphasis on 'spiders webs', ropes and meshes. These changed constantly into one another as in cannabis (and other drug) visions. Lewin in 1924 noted similar cannabis-intoxication patterns: 'coloured arabesques', 'crystals', 'stars', 'filigree lacework'. It was with the work between 1926–66 of Heinrich Klüver that analyses of these visual forms began. He noted such imagery after the ingestion of mescaline with eyes closed, or, if open, it was 'impossible to look at walls without seeing them covered with visionary phenomena'.[45] He identified four basic types of these images which he called *form constants*. They were:

lattice (honeycomb, grid, grating, filigree and so on);
web;
tunnel or funnel (alley, cone);
spiral.

Regarding the tunnel form constant, or *image constant* as he called them, Mardi J. Horowitz noted that its central element tended apparently to recede with spatial effect in some cases, giving a true tunnel-like impression.[46] The sense of moving along a tunnel is of course a major onset motif in many Near Death and out-of-body experiences.

Like Klüver, another researcher, Szuman, also found such brilliantly coloured and intensely bright forms, using self-generated illumination, to be projected against the real world when viewed with open eyes: 'These vivid visual pictures completely covered real objects.' The hallucinatory images were '. . . projected on the surfaces of the floor, the ceiling, or the wall, or they appear in space, covering the objects that lie behind them.[47]

Subsequent researchers discovered the form constants

appearing in trance states induced by sensory deprivation, crystal gazing, the electrical stimulation of the cortex, flashing lights (stroboscopic stimulation), and during migraines. In 1975, Ronald K. Siegel and Murray E. Jarvik reported on results of further, precision research they conducted on these form constants.[48] They noted that the form constants were only the first stage of a two-stage process of hallucination, in which the basic forms, ever changing and recombining, became increasingly elaborated, so that 'the simple geometrical forms give way to landscapes, faces, and familiar objects'. Even these more complex images emerging from the geometrical substratum of visionary material share many similarities. In one study, a researcher found that an astonishing 79 per cent of his subjects experienced the same developed imagery.

Siegel and Jarvik came to identify eight form constants, adding the categories line, curve (often nested curves like a partial tunnel form), kaleidoscope and 'random' to Klüver's list. They found that their subjects did not report complex hallucinatory imagery until after the lattice-tunnel constants had appeared, imagery which seemed to signal the deepening of the trance state. Their subjects, who were placed in blackout conditions during experimentation, also reported that when their eyes were open the form imagery appeared on the darkness in front of them 'like a slide show or a movie located about two feet in front of their eyes'. As the imagery developed, subjects reported that transformations often involved simple association of ideas, and was like visual thinking. Memory material became melded with the geometric forms so landscapes, buildings and people evolved out of the form constants. Sometimes mixed images, say a half animal–half human figure would appear. The representational or 'iconic' visions interchanged, combined and fragmented as readily as the geometric form constants. Viewpoints could be aerial or as if looking up from under water. Siegel and Jarvik also found specific colours to dominate at certain stages of hallucinogenic trance.

A general term for these geometric trance visuals is *entoptic* (Greek for 'within vision') phenomena, meaning visual sensations originating within the visual system anywhere from the eyeball to the brain cortex. Certain effects like *phosphenes* seem to derive from occurrences within the eyeball and cellular excitation of the retina (and possibly elsewhere within the visual system), but much of the imagery of form constants seems to originate in stimulated neuronal firing deeper within the visual system of the brain. Full iconic, representational, hallucinations seem to draw on memory imagery from deep brain function which combines with and then visually obliterates the underlying geometric structures. (It has been speculated by some experienced researchers that the memory material elicited may not only relate to the personal history of the individual, but to transpersonal cellular and even species memories.)

It is worth special note that entoptic images seem to be stronger under hallucinogenic trance than in other kinds of trance states.

A good description of the entoptic form constants element in hallucinogenic experience can be found in the report made by a non-Indian subject who took part in *yagé* sessions in Chile, supervised by Claudio Naranjo:

> I saw tiny dots, like those on a television screen, transparent dots that agitated and turned (when I fixed the gaze on one point) around a cone forming a sort of funnel, like the whirlpool that is formed when one removes the stopper. They turned, rather slowly, and this funnel opened upwards from the floor I was gazing at, and extended to the sides into my entire visual field... And in this swirl of particles lies all my visual experience. It all comes from it, this is the foundation of the scenes I saw, this was their spirit, in the same way that the dots on the television screen are the ground of all the images...[49]

In 1972, the anthropologist Gerardo Reichel-Dolmatoff reported that the Tukano Indians of Colombia decorate their homes and pottery with large geometrical designs which they say they see during their *yagé* sessions. These images from the early stages of *yagé* intoxication, include all the form constants — grids, curves, spirals and so on. The Tukano recognise that these geometric patterns give way to larger and more complex

161

imagery. 'Interestingly, the Indians themselves claim that the hallucinations are a projection and that their order is fixed,' Seigel and Jarvik comment. 'Unsurprisingly, therefore, it has been hypothesized that the individual *yagé* user projects his cultural memory onto the waving screen of these geometric motifs.'[50] Each group within Tukano society 'owns' certain *yagé* imagery, and so only certain designs can be used by certain Indians. Tukano novices in *yagé* use are trained to manipulate the hallucinatory imagery.

Now, in the cave art of Palaeolithic Europe (such as the paintings of Lascaux), the ancient Amerindian rock paintings and engravings in the Americas, and the similar rock art of southern Africa, depictions of animals, humans, and animal–human figures are accompanied by a great plethora of dots, grids, zigzags, curves and lines. No one has understood what these meant. Gradually, however, the neuropsychological and anthropological information seeped into the awareness of archaeologists studying such rock art, and a few of them began to suggest that such abstract markings might be the formalised depictions of entoptic imagery. A major proponent of this view is South African archaeologist J.D. Lewis-Williams. In 1988, he and T.A. Dowson produced an important paper, *The Signs of All Times*, in which they applied the neuropsychological information on entoptic phenomena to an interpretation of the San (Bushman) rock art of southern Africa and that of the Shoshonean Coso Indians of California, and extended the concept to the Palaeolithic cave art of Europe.[51]

The researchers chose San and Coso rock art on which to base their work because in the first case it is *known* to have had shamanic origin, and the Coso art is strongly suspected as deriving from such a context.

We have already seen how trance, kia, is integral to the lives of Kalahari people like the !Kung. Anthropologists learned that the rock paintings and engravings of these people were understood by the San to have been produced by shamans, and trance dancers would sometimes place their hands on such imagery in order to draw num from them. Ethnographic

162

information on the Coso pointed to a similar situation. The Coso artists 'painted their spirits on rocks'. In the adjacent Tubatulabal people, spirits seen in Jimson weed trance were thought to have done the paintings themselves. There seems a tradition in the area that the paintings were done, in fact, by the spirit helpers of shamans. The researcher involved with the Coso rock art, David S. Whitley, notes that the local name for shaman is *poagunt*, which derives from the cognate for supernatural power, *poa*. (This association again brings to mind the conceptual complex surrounding the Proto-Indo–European *regs*.) *Poagunt* can be translated as 'medicine man' or 'man who writes', that is, makes marks on rock surfaces. The ethnography of the area, Whitley reports, 'provides a clear indication of the shamanic origins of the art and the relationship of shamanism to dreaming and the ingestion of hallucinogens'.[52]

Lewis-Williams' and Dowson's neuropsychological model selects six main entoptic types, and identifies imagery belonging to three basic stages of trance: (a) the geometric form constants; (b) what they call 'construal' imagery, by which they mean geometric forms that the consciousness of the experient attempts to recognise or decode as representational images, so a zizag may 'become' a snake, or a string of flickering curves may turn into a line of animals, and (c) iconic or fully-fledged representational imagery emerging out of the ground of the entoptic and 'construed' entoptic forms.

The researchers recognise in the rock art images relating to entoptic imagery that not only replicate it directly but which also show form constants that have become fragmented or integrated with one another. The iconic images can also become combined, as in the classic case of the human/animal figures that appear in ancient rock art the world over. These are technically known as 'therianthropes', the best example being the Palaeolithic 'sorcerer' from Les Trois-Frères cave in France — and which relate to the already mentioned theme of the shaman turning into an animal during trance. Lewis-Williams and Dowson argue that their model applied to the configurations found in San and Coso rock art:

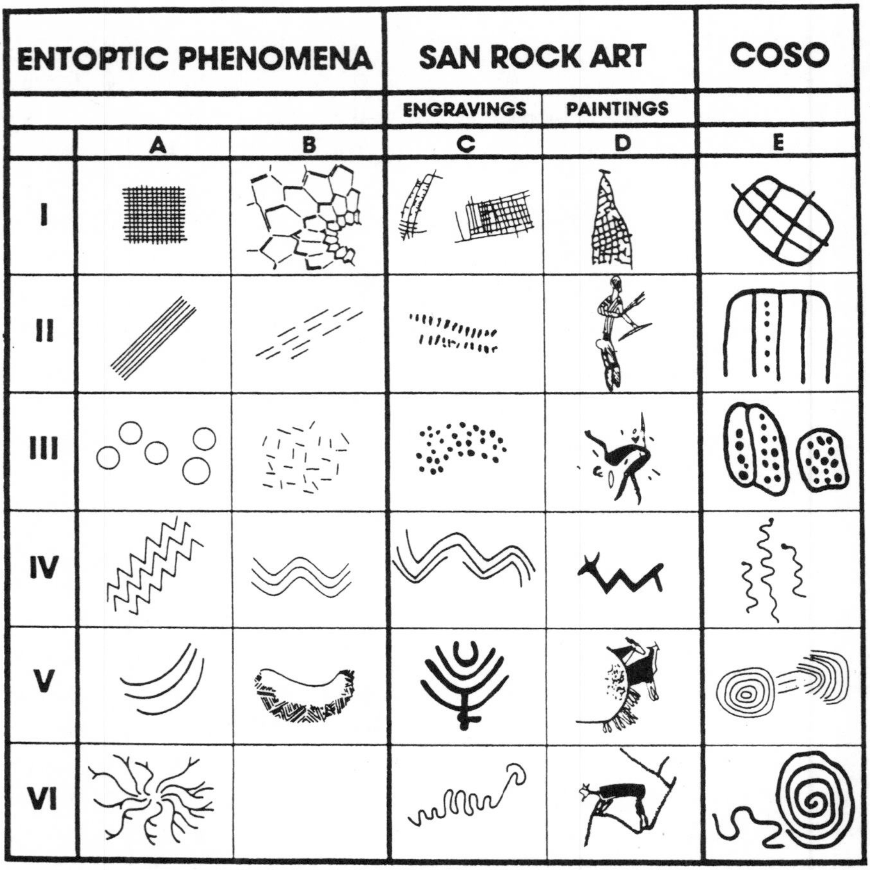

Figure 43. Six categories of entoptic phenomena compared with San and Coso rock-art depictions. (J. D. Lewis-Williams and T. A. Dowson)

... exposes the neuropsychological order underlying the seemingly chaotic integrated, superimposed, juxtaposed, fragmented, and reduplicated iconic and geometric depictions of these two arts. Far from being anarchic, San and Coso art are ordered products of identifiable stages of altered consciousness and neurologically based principles in the formation of mental imagery. The painted and engraved images are, in fact, informed by the function of the human nervous system in altered states. Because the order that results is different from the order Westerners are predisposed to seek in artistic creations, it has escaped notice.

... There is thus a strong suggestion that at least a significant component of Upper Palaeolithic art also derives from altered states of consciousness and that many of the signs depict entoptic phenomena in the various transformations we have described.[53]

Figure 44. The 'sorcerer' image from Les Trois Frères cave, France. (After Breuil and Begouen)

The researchers see the San and Coso shamans as having painted the imagery they saw projected onto the rock surfaces of the caves and rock shelters during trance, in just the way the experimenters referred to earlier saw imagery projected onto surfaces all around them when they had their eyes open, or appearing like projected slides on the darkness in front of them. The imagery may, of course, have been seen as having been put on the rock surfaces by spirits.

Not all this imagery need have been executed during trance: as forms became known and used, rote stylisation may have occurred when religious pictures were being produced. (Lewis-Williams and Dowson question, as have other researchers, whether the production of shamanic imagery marks the origins of art, especially representational art — one of the few activities that distinguishes the human species.)

One great researcher of San rock art, the late Harald Pager, noted that the paintings of the Sebaaiene Cave in the Ndedema Gorge of the Drakensberg range were visionary scenes from 'the world behind this one we see with our eyes'. As Joseph

165

Figure 45. Depiction of a painting at junction Shelter in the Ndedema Gorge, Natal Drakensburg, South Africa. The image top left is a 'trance buck' (formerly an 'ales' or 'flying buck'); images bottom right show a person on a ladder juxtaposed with a 'falling rhebok'. (After Harold Pager)

Campbell remarked about San rock art, 'The paintings had the power of a medium uniting the two worlds, of the outer eyes of the body and the inward eye of the mind.'[54]

J.F. Thackeray has used linguistic methods to further strengthen the case for southern African rock art being trance imagery. He notes the form *-hele*, which occurs in Bantu words like *mehele*, *lehele*, a rhebok, a small antelope. Antelopes were of major spiritual significance for the San; their shamans are sometimes depicted in their rock art as antelope-headed, and an odd, recurrent image is what used to be described as an 'ales' or 'flying buck', but is now beginning to be referred to as a 'trance buck'. Bantu *ihele* means a row of animals or people, one

Figure 46. Depiction of a painting at the Grootfontein site, South Africa. Antelope are shown falling off a precipice and running in line (expressed in the Bantu term ihele). *The falling antelope motif seems to be associated with 'falling' into trance. It is noticeable in this depiction how the row of antelopes develop from parallel lines — typical of a 'construal' entoptic image. The human figures depicted may be engaged in a trance dance.* (After Van de Riet, Vander Riet and Bleek)

behind the other, or objects characterised by a grid-like (lattice) pattern or structure. The Zulu term *ihelehele* means giddiness associated with height, vertigo. Thackeray sees these ideas expressed visually in southern African rock art, where lines of antelopes (these animals do tend to run one after the other) are seen streaming towards grids or nets, and human figures teeter atop ladders (literally 'high'), in association with flying trance bucks, falling rheboks (one falls into a trance), and human figures apparently in trance dances. Not only the grids and nets, but the ladder depictions would now be recognised as entoptic form constants, or fragments of such, and the flickering rows of antelopes as construal images.

Thackeray goes further and isolates a Zulu (Nguni) word form -*qab* that associates 'trance, ladders, a sense of height and the very act of painting'. The words are: *ukutiqabu*: recovering from fainting; *ukuqabela*: to climb to the top of a ladder, tree or mountain (all images of the World Axis, of course); *ukuqabela*: to paint.[56]

Form and meaning

It seems now incontrovertible that the human central nervous system during trance conditions produces universal sensory motifs that can give rise to similar imagery at all times and places where trance has been used by human beings, which is just about everywhere prior to modern times. But the fact that the brain produces a common canvas, does not mean that the beliefs, deities and rituals painted onto it are universal. So, for example, the gods and religion of the Palaeolithic hunter–gatherers who painted the walls of Lascaux or Les Trois-Frères would not be the same as those of the Kalahari Bushmen. One can look at *forms* universally, and determine the underlying neurophysiological origins, but the *meaning* those forms had for a given society would be *culturally determined*.

Harner points out that 'culture-specific factors... are of overwhelming importance in influencing both the content and structure of supernatural ideology'. Indeed, in his studies of South American hallucinogenic usage, he found that 'it seems virtually impossible to isolate the nature of the *yagé*-induced experience from its cultural context on the basis of ethnographic data alone.'[56] Kalweit comments that 'cultural and social conditioning continues to manifest itself even in an altered state of consciousness. It is very hard for the human spirit to

168

escape this conditioning... Surrounded by the shadows of its own imagination, our spirit — even while in the Beyond — conjures up countries, places, people, animals and customs which have their origin in its terrestrial environment'.[57] Dobkin de Rios writes that 'each culture will elaborate the symbology connected to the drug experience in terms of the symbols and values of its own society, while at the same time having recourse to recurrent, universal sets of symbols...'. It is, she says, 'of crucial importance' to be aware of 'the cultural patterning of visionary experience'. She observes:

> There seems to be good evidence that in a society where plant hallucinogens are used, each individual builds up a certain expectation of drug use, which, in fact, permits the evocation of particular types of visions. That is not to say that if a group of adult men claim to see serpents appear before them, they all are actually viewing the same snake, as if they were attending a movie performance. Rather, what is at issue here is the cultural patterning of categories of visions...
> ...one of the most interesting aspects of non-Western hallucinatory plant use is the ritualization surrounding their use. Although pleasurable effects are not ignored, in the main such plants are ingested within the context of complex social ritual and ceremonialism... While drug rituals are pervasive, their character and purpose vary.[58]

So, it is important not to envisage trance visions simply as some movie show experienced in a neutral frame of mind. The imagery is accompanied by powerful physical sensations and profound philosophical 'atmospheres'. The reality of the trance sensory effects — which can involve not only vision but sound, touch, a sense of motion, a dissolving of the ego (the distinction between 'I' and 'Not-I'), changes of body image — can be overwhelming. One can move in spaces that are fully three-dimensional and as 'real' as anything experienced in the outer world. Moreover, space in advanced trance states can take on bizarre extensions and twists that defy analysis. Above all, perhaps, the sense of *time* changes. Eternity can be experienced in the twinkling of an eye, or linear time can convert to oceanic dimensions, rippling with waves of eternity. The neurological cinema is simply the gateway to released structures of consciousness: who knows where the path beyond leads? The deep underlying elements that well up through the hallucinatory material, and the *exact* nature of beings and states encountered, is not truly known: they are only unreal from the perspectives of our modern Western cognitive map. Who knows if we have the right map? Kalweit sounds a similar note of caution, when he observes that a psychedelic experience begins:

> ... by seeing purely neurological patterns and personal motifs and ends with visions of cosmic archetypes and transpersonal symbols. The phosphenes, therefore, only belong to a lower (physical) stage of the visionary experience. Consequently, the theory that human symbols are no more than matrices of excitation (engrams) within the brain, or that mystical experiences are a pattern of phosphenes, is neither worthy of serious consideration nor can it be empirically substantiated.
>
> It will sooner or later in all probability be shown that mystical and parapsychic experiences, as they are assimilated by the brain, are subject to a filtering process and therefore adapt to neuroanatomical structures.[59]

My own guess is that our modern cognitive map is substantially correct, but that there are still large, vague areas around the edge — the parts that on old maps of the world were marked 'here be dragons'.

We need to learn the technology of consciousness once more, and give it a practical place in our culture, in everyone's lives. Whereas we Westerners may have glittering high technology, way beyond anything found on earth before, we are in certain ways woefully primitive in our knowledge of consciousness, of the *experiencing* of our minds. Ancient and traditional peoples lead us in that particular technology. We need to learn from them, from their methods, experience, knowledge; we need to grasp the reasons for their traditions and landscapes, and all without getting involved with their belief systems and without imposing or inventing any of our own.

CHAPTER 7

THE LINES OF THE LONE WILD GANDER

We are now in a position to appreciate properly how awesomely deep the current of trance consciousness has run in archaic and traditional, non-Western cultures, and its enormous antiquity as a recognised factor in human awareness and religion. It has been a major strand of human behaviour that, as a culture, we have now turned our backs on. Because of that, as Lewis-Williams and Dowson point out, we have been unable to see its signs in ancient rock art. We can also now understand that the human brain, whatever its relationship to mind and spirit, organises visionary experience on the common canvas of the human central nervous system, and that this imagery has been absorbed, adapted and manipulated in belief systems, social structures and roles throughout history. Thus it is possible for certain matters like shamanism, elements of rock art, or particular associations with kingship, to be viewed in a cross-cultural fashion, without getting bogged down with specific cultural belief systems. What I am going to suggest in this final chapter is that we can also do this with regard to ancient sacred landscapes, focusing on our main quarry in this book — the straight landscape line that occurs in various guises around the world. There are not only shamanic traditions, practices, cosmology and rock art — there are *shamanic landscapes* too. I suggest that this description is more accurate and informative than terms like 'ceremonial landscape' or 'sacred landscape'.

It must be stressed that I am not for one moment saying that there are any cultural affinities between, say, a British cursus and a Nazca line, nor even, necessarily, between a Nazca line

171

and an Anasazi Chaco Road. However, we have seen in Chapter 5 that there is a case to be made that all ancient landscape lines — whether physical as at Nazca, or conceptual as in the cases of Irish fairy paths, German *Geisterwege,* or Feng shui lines or 'arrows' of ch'i — seem in essence to relate to some concept or other of their being *spirit lines,* and that even relatively modern ceremonial lines, like The Mall in London, leading out as it does from a monarch's palace, are unconscious echoes of that fact. What I *am* suggesting, without prejudice regarding any individual meanings or uses to which the lines have been put in different cultural contexts, is that this exceptionally ancient and now obscure association between spirit and straight linearity in 'ceremonial' landscapes is a common denominator that occurs, like the entoptic images in rock art, because of the universality of the human central nervous system and its operation in shamanism. The concept of the straight landscape line originates, I suggest, in a funda-mental element of the shamanic experience, indeed, in what is arguably *the* central element of shamanism — *magical flight.* This is simply a particular version of out-of-body experience.

When we employ the word 'ecstasy' in general usage, we usually mean 'wonderfully happy', 'extreme pleasure' or somesuch. But the word *actually* means 'out of the senses'; essentially, out of the body. Dictionaries often define the word as meaning 'trance'. Etymologically, 'ecstasy' is a Middle English word deriving from the Old French *extasie,* in turn from the Greek *ekstasis,* a verbal noun from *existemi,* 'to put a person out of his senses'. *Ex* means out, out of. When academics use the word they use it in its proper sense, so when a religious historian like Mircea Eliade wrote of 'archaic techniques of ecstasy'[1] what is meant is old or traditional methods for inducing out-of-body trance states.

Flight of the shaman

Shamanic landscapes are where the human central nervous system has in effect left a physical mark on the land. The key physical mark from our point of view in this book is the straight landscape line, in whatever cultural form it evolved into at different times and places. To appreciate its association with shamanism, it is crucial to try and grasp the importance of the experience of shamanic magical flight, the out-of-body experience. To dismiss it as some minor, aberrant fantasy of the past is seriously to underestimate the matter. Ethnopsychologist Holger Kalweit makes the situation very clear:

> The shaman's art calls for supreme control of awareness, thought, feeling and culminates in a separation of the soul from the body... The intentional separation of consciousness... must be counted among the most mysterious attainments of the human psyche...
> The shaman... is master of death... He is 'dead' for a limited period of time... Reports about shamanistic practices frequently refer to the theme of the 'journey' in an attempt to describe how the soul leaves the body and travels through the landscape of the realm of the dead...
> The scientific study of the OBE [out-of-body experience] has only just begun. As yet we have no clear idea about its typical physiological features, nor do we know its place within the framework of higher states of consciousness. Is an OBE a unique psychic state or no more than a variant of an alternative state of consciousness? We only know that an OBE can occur in an awakened state, during sleep, in a dream, in the hypnogogic phase preceding sleep, and in other transpersonal states. One thing, however, is certain: The out-of-body state is a prerequisite for the experience of consciousness in the Beyond — an experience which has decisively influenced the religious beliefs of all cultures. Because of that, it holds a *central position* in the ethnology of religions and, as such, calls for broadly based research.[2] (My emphasis.)

Eliade points out that 'the shaman specialises in a trance during which his soul is believed to leave his body and ascend to the sky or descend to the underworld'. He goes on:

> All over the world the same magical power is credited to sorcerers and medicine men... sorcerers and shamans are able, *here on earth* and *as often as they wish*, to accomplish 'coming out of the body',.... shamans and sorcerers can enjoy the condition of 'souls', of 'discarnate beings', which is accessible to the profane only when they die.[3]

We will take a fleeting look at the modern research related to the experience in the final part of this chapter, but first we overview the shamanic history of the out-of-body experience. In the process, we will meet again some of the peoples, places and themes we have encountered in earlier chapters.

The Old World

In India, Mircea Eliade recorded that traditions of 'magical flight have a leading place... Rising into the air, flying like a bird, travelling immense distances in a flash, disappearing — these are some of the magical powers that Buddhism and Hinduism attribute to arhats, kings and magicians. There are numerous legends of flying kings...'.[6]

The mythological paradisical lands to which the shaman or king can journey belong, of course, to the geography of the mind; they are, as Eliade so eloquently put it, 'the "pure lands" of a mystical space that has at once the nature of a "paradise" and of an "interior space" accessible only to initiates'. In India as elsewhere, the power of magical flight can be obtained by a variety of trance-inducing techniques, including yoga. The importance of magical flight is stressed time and again in all methodologies, Eliade insists, and the ability is 'an integral part of a theologico-cosmological complex far more embracing than the various shamanic ideologies'. He observes that bird symbolism, found everywhere in association with shamanic magical flight, found its way into the ancient texts of India, such as the *Pancavimsa Brahmana*: 'The Sacrificer, having become a bird, soars to the world of heaven.' Joseph Campbell made a similar observation. He drew attention, for instance, to the ninth-century BC *Brihadaranyaka Upanishad*, one of several ancient texts dealing with levels of sleep, trance and consciousness:

> *Striking down in sleep what is bodily,*
> *Sleepless, he looks down upon the sleeping senses.*
> *Having taken to himself light, he has returned to his own place:*
> *That Golden Person, the Lone Wild Gander...*

174

He goes wherever he pleases, that Immortal,
The Golden Person, the Unique Wild Gander.
In the State of Sleep, soaring high and low . . .

'The Lone Wild Gander' — what more poetic image of the
free-flying soul, the ecstatic consciousness, could there be? It is
indeed an appropriate image, as Campbell put it, of 'that
remarkable out-of-body adventure'.[7]

In China too, there were deep traditions related to magical
flight. In antiquity, 'well-informed Chinese regarded "flight" as
a plastic formula for ecstasy'.[8] In legend, the first man credited
with the power of flight was Emperor Shun (late third
millenium BC). The art of 'flying like a bird' was revealed to him
by the daughters of another emperor. (Here and elsewhere, as
in the fact that Indra drank soma from Sri-Lakshmi's lips, we get
the hint that the secrets of shamanic trance were passed on in
remote antiquity by women.) 'We may note the fact,' Eliade
comments, 'that a perfect sovereign must have the powers of a
"magician". "Ecstasy" was no less necessary to the founder of a
state than his political virtues. . . And so we find that many
emperors, sages, alchemists, and sorcerers "went up to
heaven"'.[9]

Again, bird symbolism was rife. (The three types of animals
primarily used in shamanic symbolism worldwide are birds,
reindeer and the bear.) A Taoist priest, for instance, would be
referred to as 'a feather scholar', clearly indicating the shamanic
origins of Chinese magical flight.

It was also said of the Dervishes of the Islamised Turks of
central Asia that they could 'change into birds and so have the
power to fly'.[10] Many of the central Asian shamans likewise
displayed bird symbolism: the Altai shamans made their
costumes resemble an owl; the footwear of a Tungus shaman
was designed to imitate a bird's foot; the Gilyak tribespeople
used the same word for eagle and shaman, and the Yakut
shaman's apparel was decked out with a representation of a
bird's skeleton, made from iron! During his shamanic seance,
the Yakut shaman made dance movements and gestures to

Figure 47. A human figure painted on the walls of a cave at Lascaux. He seems to be wearing a bird mask, and nearby is a stick with a bird on top — a symbol of shamanism. The man appears to be in trance. Note the erection.

imitate the flight of a bird. Two birds are shown in the branches of the World Tree in its oldest Eurasian representations: in the shamanic traditions of central Asia they represented human souls, and the shaman journeyed to the Tree in order to bring back the 'soul-birds' of sick people. The antiquity of these kinds of associations are remarkable, as is shown by a figure in a Palaeolithic cave painting at Lascaux. The figure, seemingly wearing a bird-mask, is shown supine (in trance?) alongside a bird-headed stick. A bird perched on a stick is a known symbol of shamanism in documented Eurasian traditions. Bird symbolism survived even in pagan Ireland, where the powerful druid, Mog Ruith, was said to have an *enchennach* or 'bird dress', with which he could rise up 'into the air and the heavens'. Again, the father of the pagan Celtic Irish king, Conaire, was said to be a supernatural birdman.

176

We associate Siberian and other northern tradition shamanic trance with *Amanita muscaria*, Fly Agaric, ingestion, as we have seen. One of our modern images of shamanic out-of-body flight that almost certainly derives from such sources is that of Santa Claus flying on a reindeer-drawn sleigh through the night sky. In a Christmas edition of *The Ley Hunter*, the journal's cartoon character, Dod, seems to have made the right connections (Figure 48)! Rogan Taylor has suggested that the red and white scheme of Father Christmas' cloak may be an echo of the colouring of the Fly Agaric mushroom.[11]

We have already noted that the Berserkers were thought to take Fly Agaric preparations prior to their fearsome presence in battle (though there is disagreement amongst experts on this). These men were bear shamans, wearing bearskins — from whence they get their name. Nigel Pennick reports that the Berserkers were accredited with the power of *hamrammr* or shape-shifting. He remarks that one way this belief may have come about was through ideas associated with out-of-body ability, for a famous Berserker, Bothvar Bjarki, champion of King Hrolf of Denmark, was said to have fought in the king's army in the form of a bear, whilst his normal, human body lay elsewhere in trance.[12]

In addition to the flying Santa Claus, our other Western

Figure 48.

Figure 49. A fifteenth-century woodcut showing three witches flying on a pitchfork. They are turning into animal forms.

image of magical flight is the broomstick ride of the witch. Traditionally, this was the way the witch went to the Sabbat, and we have noted Michael Harner's idea that the Sabbat was in fact a magical or hallucinatory gathering rather than a physical one. In Chapter 6 we saw that the medieval witch prepared magic 'flying ointment' from plants like henbane, belladonna and mandrake. All these contain the powerful hallucinogen hyoscyamine, which 'gives the sensation of flying through the air', as La Barre notes.[13] There is the folk-rumour, aided and abetted by Shakespeare, that toads were also put into witches' brews. As ludicrous as this sounds, the ancient Maya also seem to have used toads for trance-induction, because certain species of toad contain bufotenin, which, La Barre claims, 'seems specifically to promote a feeling of flying through the air'.[14] (Indeed, it seems that this method is coming back into favour — in July, 1991, it was reported that the Vancouver authorities were considering designating a local type of toad as an illegal hallucinogenic substance, because people were picking the creatures up, and *licking* the bufotenin off them to obtain

178

Figure 50. Frigg, flying on a distaff. This mural in Schleswig Cathedral, Germany, was thought to be twelfth century, but has now been revealed as a Nazi forgery.

psychedelic trips lasting up to six hours!) Perhaps the fairytale of the princess kissing a frog who then turns into a handsome prince comes from this.[15]

The image of the broomstick is not just a romantic notion or some kind of Freudian image — though eroticism was certainly involved with the witch-trance. As atropines in henbane and other plants can be absorbed through the skin, broomsticks or staffs were sometimes used as applicators to put the ointment in contact with the vaginal membranes. Feathers might also be used. (See also Additional Notes, pp231-2.)

The riding of the broomstick is reminiscent of riding a steed, which is a reminder of the Siberian shamans riding their horse-headed sticks through the skies of ecstatic trance to the World Tree, the Cosmic Axis. The remnant of these traditions is doubtlessly the folk image of the hobbyhorse. And we should also note that Frigg, wife of Odin, was depicted riding a broomstick. Freya is closely associated with Frigg in Norse myth, and the two are generally considered to be the same mythological element, with Frigg emphasising the maternal principle, and Freya fertility. Freya was the mistress, first teacher, of *seidhr*, a form of trance divination. This was women's magic, and the *seidhonka* (or *volva* or *spakona*) would travel around farmsteads and hamlets predicting the future. The *seidhonka*'s ritual costume consisted of a blue cloak, jewels, a headpiece of black lamb with white catskins, *she carried a staff,* and conducted her divination from a high platform while seated on a cushion of chicken feathers. In the course of the divination, the *seidhonka* would go into trance and have an out-of-body experience. It was therefore clearly shamanic. The practitioners of *seidhr* also wore animal costumes, with gloves made of catskin; Freya's carriage is said to have been pulled by cats, and she has been depicted in the cloak of a *seidhkona* flying on the back of a large, striped cat. (It is thus clear where the idea of the witch's cat familiar came from.) Freya also owned a magic feather garment that enabled her to fly. She it was who taught Odin to fly, which he was able to do after donning a garment of falcon feathers. (Again we get the hint that the secrets of magical flight, of ecstatic trance, were passed on to men by women long ago.)

It was intimated in the previous chapter that it was thought in many cultures — Lapp, Amerindian and Australian aborigine — that flying shamans could sometimes be seen at night as balls of mysterious flying lights. Alistair I. McIntosh tells us that Rigo people of Papua New Guinea also had clear ideas on this matter:

> While disembodied the spirit can appear in any of three ways: as a facsimile of the physical body; in the form of a bird or flying fox (fruit bat) if further magic is used; or as a light. The size of the light varies from 'small' to 'football sized'. In motion it twinkles like many stars compacted together and is shaped like a shooting star with a tail. It can radiate several different colours — yellow, red and blue usually being the most prominent. The faster it moves the more brightly it shines.[16]

Psychologist Susan Blackmore comments on this:

> That sounds a fanciful description but remember that Muldoon claimed that at the intermediate moving speed light was thrown off behind the moving astral body, and Crookall mentions something similar.[17]

180

Sylvan Muldoon was a practitioner of 'astral travel' (as out-of-body experience used to be called) in the early decades of this century, and Robert Crookall was a scholarly investigator of the subject. Current researchers such as the American academic Keith Harary, who also has the natural ability to instigate out-of-body experiences in himself, have reported that the 'astral body' can sometimes appear as a lightball to the experient, and, on occasion, possibly to witnesses.

Throughout the world, certain images of ascent were used — the shaman's spirit could rise on smoke, ride along a rainbow, travel up a sunbeam and so on. But from northwest Europe to Tibet none was more ubiquitous than the ladder. It appears in all manner of shamanic traditions — an obvious folk representation of 'getting high'. Sometimes the ladder was placed, symbolically, against a real tree or post symbolising the World Tree, and the shaman would ascend, perhaps waving his arms like a bird's wings at the top. In other versions, notches would be cut on a post so the shaman could physically climb it, as if climbing the World Tree. It shows the remarkably universal aspects of shamanism, then, that the image of a human figure atop a ladder occurs also in southern African rock art, as we noted in passing in the previous chapter.

'Just what overpowering transpersonal experiences... informed the minds and moved the practised hands of the artists of the Late Palaeolithic, we shall of course never directly know,' Joseph Campbell wrote. 'From the Bushmen of the South African Kalahari Desert, however, whose rock art has been practised (apparently without interruption) since the close of the last Ice Age... verbal accounts have been recorded, not only of the mythology, but also of the out-of-body experiences in trance state, from which their spirited representations have been taken of an intelligible sphere, known to the eye of the mind, unseen by the light of day.'[18] He cites one of Marguerite Biesele's !Kung informants:

> When people sing... I dance. I enter the earth. I go in at a place like a place where people drink water. I travel a long way, very far. When I emerge, I am already climbing. I'm climbing threads...

> And when you arrive at God's place you make yourself small... You come and come and come and finally you enter your body again... You enter, enter the earth, and you return to enter the skin of your body... And you say 'he-e-e-e!' That is the sound of your return to your body...

Lewis-Williams and Dowson remark that snakes have symbolic value for the San people precisely because 'they go underground and then surface elsewhere as humans do when they are on out-of-body travel'.[19]

The !Kung, like all other shamanic peoples, state that the out-of-body experience is the same as death, the only difference being that in the shamanic trance the experience is, usually, temporary. The !Kung also maintain that the most powerful healers in times gone by could transform themselves into lions.

J.D. Lewis-Williams and T.A. Dowson acknowledge the out-of-body status of trance involved with San rock art. Most entoptic phenomena are simply observed by the experient, they say, but:

> ... at peak hallucinatory periods subjects begin to feel dissociated from their bodies and frequently become part of their own imagery... the subject inhabits rather than merely witnesses a bizarre hallucinatory world. We call this condition *participation*... Some rock-art depictions of human beings probably represent participation...[20]

A key shamanic element in San rock art is the 'flying buck' or 'ales' (Chapter 6). These antelope depictions are quite odd to Western eyes, but usually show a delicate creature with its legs suspended or in an upward position trailing long lines. Because they occur in association with entoptic imagery and scenes probably representing trance effects or practices, they tend now to be referred to as 'trance bucks' as we noted earlier. As Campbell put it, the flying buck represented 'the released soul of the trance dancers, as well as of the dead'.[21] Joan Halifax comments that, 'The flying deer is part of the mythology of such diverse cultures as the Samoyeds of Siberia and the Huichols of Mexico, and is associated with magical flight, transfiguration, and spiritualization.'[22]

Figure 51. Drawings of two of the many 'flying' or 'trance' bucks that occur in San rock art. The top figure appears in association with a depiction of antelope-headed men walking in a line at Procession Shelter, Ndedema Gorge, South Africa. (Harald Pager)

The New World

Stories of out-of-body feats are prevalent in Eskimo lore. Bearing in mind the Lone Wild Gander of the ancient texts of India, it is interesting to note that two geese carved from ivory were found in the grave of an Eskimo shaman dated to about AD 500 in the Northwest territories of Canada. Halifax observes that 'the goose is frequently associated with the mystic journey to the Other World'.[23]

From about 500 BC the building of mounds became an increasing feature of the Amerindian peoples of eastern and central USA, of which the shamanic Hopewell culture, and their equally shamanic precursors, the Adena, were notable examples. In northern midwest USA, such as present-day Wisconsin, many hundreds of *effigy mounds* were constructed by unknown Native American groups as part of this trend. These shaped mounds depict bears, turtles and other animals, birds, human figures and winged human figures. These are all shamanic images, and the birds and winged humans are surely

183

Figure 52. An Eskimo flying shaman, accompanied by spirit helpers. (Baker Lake Animal Print Collection, 1971; catalogue no. 13 by Jessie Oonark, Baker Lake, NWT, Canada. Reproduced by permission of the Estate of Jessie Oonark).

expressive of shamanic flight. Rock carvings from Nebraska similarly show winged humans or therianthropes. We have already mentioned the bird, usually eagle, imagery in conjunction with mushroom artefacts of the Hopewell religious culture, and Eliade noted how important the eagle feather was as a shamanistic symbol of magical flight to the North American Indian.

The Mississippian culture was developing during the latter centuries of the Hopewell era, and can be defined as a distinct type of Native American socio-religious influence from around AD 900. The societies that are loosely grouped under 'Mississippian' occupied vast areas of the Midwest and South USA. Many of their decorated shells and other artefacts show what archaeologists correctly label the 'flying shaman' theme. One particularly interesting example of this is a small sandstone tablet which was unearthed at the four-tiered Monks Mound, the largest prehistoric earthwork in North America and centrepiece of the great sacred complex of Cahokia, situated

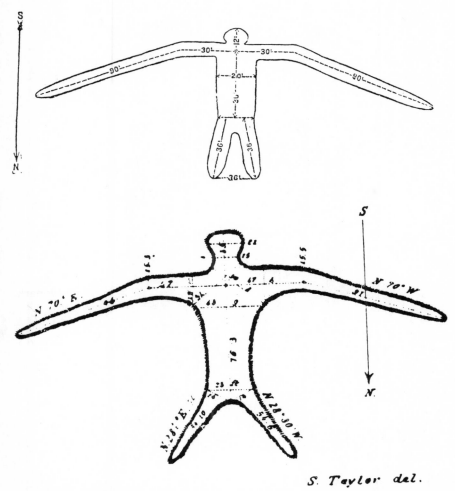

Figure 53. Nineteenth-century plans of Midwestern effigy mounds depicting winged humans or therianthropic bird-forms.

near present-day East St Louis. The great mound was the site of temples and the dwelling of the overlord or chief. The tablet shows on one side a human being in a winged costume and wearing a bird mask, and on the other side criss-cross lines that are thought to represent a snakeskin. The symbol of the snake is everywhere associated with shamanism, and certainly with the out-of-body experience, probably on account of the way the

Figure 54. Sandstone tablet depicting a person in bird costume and mask, found at Cahokia. (Author)

snake can shed its old skin. (There was a pronounced serpent cult throughout much of the Americas.)

Many of the northern Native American tribes who left such artefacts and the straight landscape lines are lost to us, and we know little about what shamanic traditions they had, though we can deduce hallucinogen usage from the information given in the previous chapter. Further south, however, in Mesoamerica and South America, the use of hallucinogens for shamanic purposes is still a surviving practice.

R. Gordon Wasson was probably the first contemporary Western researcher to take part in a Mexican Indian hallucinogenic mushroom ritual, and his account remains a classic description of the hallucinogenic out-of-body experience conducted in a traditional setting.

> Your body lies in the darkness, heavy as lead, but your spirit seems to soar and leave the hut, and with the speed of thought travel where it listeth, in time and space, accompanied by the

186

shaman's singing and by the ejaculations of her percussive chant... the bemushroomed person is poised in space, a disembodied eye, invisible, incorporeal, seeing but not seen. In truth, he is the five senses disembodied, all of them keyed to the height of sensitivity and awareness, all of them blending into one another most strangely... As your body lies there in its sleeping bag, your soul is free...[24]

The song of an Eskimo shaman echoes Wasson's 'disembodied eye':

My body is all eyes.
Look at it! Be not afraid!
I look in all directions!

The ethnographic information on hallucinogenically-induced out-of-body experience in South America is considerable, as the following brief examples illustrate. In 1858, the Ecuadorian geographer Manuel Villavicencio described the effects of the *Banisteriopsis* preparation, *ayahuasca*, when he was with the Zaparo Indians as causing 'vertigo and spinning in the head, then a sensation of being lifted into the air and beginning an aerial journey... I can say for a fact that when I've taken *ayahuasca* I've experienced dizziness, then an aerial journey in which I recall perceiving the most gorgeous views...'. In 1953, Avencio Villarejo felt similar sensations 'of being suspended in the air' when he took *ayahuasca*. When anthropologist P. Reinburg took *yagé* in 1921 it felt to him 'as though my body has disappeared; I am nothing more than a mind observing with interest...'. Hans Peter Duerr in his *Dreamtime* (1975/1985) observes that *yagé* 'seems to be specifically a "drug for flying"'. Harner reports that the Jivaro Indians of the Ecuadorian Amazon actually use the term 'trip' to describe the sensation of flying during *ayahuasca* sessions, the same term which of course became the spontaneous description of the psychedelic experience amongst Western youth![25] When a Campa Indian of eastern Peru takes *ayahuasca* he finds that 'his head spins, he thinks he is flying through the air'. Gerald Weiss noted that during a Campa shaman's seance, the shaman might commence a soul flight even while he is singing, and go to some distant place to return later. 'Some shamans move from sight of the rest of the group during the ceremony and then pretend to disappear bodily on such a flight... The soul-flight of the shaman is an optional concomitant in any case, and in its usual form is a personal experience that does not intrude upon the actual performance of the ceremony.'[26]

We only have to think for a moment of the unknown generations of Amerindians going through such experiences. How can we doubt that the recurring Amerindian sacred landscape motifs of straight lines and effigy earthworks relate to them? That such landscape imagery proves so intractable to us is because we no longer know of the out-of-body experience in any sort of cultural sense. It is when we get to the Andean lines, and especially, perhaps, the Nazca geoglyphs, that we can at least see the clearest juxtaposition of ethnographically traceable traditions of hallucinogen use and physical markings on the ground, and so Nazca provides the cue for us to think a little more directly about the nature of the shamanic landscape.

Shamanic land markings

There are two kinds of characteristic physical markings found in shamanic landscapes — effigies of one kind or another, and some form of linear marking such as a ceremonial track, road or avenue. These elements are now found only rarely to survive together as, fortunately, is the case at Nazca. And there are variations. For instance, the line may be indicated merely by the alignment of earthworks, mounds, or other sacred spots, and we have seen (Chapter 1) that such a ley-type alignment can be open to dispute as to whether it is a chance effect or not. Sometimes the shamanic landscape has lines that are only conceptual — they exist only in the collective mind of the culture occupying the landscape — as with the fairy paths of Ireland, or the engineered geomantic landscapes of old China. If the culture disappears and leaves no documentation, the conceptual lines disappear with it. Fortunately, at Nazca, we have indisputable lines and effigies engraved on the pampa, in a cultural matrix where hallucinogen ingestion is known to have been an inherent behavioural pattern.

188

Terrestrial effigies and lines, at Nazca or anywhere else, had outward, socio-religious uses relevant to the society which constructed them. Collectively, such markings are an outward sign of a shared belief regarding inner reality; they are literally sacramental. So, the effigies may have been mounds linked with the burial of the dead (though by no means always); the lines may have been processional routes, demarcated lines of pilgrimage, sacred tracks or geometrically-defined areas of sacred space. In Chapter 3 we saw just how complex the social, ceremonial and spiritual concepts associated with *ceques* had become. But though there is a ground-level, physical usage of such lines, it is linked to a spiritual worldview, and the lines and, particularly, the effigies, also signal their presence vividly from the air, from above. Because this is so obvious at Nazca, we noted in Chapter 3 that Erich von Daniken could invoke typically late twentieth-century notions like spaceships. But there is another explanation, one more authentically in tune with a shamanic society: the ceremonial landscape markings were linked with the idea of out-of-body travel during (particularly) hallucinogen-induced trance states. They related to the supposed aerial perspective of what was believed to be the temporarily disembodied mind of the shaman during its travels.

I am by no means the first to make this suggestion. Although I arrived at the conclusion independently,[27] I came to discover that anthropologist Marlene Dobkin de Rios had long pre-empted me. (The first suggestion that 'astral travel' and 'leys' might be linked was first put forward by one Dan Butcher in an early issue of *The Ley Hunter* journal, however, early in the 1970s.) In 1977 Dobkin de Rios pointed out that three New World areas of giant land effigies — the Adena/Hopewell region of the USA, the Olmec territory of Mexico, and the Nazca geoglyphs of Peru — occurred in areas where plant hallucinogens were known to have been used in a shamanic context. (The Olmec site at San Lorenzo on the Gulf Coast is situated on ridges that are so massive they were initially assumed to be natural, but in fact comprise a huge earthwork depicting a flying bird three-quarters of a mile long and comprehensible only from the air.) She suggested that these giant land markings were constructed 'due to shamanistic, out-of-body experiences, the so-called aerial voyage...'[28] The recurring 'flying god' motif found on artefacts left by the region's earlier Paracas culture is also suggestive. Elsewhere, Dobkin de Rios has identified the use by the Nascan culture of the hallucinogenic cactus 'San Pedro' (*Trichocereus pachanoi*), which is depicted on Nasca and Paracas pottery, as well as ancient Peruvian temples; species of *Datura*, and *wilka* snuff.[29] This may not be the full inventory of available psychoactive plants in the area, as Dobkin de Rios points out.

Dobkin de Rios suggests that the terrestrial effigies may represent shamanic spirit helpers or familiars deployed as supernatural signs to the gods or spirits and perhaps warnings to potentially hostile shamans from elsewhere (she has found that in shamanic cultures there is a considerable amount of rivalry and feuding between shamans of different groups). The effigy markings were thus 'power symbols and icons'.[30] She envisages a Nasca society which had shaman-leaders 'enmeshed in a world view focusing on power and dominion of man over nature'.[31] She argues that the geometrical elements of the pampa markings, however, could be entoptic-related.

The making of the geoglyphs would have also had the effect of reinforcing the authority of the shamanic theocracy, as well as providing a socially-cohesive activity.

Archaeologist Evan Hadingham came to similar but less directly stated conclusions in his book *Lines to the Mountain Gods* (1987). He, too, noted the hallucinogenic history and prehistory of the region (particularly the use of San Pedro cactus by a modern shaman working on the geoglyphs) and its depiction on Nasca and Paracas ceramics. He asked: were the 'giant animal images inspired by shamanism?' Regarding the *lines*, he suggested that after the decline of the ritual centre of Cahuachi, the:

> ...focus of ritual activity apparently shifted... to dozens of ray centres widely scattered on the open pampa. Reaching these...

190

frequently involved hours of arduous walking from the nearest valley along the straight-line pathways. It is likely that such shrines were intended mainly for rites and offerings by individuals.

Indeed, if there is a common thread connecting all the Nazca earth markings, as well as those from California and the Midwest, it is surely related to the basic theme of shamanism: the solitary priest who makes personal contact with otherworldly powers.[32]

Hadingham felt that though the unicursal figurative markings may have been for group activities such as dances, the ray centres, and thus presumably the lines, 'were intended for rituals of an essentially private and solitary kind'.

I agree with Dobkin de Rios about the likely meaning of the figurative geoglyphs, the 'biomorphs'. (One might also add that the existence of some examples of 'X-ray' depictions in a few of the geoglyphs further confirms their shamanic nature.) The reason for the straight lines, however, have perhaps not been given enough thought. I suspect that is because their explanation may be so simple it is too obvious to see!

My suggestion is that the lines are surely *lines of magical flight* marked on the ground, vaguely similar to the flight routes airlines plot across an area. Figure 55 depicts the plotted flightpaths of just one airline over part of Germany, for instance: the flight plots of all traffic around a given airport might well appear as complex as any part of the Nazca pampa! Certainly, the lines marking the shamanic flightpaths were used ritually on the ground too in their exoteric functions to do with ritual and socio-religious requirements, but, if the Cuzco *ceques* are anything to go by, they were still understood as being primarily features of the spirit landscape. Esoterically, in their essence, *the paths were the physical correlates of the routes of shamanic flight in the spirit landscape;* lines either marking the designated ways over that landscape for the disembodied mind of the shaman, or recording where the shaman's spirit had travelled, or both. They would be sacred ways precisely because of that belief; one would walk in the way of the spirit.

We have to try to envisage a worldview in which there was a spiritual version of the terrestrial environment — the Elysian Fields, Eden, the paradisical land, Plato's 'True Earth', the Land

191

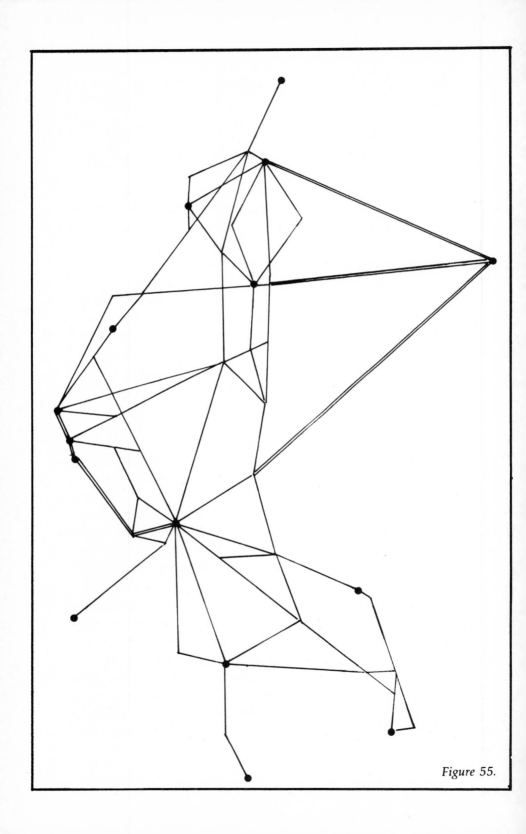

Figure 55.

of the Dead — that can be journeyed to and through only in ecstatic trance or at death. The Land of the Dead, in virtually all traditional cultures, *occupies the terrestrial landscape, but in a different dimensional space*. The mundane sky similarly is a correlate of that which arches over the spirit realms. There was an underworld too, a spiritual replica of the subterranean reaches of the physical world, where the dead were located in some cosmologies — though Eliade considered the theme of the underworld to be a relatively recent innovation in shamanism.

The sacred places of the physical world were where traffic between the worlds was possible. At Nazca, I suggest the ray centres would have served that function, and specifically with regard to out-of-body flight. In the simplest, shamanic societies, the sacred place was the location of the symbolic World Tree or omphalos, World Navel. This was where one gained access to the spirit world. Such locations were monumentalised in more complex societies, ultimately becoming temples.

This explanation for the lines is as simple and direct as the features themselves; *flight is the straight way over the land*. Terrain oblivious. The whole message is encapsulated in the saying 'as the crow flies'. Another saying makes the same point, 'as straight as an arrow'. Indeed, the arrow was an ancient symbol of magical flight.[33] In Greek legend, for instance, Abaris (linked with Apollo), carried a golden arrow as he moved through the land, healing and divining. In some legends, he flew through the air on his golden arrow. The arrow is a key symbol of magical flight in Siberian shamanism, too. The Koryak shaman left his body along the path traced by an arrow. The Samoyed shaman held two arrows point upwards during his seance. When healing a sick person, the Buryat shaman would place an arrow on the ground near the patient's head. From its point a straight red thread was run out through the entrance of the yurt or tent to a birch pole set up outside (birch was associated with the World Tree in Siberian shamanism, and Fly Agaric has a symbiotic relationship with birch). The thread was the route for the sick person's spirit to return to its body.

This theme of string or thread is a common one, and is another version of a 'line' that facilitates passage of spirit. We recall that the !Kung trance dancer when out-of-body 'climbed threads' to heaven. Tunguska tribes believed that an invisible thread connects the human being with the god of fate *in a straight line*.[34] Some traditional peoples believe that the soul is connected to the body by a supernatural thread or line. (Modern Spiritualists have taken for granted that there is a 'silver cord' connecting the 'astral' and physical bodies.) The Rigo, for example, conceive of a 'fishing line', which remains taut and extends indefinitely as the spirit travels beyond the body.[35] Different tribes of Australian aborigines have varying traditions about a thread, issuing variously from the mouth or penis, linking body and spirit during *miriru*, the out-of-body state. One tribe, the Rai, believe in an invisible 'rope of air' on which they can travel in spirit through the air or under the ground. I suspect that such concepts of threads and ropes are direct equivalents of the shamanic landscape lines — they are linear passages of spirit. They have their complement in the traditions where knots and tangles of thread block the passage of spirit (Chapter 5).

The relic of another version of the same basic motif which surfaces in various Amerindian traditions is that of a 'path'. The shaman of the Thomson Indians, British Columbia, for instance, takes 'the old path that the ancestors used in times past to reach the land of the dead'.[36] The Road of the Dead is a common theme — in some traditions it remains open only for a very short, special time. Again, the Mazatec shamaness implores at the beginning of a mushroom ceremony: 'Let us go along the good path . . . The path of the Master of the World. Let us go in a path of happiness.'[37] In Navajo initiation dances, the medicine-man sprinkles a path of meal 'for the gods to tread'.[38] There is the straight 'peyote path' in the ceremonial layout of peyote altars, and so on. There are many more traditions and songs related to paths. And, of course, we must not forget that an Indian informant proclaimed that the Anasazi roads around Chaco Canyon may look like roads, but were not roads

(Chapter 3). There was also the Navajo legend that the Anasazi could travel the Chaco 'roads' in *invisibility*.

The idea that the straight lines of the Amerindians, and therefore by implication the linear elements of shamanic landscapes throughout the world, could relate to the universal experience of magical spirit flight is in keeping with the whole shamanic worldview. Nevertheless, though one can pick up some direct hints in Amerindian traditions — like the Selk'nam Indians of Patagonia who state that in an out-of-body experience the 'eye' leaves the body of the shaman *'and flies in a straight line* to the desired location' (my emphasis), trailing behind it a fine thread[39] — to confirm it as valid really requires a direct statement on the matter from an Amerindian society which has straight paths in its territory and is still conducting shamanic out-of-body activities in a relatively unbroken tradition from ancient times.

I felt the chances of such a confirmation were unlikely in the extreme, but by happy coincidence something approaching that requirement has come about.

In December, 1990, a remarkable film was broadcast by the BBC. It was made by Alan Ereira and was called *From the Heart of the World*. It dealt with the Kogi Indians of Colombia, who we mentioned in passing in Chapter 3. These people are the vestiges of the pre-Colombian Tairona civilisation which occupied the Sierra Nevada de Santa Maria, a huge mountain complex that rises in a distance of only 26 miles (42 km) from the tropical conditions of the coast to its snow-capped peaks, containing ecological niches and climatic zones comparable to all the main ones to be found on earth. It is the earth in microcosm. The Kogi, a Chibcha people, are one of three surviving indigenous groups in the Sierra, but they are the least acculturated; indeed, they represent the most complete cultural survival of pre-Columbian America.

The geographical isolation of the Tairona civilisation ensured insulation from the Incas and Aztecs, but it was part of a cultural complex that nevertheless stretched through northern Columbia and into Central America.

Around AD 1600, a concerted attempt by the Spanish to Christianise and subjugate the Indians led to an uprising by the Taironas followed by bloody retaliation from the Spanish. Decimated, the surviving Indians withdrew deep into the Sierra.

Ereira estimates the Kogi to number about 11 000 today. Little is known of them; they keep themselves remote from the world around them, which, in these parts of Colombia, are peopled by tomb robbers, narcotics traffickers and guerillas, amongst others. The dense forest and rugged topography help to keep the Kogi undisturbed in their mountain fastness — indeed, the region is the location of the legendary El Dorado.

Geraldo Reichel-Dolmatoff conducted the best early academic studies of the Kogi, but even that was with relatively limited contact. He showed the Kogi cosmology to be essentially the shamanic 'three-world' model, though elaborated into a nine-world system. The Cosmic Axis in the Kogi system is represented not by a World Tree, but by a Cosmic Spindle, which is symbolised by the ceremonial house or *nuhue* in each Kogi village. The nine worlds of the cosmological scheme are pictured as discs on the shaft of the spindle, and are all thought of as 'Earths' — '...we came up earth upon earth. Earth, another earth, another earth... But we are only in the middle.'[40] The shaft of the spindle represents the masculine principle; the disks, the 'earths', are feminine.

The Kogi think of their domain as the Heart of the World, and its meteorological zones contain representatives of the world's flora and fauna. They are the stewards of this Eden: they are the Elder Brother. We, troublesome, rapacious and polluting as we are, are the Younger Brother.

Kogi society is orderly, hierarchical in fact, a smaller and modified version of the proto-state which the Tairona civilisation was. The ruling level is made up of the *Mamas*, a name which effectively means Enlightened Ones. They are the educated people, the judges and priests. There are female as well as male Mamas, but the general ordering of society is largely a male preserve, though women are respected. The mass of ordinary people are best described as vassals. They are taught and governed by the decree of the Mamas. To accomplish this, and to attend to the maintenance of the Kogi towns and villages, and the network of roads which interlink across the Sierra, the Mamas work through two intermediate levels of the social hierarchy, the *comisarios* who are assisted by the *cabos*. These will, if necessary, use physical force to ensure that a vassal attends to a duty. It is not a society that Westerners would approve of, but it seems essentially fair after its fashion.

The Mamas are the seers. They are chosen by a process of divination which is deeply integrated into Kogi life. In olden times, and ideally, the potential Mama (*moro*) is selected at birth. The child is taken to a cave or dark forest abode. He is looked after by a cabo and weaned by his mother. The child is brought out only at night, and then with head covering to prevent him seeing the moon or stars. As the child grows, he is fed only sparingly, and with special foods. He is massaged. By this incredibly intensive regime of sensory and social deprivation, and semi-starvation, the child learns to tune into *aluna*. This is the Spirit Earth that lies behind manifest creation. Ereira describes the Kogi concept of aluna as 'The life force... the intelligence of being...'. It is the Mother. It was there before creation. It is 'a spirit-world mirroring everything material'.[41] The mind is aluna. Reared in such a way, the child begins to sing. 'All by itself, it begins to sing... And then this child that has been reared in the spirit world begins to hear the inner music of the universe, and he begins to act in accordance with what he hears. He begins to dance'.[42] He also develops the ability to see and talk 'in aluna' with the 'fathers and masters of the world', the ancestors and spirits. And so the child grows. Mama Bernado, who told Ereira of these things, was not taken as a baby for training but as a child. His confinement lasted nine years.

In its teens, the *moro* will undergo further teaching at the hands of the Mamas, or the training will be discontinued if the child does not seem fully suitable for further progress as a Mama.

The Mamas live and act in the physical plane, but they

simultaneously see and act in the Spirit Earth, in aluna. Ereira was informed: 'When the Mama looks, he sees the spirit world. He sees that rock, but he also sees the spirit rock. He sees that river, but he also sees the spirit river. . . .'. Everything happens through aluna, and the Mamas try to keep accord between the Spirit Earth and the physical plane.

Clearly, this process whereby the Mamas are trained is the key mind-altering element in Kogi society. But all adult male Kogi also chew coca continuously — it was one of the commandments of the Mother. They use a container called a poporo which represents the womb and cervix. Powdered shells are mixed with the coca, and a stick is placed in the mixture in the poporo, withdrawn and sucked. It is then wiped off around the rim of the poporo, and over time a thick lime 'calc' is built up. This usage of coca is unlikely to produce hallucinogenic effects, but does act as a stimulant and medicine, and perhaps induces a generally dreamy state. The Taironas were consummate workers in gold, and hundreds of the small figurines, some therianthropic, have been recovered from ancient tombs (mainly by tomb robbers). They were for wearing on the body and for hanging on trees at sacred places. On some of the gold objects there are mushroom-shaped forms which have been interpreted as hallucinogenic mushrooms, and it has been posited that the Tairona civilisation experienced 'a hallucinogenic mental explosion'.[43] The Mamas sometimes also fast and go without sleep for several days at a time. Dance, drumming and singing is also practised. Ereira notes in his book, *The Heart of the World*, that the dancing has a 'dreamy' aspect to it.

The Mamas have become aware that there is trouble in their Eden. The world is heating up, the snows on the peaks are retracting, and the high tundra is drying out. The mountain is rocky where it had been covered by snow only a few years previously. The lakes are diminishing, the flow of rivers reducing. On the model of the whole earth, which is effectively what the Sierra is, this is equivalent to what is happening at the poles. The Kogi see it and know it forewarns of serious developments: the reducing water supply will inevitably affect the whole of the Heart of the World. (To the Kogi, water is not only the lifeblood of the physical planet, it also has great metaphysical significance — it is memory and potential.) These ominous signs are the fault of the Younger Brother, who knows not how to behave in accordance with the laws of the Mother. Because of this situation, and because of Ereira's attitude which they appreciated, the Kogi decided to speak to Younger Brother through television, and explain to him the problems he is causing, and tell him that things have to be changed. With considerable difficulties, well-described in his book, Ereira and his colleagues made the film. It was the first time the Kogi had ever allowed themselves to be filmed.

Watching the film, my attention was particularly alerted when the cameras showed the ruins of the so-called The Lost City of the Taironas, one of many remarkable stone-built cities of the Sierra known of in Spanish times but most of which have now been reclaimed by the forest, lost to all but the Kogi. The old city was linked to a system of paved roads or· paths — straight paths. All the cities had been so linked. Archaeologists know of about 200 miles (320 km) of roads across the Sierra, but do not know the full extent. Further, at the entrance to the Lost City stands a standing stone nicknamed the 'Map Stone' because it is criss-crossed with incised lines like some kind of map. Could they relate to the roads? The Kogi understand the roads to have been built by the ancestors, and 'they are sacred, and must be maintained, and must be walked'.[44] Indeed, Ereira and his team found the roads to be in regular use, as the Indians moved about their daily business. However, Ereira's commentary to the sequence on the Map Stone was intriguingly oblique:

> The Mama has to walk in a world visible only to the mind's eye, the world of *aluna* . . .
>   . . . the stone paths of the ancestors are traces of the spirit paths which the Mamas walked, in a space we do not understand. These are the paths in the Map Stone. They do not match the material pathways; they are lines of thought, not lines on the ground. But there were points where the two worlds used to meet . . .[45]

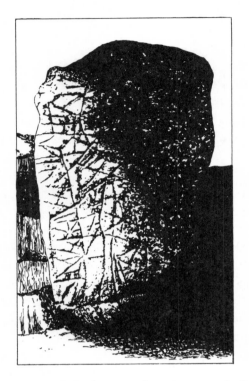

Figure 56. The mysterious 'Map Stone' at the entrance to the Lost City of the Taironas. (Drawn by author from a photograph by Alan Ereira)

Could this be a coded reference to out-of-body travel? Through a fortuitous coincidence, I learned that this might just be the case, so I wrote, a little apprehensively, to Ereira, realising that if I was wrong, my query would look bizarre, to say the least. I asked if the Kogi paths 'relate to the Mamas' out-of-body journeys — spirit travels in a spirit version of the physical world?' Ereira kindly did not keep me in suspense long. Yes, the Mamas had told him precisely this: 'Your explanation — "spirit travels in a spirit version of the physical world" — is perfectly clear and describes the Mamas' work in a way which they themselves would recognise.' (Ereira, personal communication.) Ereira drew my attention to a sequence in the film where vassals are shown cleaning a path in one Kogi town,

200

supervised by the Mamas. (The vassals had, Ereira informed me, experienced drumming and instruction the previous night in the nuhue, to instil in them the importance of the job they had to do.) The path ran from a river in a straight line to the centre of the town, where it seemed to disappear under a building. Ereira told me that it was explained to him quite carefully that this was the physical trace of a spirit path which continued straight on, but only in *aluna*, to another river. The cleaning of the path was a physical, we might say symbolic, act, which the supervising Mamas were transforming into a cleansing in *aluna*. 'The Mamas see part of their work as being concerned with travel in the other worlds,' Ereira confirmed. He added wryly that it required 'a certain adjustment of perspective' for him to think 'of relatively mundane work such as path-cleaning as an out-of-body experience'!

The town where the path was being cleaned was, so the Kogi claimed, pre-Tairona, and the path was one of its oldest features.

Later, I was able to read in Ereira's book that the Kogi maintained that 'The Mamas used to travel in *aluna* and meet other people from other places there. But as the years passed, there were fewer and fewer people who reached the spirit world to talk with them. Now there is no one. It is deserted.'[46]

All this immediately puts the curious practice of *ritual sweeping* into place (Chapter 3). We recall that Gary Urton witnessed the ritual sweeping of the town square in an Andean community. The square was used for mundane activities most of the time, but to prepare for a religious festival, *to create symbolically sacred space*, the kinship groups were allotted strips across the square to sweep ritually. Now presumably just a rote ceremony, we can suspect that it derives from a time when such cleaning, linear sweeping, was indeed the physical expression of a process occurring in the spirit world. Further, we noted that from her studies at Nazca, Helaine Silverman suspected, as did Urton, that the pampa lines had also been ritually swept in their heyday. She learned from Phyllis Pitluga that 'on the pampa

201

some lines are more easily seen than others' which Pitluga had no problem in attributing to 'the practice of sweeping the lines by ancient peoples'.[47]

We should not suppose that ritual sweeping is just an Andean phenomenon — it occurs in ancient traditions of the Indo–European world, too. For instance, several survivals occur or are documented in folk ceremony in Britain. The annual 'Plough Stots' at Goathland, North Yorkshire, involves a team of sword dancers who progress to a crossroads. They are followed by a man dressed as a woman, a 'Betty', who carries a broom and ritually sweeps the road behind the sword dancers. In villages near Sheffield the Old Tup folk ceremony was performed at Christmas. Old Tup was a kind of hobbyhorse, but with a sheep's head which had horns fastened to it. One of the players of the folk drama acted out the stabbing of Old Tup, who is then revived by another character, the 'Doctor'. They were accompanied by 'Our Old Lass', a man with a blackened face who carried a broom. The shamanic elements of such ceremonies are clear: the death–rebirth theme, the hobby horse or its equivalent, ritual transvestism, and, as we can now perceive, ritual sweeping.

But, staying with the Nazca lines, we can strongly suspect that they, or some of them at least, were, surely, seen as being the physical correlates of spirit paths in a spirit landscape, paths defined by the shaman's soul during its out-of-body journey. In his book, Ereira suggests, almost certainly correctly, that the Kogi concept of *aluna* was probably part of a complex of similar ideas permeating the whole Amerindian world, a worldview created or reinforced by the use of many shamanic techniques, not least the ritual ingestion of hallucinogens.

In general, then, we can say that the shamanic landscape line is the superimposition of inner space onto the outer world, and where that superimposition occurs, we have 'sacred space'. The course of the out-of-body, usually 'flying', spirit was seen expressed in the 'otherness' of the mystical straightness of the line (in its purest form). (See Additional Notes, p.232.)

In a curious way, I suspect that this association of straightness and spirit (which in some evolutions, took forms involving less exacting linearity), was reinforced by the occurrence in nature of the straight beam of light. Light is the metaphor *par excellence* for spirit. There are few more numinous scenes in nature than rays of sunlight stabbing through gaps in clouds, and streaming to earth. Even today, such a scene stirs a deep sense of the sacred in us. I suspect that this association of spirit — lightbeam — straightness was what was being expressed in the monuments (such as Ireland's Newgrange) and caves (such as those of the Chumash Indians of California) which were used to admit sunbeams at certain points of the year.

At the deepest levels of trance there is an experience involving the merging or meeting with a shining deity or cosmic light source. As Joan Halifax puts it: 'The journey's mythic end is the sun. The shaman flies through the Sun Door to the realm of eternally awakened consciousness... the realm of the immortal. The solar region is beyond time and space.'[48] To the early Indo–European, this was *Diw*, the Shining One.

Spirit and spirits did not always take straight courses, and the straight line may relate specifically to the *flight* of the shaman's soul, not when it is travelling in animal form, nor the routes of other kinds of spirits. As Halifax states: 'In some shamanic cultures, the path of initiation is an invisible one. Scrolls, labyrinths, meandering trails, and straight lines, all roads of varying meaning...'[49]

Evolution of the line of magical flight

The belief in *aluna* surely springs out of the universality of experience engendered by the human central nervous system when suitably stimulated. And we have seen just how universal the out-of-body experience was. This factor is further reinforced by a cross-cultural study by Dean Shiels who traced no less than 67 indigenous societies throughout every continent in the world who had traditions relating to out-of-body experience.[50]

Depending on the cultural destiny of a given society, the experience was transformed into all kinds of beliefs and social structures. In Chapter 4, for instance, we learned of the curious proto-Indo–European linguistic relic of *regs*, the root of words to do with kingship and government, arguably with a king's *mana* or supernatural power, and with straightness, both spatial and moral. We found that Indo–European mythology enshrined personages such as Odin who combined shaman and sovereign. In Chapter 6, we noted that it has been argued that the idea of the thunderbolt-wielding skygod, of which there are so many examples in Indo–European mythology, may be related to hallucinogenic experiences, specifically involving the Fly Agaric mushroom. Sovereigns, soma and shamanism were shown to be deeply intertwined. The fact that linearity also got into the conceptual brew is explained, I maintain, by the fact that shamans, and, later, kings, *flew* (see above), and flight is the straight way over the land. We can envisage a kind of evolution in which, for public, exoteric, consumption, this came to be conceptually presented as the king sending out his will or personal *mana* over the realm. Sometimes symbolically presented as ceremonial straight ways associated with kingship, and other times as ceremonial processions, perhaps associated with territorial symbolism such as the ritual confirmation of boundaries, this gave rise to the creations of markers and shrines. Recall Eric Partridge's definition of the *regs*, 'to lead or guide straight... a movement straight from one point to another...'[51] Similarly, the Kogi were instructed by the Mother to walk the straight paths, paths that were defined by the out-of-body spirit travels of the Mamas.

We are dealing with deep roots of human experience.

This conceptual process leading (away) from the experience of the shaman's magical flight to ceremonial constructs built on it, has, in a curious way, been continued by the modern, New Age notions of 'energy lines'. We can put together a simplified model of the evolution of the line of magical flight something like that expressed in Table 2, though it is not suggested that such developments occurred in such a neat chronological manner nor all of them in any one society. There were overlaps, stultified developments, regressions and so on, and different cultures took different courses.

Table 2

EVOLUTION OF THE LINE OF SPIRIT FLIGHT
(Simplified Hypothetical Model)

Feature	Socio–religious Context (ASC = Altered State of Consciousness)
Non-physical line of spirit flight; movement in the spirit world; journey to the land of the ancestors, of the dead	Shamanism (solitary; direct ASC experience) *Tribal society*
Physical markings of course of spirit flight; alignments of shrine sites; minimal linking of sacred places; sightlines	Shamanism; shamanic seance; communal spirituality; (varied levels of direct ASC experience) *Tribal society*
Ritual pathways, tracks; pilgrimage routes; avenues of the dead	
Spirit paths; conceptual lines of power	Shamanic religion; social structuring of ritual; embellished belief systems; (varied ASC experience levels) *Tribal/proto-state*
Sacred boundaries; sacred ways	
Ceremonial processions; ceremonial ways	Priests, theocracy; formalised religion; (diminishing and controlled ASC experience) *Proto-state;*
Sacred/secular boundaries; sovereignty	
Secular boundaries; territory	Kingship; divine king; *Proto-state;*
Royal or imperial roads; triumphal ways; death roads; ghost paths; marked meridians; imperial spirit ways	Monarchy; rote belief systems *State;*
Symbolic palace layouts; symbolic city layouts; ceremonial architecture; architectural lines-of-sight	Secular government; secularised religion; secularised monarchy; rote beliefs; 'folk superstition' *State*
Beating the bounds; folk dancing, traditions; rote ceremonial processions public processional ways	Dominance of rationalism; industrialisation; break of conceptual continuity *State*
Field documentation; reports Research; theories: 'Roman survey', 'traders' tracks', etc.;	Secular Western state; Official state religion
Fantasies: 'grids', 'energy lines'; 'intergalactic leylines', etc.	High-tech society; spiritual famine

205

Thus, the long fall from experience to conceptualisation runs its course: from earliest times spirit was associated with supernatural power, *mana* by whatever other name, and that concept, as we have indicated earlier, has in turn been gradually going through transformation into energy since Victorian times so that now the flight of the soul has finally been replaced by a 'spiritualised' image of the circuit-board: the circuitry is formed by 'energy lines' and 'grids' and the circuit board is the landscape, the body of the earth.

This electronic analogy is not a casual one. The inherent materialistic tendency of the modern world is bringing the experience of expanded consciousness, at a cultural level, to the brink of being replaced by computerised 'virtual reality', in which a person wearing a special audio-visual headset and an electronic body stocking is projected into a three-dimensional 'cyberspace', computerised reality, in which body movements are electronically coordinated with actions in the cyberspace program, so that the person participates in a computer-created experience or adventure. It is an electronic analogue of the hallucinogenic experience. It is a system that has developed out of military computer-simulation technology. As war becomes a video game and televisual experience, so the experience of our souls is taken in charge by the computer.

The drift of our culture to total materialism has therefore reached literally inside our heads, and electronic circuitry takes over from the limitless potential and natural realities of the nervous system. Cyberconsciousness. Ironically, the New Agers dowsing 'energy lines' are the very opposites of the spiritual catalysts they suppose themselves to be. The irony is cruel: the actual out-of-body experience is about to be replaced by a cyberspace counterfeit, and the lines of spirit travel across the land have become the fantasised 'energy lines' spawned by the newly-minted electronic archetype that has been constellated in the Western psyche over the course of the twentieth century.

Those lines lead further and further from *aluna*. While it may be argued that the belief systems of the Kogi, Siberian shamans and the rest are equally fantasies, the vital difference is that they are or were based on the actual experiences of deep human consciousness, of inner, spiritual revelation and realities. The modern fantasies are no such thing, and belong more to Hollywood and Disneyworld than the inner potential of the human central nervous system.

In at least a metaphorical sense, we are becoming increasingly 'brain dead'.

Landscape or Mindscape?

Let us finally direct our attention to the nature of the real, human experience of out-of-body travel. Two key questions present themselves.

First, if the experience was so universal, and viewed as being so important in the past, why do we have no experience of it today?

The answer is that we do. Modern researchers have gradually come to realise this from, particularly, deathbed observations, and the reported experiences of people who recover from accidents or illnesses in which heartbeat and breathing stops for a short period — the 'Near Death Experience'. In this a person might find himself looking down on his body, usually in a calm, detached manner, perhaps observing medical staff rushing to resuscitate him. He may experience a rapid-sequence 'life review'. Then, typically, he finds himself travelling along a tunnel, floating or flying with increasing speed towards a light at the far end. In the usual sequence, reported worldwide, the person undergoing the Near Death Experience emerges into a paradisical summerland, and a luminous figure is encountered, often a dead relative or a personage from the person's religious belief system. In some cases, a further dimension of the experience occurs in which there is a transcendental union with a divine light, the godhead. But, inevitably, as it is a *near* death experience, at some point a voice tells the person that their time is not yet, and there is a swift, and sometimes violent, return to the body.

There is no difficulty seeing the elements of the shamanic journey in the Near Death Experience, and, indeed, universal entoptic phenomena such as the ubiquitous tunnel. It is interesting that most people who return from such an experience find their lives and worldview transformed: they fear death less, and become less materialistic in their outlook. A few even seem to acquire unusual healing or psychic abilities. This is a classic shamanic pattern.

That such experiences hold a deep, nowadays inarticulated, significance for us seems to be indicated by the fact that one of the first books to present the Near Death Experience in a publically-accessible, comprehensive fashion, Raymond Moody's *Life after Life*[52], sold around 10 million copies.

In past cultures, there used to be texts for initiatory out-of-body procedures and the process of physical death — the same text was relevant to both circumstances. Classic among such texts were the Egyptian and Tibetan *Book of the Dead* and there was the medieval European 'art of dying' — *ars moriendi*.

Researchers Stanislav Grof and Joan Houston had the occasion during their work to administer LSD to a volunteer who later underwent a natural Near Death Experience. The man reported that he found his Near Death and psychedelic experiences exceedingly similar. 'Without the [LSD] session,' he said, I would have been scared by what was happening, but knowing these states, I was not afraid at all.'[53] Aldous Huxley even took LSD as he was dying.

Another way in which out-of-body experience is with us today is in its spontaneous occurrence in people. It often happens in association with sleep: a person 'wakes up' in a dream and then finds themselves out-of-body, or they 'exteriorise' as they are dozing off. Other times, the experience can be triggered by fatigue, physical or psychological shock, drugs, illness (especially fever), or extreme pain — the conditions effectively sought in ancient initiatory experiences. Even astronauts, apparently, perhaps because of weightless conditions, have found themselves not only out of their bodies, but outside their spacecraft as well![54] These spontaneous cases appear, from the research and surveys that have been conducted at various times, to occur to a surprisingly large number of people in contemporary society.

The third, least recognised and most bizarre way in which moderns experience out-of-body conditions is by being 'abducted' by a 'UFO'. Typically, the person, usually alone and at night, in bed or lonely spot in the country, feels as if he or she is 'floated' along an energy beam and brought to a strangely illuminated interior usually designated as a 'craft', surrounded by strange entities, subjected to invasive physical examinations, and perhaps shown cosmic or paradisical scenes out of the alien spacecraft's window or where the spaceship takes them to. The 'abductee' is later returned to their bedroom or locale, and usually has no recollection of how they got back. Such amnesia is often sensationalised by writers as 'missing time'. These out-of-body experiences are shaped by the modern myth of the machine, hence impersonal alien space technology and entities are encountered. The machine is inside our alienated souls; the gods are dead.

Because we do not have a modern shamanic tradition, and are, as a culture, becoming increasingly out of touch with the functioning of our psyches, these three types of experience are not usually put into a broader context either by the experients or people researching their cases. There is no place for them in the modern Western worldview. No one *officially* believes the out-of-body experience actually happens. Nevertheless, it *does* happen, and should be no more labelled 'occult' than is sleeping, eating or any other human function. This ages-old human experience is still with us.

The second key question is, when the shaman, or anyone else, has an out-of-body experience, does the 'soul' really travel in the physical environment; does anything *actually* leave the body? The answer to this is much more difficult.

At first glance, it seems a ludicrous question — the universality of the experience assures that it is authentic, and so something surely *has* to leave the body. But research over the last two decades or so makes this questionable.

An important researcher in psychophysical matters has been Celia Green. In 1968, she coined the term 'ecsomatic' for the out-of-body experience, and conducted some telling research on the phenomenon.[55] She also introduced the term 'metachoric'[56], by which she meant an experience in which a person's entire visual field becomes hallucinatory during waking consciousness. So, for example, one might be walking down a street and suddenly see dead Uncle George standing on the corner. A ghost? The metachoric theory would say 'No'; rather, the *entire street scene* had been reproduced by one's mind in a flash, looking indistinguishable from the original, actual scene, except that it contained the image of Uncle George. The hallucinatory view was seamlessly merged with reality. Not surprisingly, this theory was not taken up very widely — it seemed too outlandish to take seriously. But then fate took a hand.

In 1913, Frederick Van Eeden had published a paper[57] which incorporated a section on what he called *lucid dreams*, by which he meant those in which the sleeper obtains full critical consciousness without disturbing the sleep state. In short, being awake within a dream. Other early researchers had also noted this paradoxical state, but Van Eeden's paper was reprinted in a seminal work in 1969, *Altered States of Consciousness*, edited by Charles T. Tart.[58] This, along with another important work by Green, *Lucid Dreams* (1968),[59] caused a few sleep and dream researchers to begin looking at this unlikely-sounding phenomenon. Most of their colleagues were uninterested or downright suspicious. In 1975, however, British researcher Keith Hearne, working with Alan Worsley, a subject who regularly has lucid dreams, found a way of proving the reality of lucid dreaming.

In the course of a normal sleep cycle, we dream at spaced intervals, the dream periods getting longer towards the end of the cycle. Dreaming is indicated by Rapid Eye Movements (REMs), a rolling, jerking movement of the eyeballs beneath the closed lids — to some extent as if the dreamer is moving the eyes in response to action happening in 'front' of them. Certain physiological changes also take place during dreaming. An interesting one is that men tend to get erections, which might explain the appearance of erect phalli on cave art figures. While usually interpreted as symbolic of fertility, these may in some cases represent shamans in trance — see Figure 47, for example. Women experience increased vaginal blood flow. (Both these factors may have some relevance with regard to reported 'experiments' or 'examinations' by 'aliens' on reproductive organs during 'abduction' experiences.) Another, important physiological change during dreaming is that the sleeper is effectively paralysed, with only respiratory and eye muscles functioning normally. This allowed Hearne to hit on the idea of arranging with his subject a sequence of eyeball movements to be signalled when he was next having a lucid dream. Worsley was wired up to electronic monitoring equipment in the dream laboratory and, sure enough, the all-important eye-movements signal was picked up.[60] The polygraph traces showed the other measurements indicating that Worsley was in a sleep state when he signalled. It had been proved possible to signal to the outside world from within a dream.

Since then, work on lucid dreaming has moved forward in leaps and bounds, and is taking place in a few university contexts. It is revealing the way consciousness works in dream states: how vivid imagery can be conjured into awareness, how memory material, entoptics and inner and outer sensory signals can all be merged together producing coherent imagery, how the mind can use puns and word-links to move from scene to scene in a dream, how self-generated illumination in dreams is used, and so on. It is also now known that the human mind *can* indeed produce perfect replicas of the outside world. During lucid dreams, subjects have even experienced getting up in the dream laboratory and seeing everything as perfectly 'real', when they were, in fact, securely asleep, if lucid, all the time. This type of experience is called the 'false awakening'. Some people have woken up, got out of bed, washed, dressed, and even had breakfast before the fact that it was a lucid dream became apparent. Clearly, such experiences come close to out-of-body conditions. Researcher and experient, Stephen LaBerge, of Stanford University, once 'rolled' out of his sleeping body, as if having an out-of-body experience, and moved around a metachoric version of his bedroom and saw a metachoric version of his body on the bed.[61] But he was able to determine that he was having a lucid dream. Clearly, the human mind is so brilliantly creative it can indeed conjure up a metachoric reality in an instant, as Celia Green had predicted.

A characteristic sensation in lucid dreams is that one is flying — again indistinguishable from out-of-body experience.

It is important for those who have not experienced lucid dream states to be disabused of any notion that we are talking about some nebulous, unrealistic dream effect. Lucid dreaming provides one with sensations and an 'environment' as 'real' as anything experienced in waking life. One of my own experiences in 1989 may help illustrate this.

I had gone to sleep late evening. At what I later checked to be about 5 a.m., I had a dream in which I was in the darkened chambers beneath an Egyptian temple, looking for a way out. It actually looked a little like an underground car park, but I 'knew' it was beneath a temple! I found a dark, open doorway and ran through it. As I ran down the long dark corridor beyond, it began to dawn on me that I was experiencing the typical entoptic 'tunnel' configuration. Immediately, I was running in a landscape that was illuminated by the sun rising or setting just outside my frame of vision to the left. I was still in a dream stage, but was becoming increasingly aware and the dream was becoming correspondingly more vivid. Ahead of me was a monumental, marble trilithon (two uprights and a lintel), about 40 feet (12m) tall. Others stood in line beyond. As I ran towards it, I 'took off' and flew Superman-style — head-first, arms outstretched ahead — through the line of trilithons. I flew at increasing speed. Each time I passed through a trilithon, the lefthand upright flashed a shadow across me, as the sun was in that direction. The shadow flashes became faster, faster, faster, faster . . . And then I broke out of the avenue of trilithons and soared upwards into a perfect azure sky. As I did so, I became fully conscious — to the same degree as in waking life (in fact more vividly so, judging from my normal mental state!). Upwards I flew, into what I experienced as fully three-dimensional space, then, arching backwards, I 'looped the loop'. The sensation was fully physical, breathtaking, exhilarating. Then I levelled out and floated at a moderate speed about 50 feet (15m) or so above the countryside. I followed a long straight path that emerged from a grassy hillock. As I passed above a stile on the path I made sure to scrutinise it with care, and observe its foreshortened aspect from my aerial position, how its perspective changed correctly as I flew by, and, indeed, as I looked back at it over my shoulder. Ahead and around was a vast, sunlit landscape, with blue-distant hills. It reminded me of the mellow, rolling landscape of Herefordshire. This was the True Earth, the Spirit Earth — or, at least, the version copyright of Paul Devereux's nervous system!

There is not space to go into the whole experience here. Suffice it to say that I passed over roads and houses that looked perfectly normal. I also spied down, unseen, on what were apparently human beings, but they were dressed in strange one-piece, sage-green tunics. One grey-haired man rode a tricycle that had, to my eyes, unfamiliar engineering.

Towards the end of the episode, I floated, upright now, past some trees. I tried to memorise the shape of the leaves, though I found I was no better at that in this curious state than in my normal waking state. I reached out. Could I feel, touch them? I grabbed a handful of foliage as I passed slowly by. To my frank amazement, and then unease, I found I could. I could feel the texture of the leaves, and the resistance of the branch of foliage as I held on to it while I continued floating by. When I let the leaves go, the branch sprang back. At this time, I was not aware that *all* one's senses could accompany one into the 'Otherworld', and I started to question where I really was. My goggle-eyed wonderment was beginning to give way to more conservative concerns, and I felt it was time to get back to normality. How? I seemed to be in another reality, not a dream. Because the landscape I was flying over was 'real' — it had a stable geography — I was able to find my way back to the straight track, and saw the low conical hill beyond. Where the hell could I go to get back? I could not see the 'Egyptian temple' the adventure had started out with. Despite the reality of the situation, I still reasoned (actually, by now, hoped) that I was within a lucid dream, so, taking an ultimate reality test, which is a euphemistic way of saying I took a bit of a risk, I flew full-pelt and head-first into the side of the hillock. There was a fleeting blackout, and I calmly opened my eyes in bed.

There was no sense of 'waking up'. I simply blacked out in one reality and opened my eyes in another one, one no more 'real' than that which I had left. I checked the time. I realised I must have had a lucid dream. Though I was shocked at the vivid reality of it, I was also alert to the fact that I had seen a 'fairy hill', an old straight track, and a landscape that looked like Herefordshire, Alfred Watkins' home county (Chapter 1). The product may have been flawless, but I had a suspicion who the designer was.

Subsequent experiences have convinced me that the mind can indeed produce perfectly 'real' environments. The space is fully three-dimensional (though can take on some interesting distortions at times) and the scenes are convincingly illuminated. Some lucid dreamers report odd errors (like a glass breaking a little too late after it has been dropped), so the counterfeit nature of the reality sometimes shows itself briefly.

Alan Worsley is reportedly working on moving into lucid dream states straight from waking consciousness, without any intervening sleep. En route, he is encountering 'entities' that bear a striking resemblance to the 'aliens' reported in 'abduction' cases.[62] Researchers have recorded REM occurrence in normal, eyes-open subjects who had their eyelids taped open, and some people normally sleep and dream with their eyes open. (I do so myself on occasion, and I remember one memorable waking dream in which an eagle figuring in it underwent a remarkable metamorphosis into the doorknob and fingerplate my half-open eyes were actually directed at as I awoke!) So 'abductions', especially as they are so often initiated in bedrooms, are almost certainly a form of lucid dream altered state. Such states can be triggered naturally during sleep, or because of intense psychosocial pressures, physical weakness or fatigue, sensory deprivation or monotony, or external geophysical effects — any of the types of conditions we have already noted are contained in the techniques for producing shamanic ecstasy.

A seeming example of a geophysical trigger is a case that apparently took place on the Yakima Indian reservation in Washington State, USA, in 1967. The reservation has a history of being plagued by 'earth light' phenomena (it is also adjacent to the part of the Cascade mountains where Kenneth Arnold had his famous 'flying saucer' sighting in 1947). Five people were stranded at night on the reservation when their car broke down at an isolated location. They encountered one of the strange lights, and all suffered amnesia. The only thing one witness could recall was 'seeing himself and the others frozen, looking up, from a perspective as if he were out of his body'.[63] It is worth noting that several reported 'abductions' have started with the abductee first of all coming into close contact with a light ball.

A modern monotony trigger is driving; it seems many abductions are reported during road journeys. We only have to think about this for a moment. A long car drive can quite definitely generate a light trance state, as any experienced driver will know. This is especially true at night. Furthermore the road ahead (again especially at night), forever rushing up to the driver, provides a powerful visual reinforcement of the 'tunnel' form constant, the very entoptic image associated with the onset of the out-of-body experience, particularly in America with its long straight roads. Indeed, the famous poster for the film, *Close Encounters of the Third Kind*, was of a nightime road stretching ahead!

Obviously, if abductions are a form of spontaneous metachoric experience, then any amount of perfectly 'real'-looking, bizarre, hallucinatory material can be released into it; and this

215

would be recoverable even by regression hypnosis — *the experience itself is real to the person involved.* It is spontaneous shamanism occurring in an unprepared person, living in a society essentially hostile to such experiences, and with a worldview that is materialistic and machine-oriented. Hence hostile alien beings and machinery. Hence abductions to a location 'out there', beyond the body.

Susan Blackmore, a psychologist who herself had a remarkable three-hour out-of-body experience[64] has come to the conclusion, after years of research, that nothing leaves the body during such an experience. 'Rather,' she says, 'I think it is all a question of changing the perspective from which the brain models the world... Normally this is a model built as though there is a person inside the head — of course this is an illusion but a very convenient one for getting around the place. Why should this ever be given up? I suppose that it is either when the normal perceptual model cannot be built (near-death, hypoxia, shock, etc.), when it doesn't have enough information from the senses (meditation, sensory deprivation) or when there is a damned good reason not to want to have a body centred view (extreme pain, fear)...' (Blackmore, personal communication). Her view that we are indeed dealing with metachoric experiences rather than actual exteriorised consciousness in out-of-body states is echoed by some other leading scholars dealing with lucid dreaming and other altered states.

On the other hand, I bluntly asked one researcher, who also regularly experiences out-of-body states, if there were differences or not between lucid dreaming and out-of-body experience. He drew a line on a table napkin. Stabbing one end with his pen, he said that at one end of the continuum we have normal dreams, then as we pass along the continuum we have a range of increasingly vivid states of dream and trance consciousness. At the other end of the continuum, he went on, tapping the other end of the line, we have the highest forms of lucid dream. But there may also be an experience, he suggested, sweeping his pen off the napkin, in which consciousness does in some mysterious way separate from the body — that is, if one assumes consciousness is attached to the body in the first place. 'But I'd not put that in a paper,' he grinned.

I have had at least one out-of-body experience that I find difficult to accept did not involve a genuine exteriorised state, but I have to admit I cannot rationally explain why it was any different to other, equally realistic experiences that I am satisfied were lucid dreams. There have been some experiments where volunteers have tried to see targets placed out of their physical sight during out-of-body sessions. There have been a few, but only a few, fairly convincing positive results, but it seems most researchers do not consider them as being totally conclusive as yet. There are also a limited number of reported instances observed by anthropologists working in the field, where Indians in hallucinogenic trance states seemingly brought back authentic and later provable information from a distance.[65] If it ever can be proven to Western requirements that the mind can move through the external environment, then, without doubt, current models of reality will be shaken to the core. The whole current Western concept of consciousness would have to be reassessed, and with it the entire philosophical base of our culture. *The idea of genuinely exteriorised consciousness will therefore be resisted with determined tenacity.*

Having said all that, it has to be admitted that as more is learned about the mind, the metachoric view is strengthened, and researchers like Blackmore, who have experienced what they are talking about, have no particular axe to grind; their research simply indicates the way the brain-mind works. And that is marvellous enough. It may be, too, that *psi* or ESP faculties become more active during sleep states,[66] which could explain concrete information being obtained as though by an exteriorised mind. (If true, this will also challenge the official modern worldview.) Furthermore, if one looks back to the wisdom of the ancient sages who wrote the *Upanishads*, who wrote of the Lone Wild Gander, it can be seen that in their remarkable knowledge of human consciousness they make it pretty clear that the wandering spirit does so within the mind, and not externally. The *Mandukya Upanishad* speaks of the 'inwardly cognitive, experiencing in exquisite solitude luminous enjoyments'; the *Brihadaranyaka Upanishad* tells us that 'When, on falling asleep, one takes along the material of this all-containing world, tears it apart and builds it up, oneself, and by one's own light dreams: that person becomes self-illuminated.' The Lone Wild Gander, we recall, soars high and low 'in the state of sleep'. The modern researchers therefore seem in accordance with the ancient sages.

Blackmore feels that the out-of-body experiences are in fact a kind of clinging to self, in a sense a hinderance along the way to deeper and more profound mystical consciousness.

It is these more profound states that the mystics of all ages emphasise. The Upanishads likewise make this clear. In a sense, not only are metachoric worlds illusory, so is our so-called 'real world'. It is a construct put together in the brain from raw energy data impinging on our senses. All altered states are *exceptionally* malleable by set and setting, cultural expectations and influences. The experience of the 'real world' is similarly massaged by cultural expectations. Culture is a sustained hallucination, and never more so than with our international media massages. All is *maya*, all is illusion. There is only Mind, the godhead, the Void of All-Knowing beyond time, space, life, death; beyond considerations of 'inner' or 'outer' — beyond all dualities. Each of us individually builds an ego like a psychic coracle to navigate the cosmic ocean of Mind at Large. In altered states that construct is pulled out of shape and, in deep experiences, dissolved: the out-of-body experience is an early indicator of that process. In the shamanic trance, the shaman 'travels' in the spirit worlds, but ultimately merges with a shining god or a cosmic light.

But this is deep, metaphysical stuff we need follow no further here. Within the realm of dualities, we can say that the jury is still out regarding whether or not 'anything leaves' the body during the out-of-body, the ecsomatic experience. Ultimately, whatever the final outcome may be, it does not affect the matter of shamanic landscapes. Whether a shaman actually flew over

218

the physical surroundings of a society, or whether it occurred 'only' in a metachoric sense, the effect was the same. I cannot help but think of my lucid-dream version of 'Herefordshire', and the elements in that experience which were built from my involvement with ley hunting. It drove home to me how such experiences, had in a society which firmly believed that spirit flight occurred in the spirit version of the physical world, would be moulded and equipped with the gods, spirits, procedures and 'power places' that went with that society's cosmology. If I had shamanic out-of-body experiences in such a society, would I not see those spirits? Indeed, would I not fly over a metachoric landscape that looked just like the one in the physical environment, if that is what I believed I was doing? And where I entered that landscape to seek entrance to the Underworld, or where I met spirit helpers, and so on, would I not readily transfer those places to the real landscape? Would not the paths of my spirit across the landscape of the metachoric 'True Earth' be translatable onto the physical surface of the mundane landscape? Are the landscape lines not the terrestrial analogue of the tunnel entoptic form constant that heralds out-of-body experience?

Is it not now clear from all that we have discussed in these pages that our minds carry the blueprint of the spiritual earth? If only our own culture could again find those wellsprings of the psyche. If only it could find them and translate such timeless patterns from our minds to the physical earth; from aluna as the Kogi Mamas would say. If only we could allow the spiritual earth to leave its physical mark, as the shamanic peoples of the past once did.

EPILOGUE

Landscape lines, leys, alignments, are *traces*. They are variously-evolved features that had their origins in the ecsomatic experience at the heart of shamanism. They may have become, conceptually, lines of power, then energy; they may have become physical tracks, ritual pathways, avenues of the dead or whatever, but they are in essence simply traces of an effect of the human central nervous system transferred to the land. That effect, as we have discussed, is the remarkable ability of the human mind to roam experientially, if not actually, beyond the body.

That means there are two kinds of 'ley hunting' available to the modern alignment researcher: outer and inner. The outer involves studying ancient shamanic landscapes — on maps, air photos, and in the field. We need to look at them, find out all we can about them, learn from them. But there is an inner geography too, as we have seen in these pages. There is the Spirit Earth overlying the physical lineaments of the land; Wordsworth's 'something far more deeply interfused'. It can be seen only through the lens of the mind. We need to explore that inner landscape as well.

The out-of-body, ecsomatic, state, the essence of the shamanic experience, needs to be brought back from its cultural exile and given much greater attention in our modern times. It is a practical way for us to get back inside our psyches again. By visiting the Spirit Earth, repeatedly, consciously and in culturally recognised and approved ways, we would rediscover the perennial protocols for inhabiting the physical earth, for correcting our worldview.

This work is already going on at university levels on the one hand, and in hole-in-the-corner occult practice on the other. I feel it needs to be wrested from both camps and brought into the light of day as a technique and experience commonly available. Otherwise, most people's experience of the ecsomatic state has to await a spontaneous occurrence of the phenomenon, perhaps a Near Death Experience, or possibly only at the end of their lives. It would be better, would it not, to try to master the condition in less extreme circumstances?

Many techniques exist for achieving the ecsomatic state, and they have been described in various books, and are taught by various practitioners. I am personally trying to evolve a means that will be effective for most people, without the need for advanced psychophysical abilities. Those working in various branches of consciousness studies, including the lucid dream researchers, are similarly developing techniques and aids.

If the ecsomatic state was culturally sanctioned and respected, if our politicians, bankers, industrialists and others regularly experienced the state, as is technically feasible for them so to do, then slowly but surely our modern Western worldview, so wanting and dangerous in many respects, would be modified and made more whole. We could make the whole earth a shamanic landscape.

REFERENCES

Chapter 1: The Rise of a Heresy
1. John Michell, *The New View Over Atlantis*, Thames & Hudson, 1983.
2. M. Behrend, N. Pennick and P. Jones, *W.H. Black, Pioneer Geomantic Researcher – Selected Works*, Institute of Geomantic Research 1976.
3. Alice Dryden (ed.), *The Memorials of Old Leicestershire*, George Allen, 1911.
4. W. Done Bushell, 'Among the Prescelly Circles', *Archaeologia Cambrensis*, 11, 1911.
5. Allen Watkins, *Alfred Watkins of Hereford*, Garnstone Press, 1972.
6. Alfred Watkins, *The Old Straight Track* (1925), Garnstone edition, 1970.
7. R.J.C. Atkinson, 'Archaeologists vs. Ley Hunters', *The Ley Hunter*, 90, 1981.
8. Jonathan Mullard, 'Over Old Ground', *The Ley Hunter*, 100,1986.
9. Alan Wharam, *The Ley Hunter*, 103, 1987.
10. Ron Shoesmith, *Alfred Watkins – A Herefordshire Man*, Logaston Press, 1990.
11. Nigel Pennick in *Lines on the Landscape* (Nigel Pennick and Paul Devereux), Hale, 1989.
12. John Michell, *A Little History of Astro-Archaeology*, Thames & Hudson, 1977 and 1989.
13. Josef Heinsch, *Principles of Prehistoric Sacred Geography* (originally read as a paper at the International Congress of Geography, Amsterdam, 1938), translated by M. Behrend, Zodiac House, 1975.
14. Ibid.
15. Michael Behrend in the Preface to his translation of a collection of Kurt Gerlach's papers, *Leys of the German Empire*, Institute of Geomantic Research, (undated, but post-1976).
16. Ibid.
17. Philip Heselton, *Tony Wedd – A New Age Pioneer*, Northern Earth Mysteries, 1986.
18. Paul Devereux, *Earth Memory – The Holistic Earth Mysteries Approach to Decoding Ancient Sacred Sites*, Quantum, 1991.
19. Philip Heselton, *The Elements of Earth Mysteries*, Element, 1991.
20. John Michell, *The Old Stones of Land's End*, Garnstone, 1974.
21. Paul Devereux, *Earth Lights*, Turnstone Press, 1982.

222

22. Paul Devereux, *Earth Lights Revelation*, Blandford Press, 1989 and 1990.
23. Paul Devereux, *Places of Power*, Blandford Press, 1990.
24. Paul Devereux and Ian Thomson, *The Ley Hunter's Companion*, Thames & Hudson, 1979, (re-issued in digest form as *The Ley Guide*, Empress, 1987).
25. Brian Larkman, 'The York Ley', *The Ley Hunter*, 100, 1986.
26. Nigel Pennick in *Lines on the Landscape*, op.cit.
27. Ibid.
28. Paul Devereux, 'London Leys and Lines', in *Legendary London* (J. Matthews & C. Potter eds.), Aquarian, 1990.
29. John Palmer, *Blue Stones*, unpublished manuscript.
30. Nigel Pennick in *Lines on the Landscape*, op.cit.
31. E.J. Eitel, *Feng-Shui (The Rudiments of Natural Science in China)* (1873), Cockaygne edition, 1973.
32. W.Y. Evans-Wentz, *The Fairy Faith in Celtic Countries* (1911), Colin Smythe edition, 1977.
33. Guy Underwood, *The Pattern of the Past* (1969), Abacus edition, 1972.
34. Arthur Lawton, *The Mysteries of Ancient Man*, private, 1939.
35. Tom Graves, *Dowsing – Its Techniques and Applications*, Turnstone Press, 1976 (re-issued as *The Diviner's Handbook*, Aquarian, 1986).
36. Tom Graves, *Needles of Stone*, Turnstone Press, 1978 (re-issued as *Needles of Stone Revisited*, Gothic Image, 1986).

Chapter Two: Other Lines of Enquiry
1. Alex Gibson and Roy Loveday, 'Excavations at the Cursus Monument of Aston-upon-Trent, Derbyshire', in *Midlands Prehistory* (A. Gibson ed.), BAR British Series 204, 1989.
2. Chris Fletcher, 'The Aston Cursus as a Ley', in *The Ley Hunter*, 112, 1990.
3. Peter Topping, 'Excavations at the Cursus at Scorton, 1978', in *Yorkshire Archaeological Journal*, Vol. 54, 1982.
4. J.F.S. Stone, 'The Stonehenge Cursus and its Affinities', in *The Archaeological Journal*, 1947.
5. Patricia M. Christie, 'The Stonehenge Cursus', in *Wiltshire Arch. and Nat. Hist. Magazine*, 58, 1963.
6. R.J.C. Atkinson, 'The Dorset Cursus', in *Antiquity*, 29, 1955.
7. Richard Bradley, *The Dorset Cursus: The Archaeology of the Enigmatic*, Wessex Lecture III, Council for British Archaeology Group 12, 1986.
8. Ibid.
9. Ibid.
10. D.P. Dymond, 'Ritual Monuments at Rudstone', in *Proc. of the Prehistoric Society*, 32, 1966.
11. For the full study, see 'Prehistoric Lines in Britain' by Paul Devereux, in *Lines on the Landscape*, op.cit.
12. Andrew Fleming, 'Coaxial field systems: some questions of time and space', in *Antiquity*, Vol. 61, No.232, July 1987.
13. Andrew Fleming, *The Dartmoor Reaves*, Batsford, 1988.

14. Fleming 1987, op.cit.
15. Ibid.
16. John W.M. Peterson, 'Why did the idea of coaxial field systems last so long?', in *Antiquity*, Vol.64, No.244, September 1990.
17. H.H.E. Loofs, 'The Mok Khalan alignment in southern Thailand and associated archaeological remains', in *Journal of the Malaysian Branch of the Royal Asiatic Society*, Vol.L, Part 1, 1977.

Chapter 3: The Amerindian Legacy
1. Laetitia Sample, 'Trade and Trails in Aboriginal California', in *Reports of the Univ. of California Archaeological Survey*, 8, 1950.
2. S.A. Barrett and E.W. Gifford, 'Miwok Material Culture', in *Bull of the Public Museum of the City of Milwaukee*, 4, 1933.
3. Chris Kincaid (ed.), *Chaco Roads Project Phase I*, US Dept of the Interior, Bureau of Land Management, 1983.
4. Kendrick Frazier, *People of Chaco*, Norton, 1986.
5. Ray A. Williamson, *Living the Sky*, University of Oklahoma Press, 1984.
6. Cited by Pennick in *Lines on the Landscape*, op.cit.
7. Thomas L. Sever, 'Remote sensing applications in archaeological research; tracing prehistoric human impact upon the environment, doctoral dissertation, University of Colorado, University microfilms, 1990.
8. Cited by Benjamin P. Robertson in Kincaid, 1983, op.cit.
9. Alan Ereira, *The Heart of the World*, Jonathan Cape, 1990.
10. Victor Von Hagen, *Highway of the Sun*, Little, Brown & Co., 1955.
11. Evan Hadingham, *Lines to the Mountain Gods*, Random House, 1987.
12. A.F. Aveni, 'Order in the Nazca Lines', in *The Lines of Nazca* (A.F. Aveni ed.), The American Philosophical Society, 1990.
13. Ibid.
14. Ibid.
15. Tom Zuidema, cited in ibid.
16. Presented in a paper by Tony Morrison at The Ley Hunter *Moot*, York, 1985.
17. Gerald Hawkins, *Beyond Stonehenge;* Hutchinson, 1973.
18. *The Lines of Nazca*, op.cit.
19. A.F. Aveni, 'Epilogue' in *The Lines of Nazca*, op.cit.
20. Persis Clarkson, 'The Archaeology of the Nazca Pampa, Peru: Environmental and Cultural Parameters', in *The Lines of Nazca*, op.cit.
21. Ibid.
22. T. Zuidema, 1982, cited by H. Silverman in 'The Early Pilgrimage Center of Cahuachi and the Nazca Lines: Anthropological and Archaeological Perspectives', in *The Lines of Nazca*, op.cit.
23. Tony Morrison, *Pathways to the Gods*, Michael Russell, 1978.
24. Silverman, 1990, op.cit.
25. Ibid.
26. Ibid.
27. Gary Urton, 'Andean Social Organisation and the Maintenance of the

Nazca Lines', in *The Lines of Nazca*, op.cit.
28. Aveni, 'Epilogue', in *The Lines of Nazca*, op.cit.
29. Helaine Silverman and David Browne, 'New evidence for the date of the Nazca lines', in *Antiquity*, Vol. 65, No.247, June 1991.
30. Aveni, 'Epilogue', in *The Lines of Nazca*, op.cit.
31. Morrison, 1978, op.cit.
32. Hadingham, 1987, op.cit.

Chapter 4: The King and the Land
1. Joseph Campbell, *The Way of the Animal Powers*, Harper & Row, 1988.
2. Ibid.
3. Neville Drury, *The Elements of Shamanism*, Element, 1989.
4. Joan Halifax, *Shaman – The Wounded Healer*, Crossroad, 1982.
5. Ibid.
6. Holger Kalweit, *Dreamtime and Inner Space*, Shambhala, 1988.
7. Marlene Dobkin de Rios, *Hallucinogens* (1984), Prism edition, 1990.
8. Michael Harner (ed.), *Hallucinogens and Shamanism*, Oxford University Press, 1973.
9. Mircea Eliade, *Shamanism – Archaic Techniques of Ecstasy* (1951), Princeton University Press Bollingen edition, 1964.
10. Ibid.
11. Ibid.
12. Gerald Weiss, 'Shamanism and Priesthood in Light of the Campa Ayahuasca Ceremony', in *Hallucinogens and Shamanism*, op.cit.
13. Eliade 1951/1964, op.cit.
14. Harold Bailey, *Archaic England*, Chapman & Hall, 1919.
15. J.P. Mallory, *In Search of the Indo-Europeans*, Thames & Hudson, 1989.
16. Ibid.
17. Colin Renfrew, *Archaeology and Language: The Puzzle of Indo-European Origins*, London, 1987 (cited in Mallory, ibid.).
18. John Robb, 'Random causes with directed effects: the Indo-European language spread and the stochastic loss of lineages', in *Antiquity* 247, June 1991.
19. Mallory, 1989, op.cit.
20. Ibid.
21. Eliade 1951/1964, op.cit.
22. Ibid.
23. Mallory, 1989, op.cit.
24. Jim Kimmis, in a paper to Institute of Geomantic Research Symposium, Cambridge, 1979.
25. Jim Kimmis, 'The King's Highway', in *The Ley Hunter*, 89, 1980.
26. Eric Partridge, *Origins* (1958), RKP edition, 1961.
27. Marion Wenzel, *House Decoration in Nubia*, Duckworth, 1972.
28. Paul Devereux, 'Straight Walking', in *The Ley Hunter 102*, 1986; also in *Lines on the Landscape*, op.cit.

29. Caitlin Matthews, *Arthur and the Sovereignty of Britain*, Arkana, 1989.
30. Alwyn and Bryn Rees, *Celtic Heritage*, Thames & Hudson, 1961.
31. John Michell, *New Light on the Mysteries of Glastonbury*, Gothic Image, 1990.
32. James Frazer, *The Golden Bough* (1922), Macmillan edition, 1932.
33. A & B Rees, 1961, op.cit.
34. Anne Ross, *The Pagan Celts* (1970), Batsford edition, 1986.
35. Ibid.
36. John Palmer, *Blue Stones*, op.cit.
37. William Howells, *The Heathens*, Doubleday, 1948.
38. Mallory, 1989, op.cit.
39. Frazer, 1922/1932, op.cit.
40. Ibid.

Chapter 5: Spirit Lines
1. R.J.C. Atkinson, 'The Dorset Cursus', in *Antiquity*, 29, 1955.
2. Richard Bradley, 1986, op.cit.
3. David Keys, 'Godmanchester's Temple of the Sun', in *New Scientist*, 2, March 1991.
4. Peter Harbison, *Pre-Christian Ireland*, Thames & Hudson, 1988.
5. John Palmer, 'The Deathroads of Holland', in *The Ley Hunter*, 109, 1989.
6. John Palmer, 'Deathroad', in *The Ley Hunter*, 113, 1990.
7. John Palmer, 'Deathroads III', in *The Ley Hunter*, 114, 1991.
8. A.F. Aveni, in *The Lines of Nazca*, op.cit.
9. Weston La Barre, 'Anthropological Perspectives on Hallucinations and Hallucinogens', in *Hallucinations*, R.K. Siegel and L.J. West (eds.), John Wiley, 1975.
10. John Fire/Lame Deer and Richard Erdoes, *Lame Deer – Sioux Medicine Man*, (1972), Quartet edition, 1980.
11. Weston La Barre, *The Peyote Cult*, University of Oklahoma Press, 1989 edition.
12. Ibid.
13. Cited by Evan Hadingham, 1987, op.cit.
14. Deb Saward, 'The Rösaring Road', in *Caerdroia*, 18, 1986.
15. W.F.J. Knight, 'Maze Symbolism and the Trojan Game, *Antiquity*, Vol. VI, No.24, December 1932.
16. Nigel Pennick, *Practical Magic in the Northern Tradition*, Aquarian, 1989.
17. K. Branigan (ed.), *Atlas of Archaeology*, Macdonald, 1982.
18. E.J. Eitel, 1873/1973, op.cit.
19. Stephen Skinner, *The Living Earth Manual of Feng-Shui*, RKP, 1982.
20. Evelyn Lip, *Feng-Shui* (1979), Heian edition, 1987.
21. See p.60, ibid.
22. Dermot Mac Manus, *The Middle Kingdom* (1959), Colin Smythe edition, 1973.
23. W.Y. Evans Wentz, 1911/1977, op.cit.

24. Marlene Dobkin de Rios, 1984/1990, op.cit.
25. Ibid.
26. Mircea Eliade, 1951/1964, op.cit.

Chapter 6: Trance, Dance and Magic Plants
1. Weston La Barre, in Hallucinations, op.cit.
2. Michael Harner, *The Way of the Shaman* (1980), Bantam edition, 1982.
3. Mircea Eliade, 1951/1964, op.cit.
4. Ibid.
5. Weston La Barre, 1989, op.cit.
6. Ibid.
7. Marcel Granet, cited in Eliade, 1951/1964, op.cit.
8. Richard Katz, *Boiling Energy*, Harvard University Press, 1982.
9. Harner, 1980/1982, op.cit.
10. Eliade, 1951/1964, op.cit.
11. Paul Devereux, *Places of Power*, op.cit.
12. Alberto Villoldo and Stanley Krippner, *Healing States*, Simon & Schuster, 1986 and 1987.
13. Paul Devereux, *Places of Power*, op.cit.
14. W.Y. Evans Wentz, 1911/1977, op.cit.
15. Jim Swan, 'Sacred Places in Nature', in *Shaman's Path* (Gary Doore, ed.), Shambhala, 1988.
16. Holger Kalweit, 1988, op.cit.
17. Paul Devereux, *Earth Lights Revelation*, op.cit.
18. See Persinger's work, cited in ibid.
19. Marlene Dobkin de Rios, 1984/1990, op.cit.
20. Richard Katz, 1982, op.cit.
21. Weston La Barre in *Hallucinations*, op.cit.
22. Charles Musès, 'The Sacred Plant of Ancient Egypt', in *Gateway to Inner Space* (Christian Rätsch ed.), Prism, 1989.
23. Marlene Dobkin de Rios, 1984/1990, op.cit.
24. Weston La Barre, 1989, op.cit.
25. W. Reininger, 'Remnants from Prehistoric Times', in *The Book of Grass* (George Andrews and Simon Vinkenoog eds.), Grove Press, 1967.
26. Marlene Dobkin de Rios, 1984/1990, op.cit.
27. Ibid.
28. Weston La Barre, in *Hallucinations*, op.cit.
29. Ibid.
30. Nigel Pennick, 1989, op.cit.
31. Mircea Eliade, 1951/1964, op.cit.
32. Weston La Barre in *Hallucinations*, op.cit.
33. Michael Harner, 1973, op.cit.
34. Bouguet, cited by Harner in ibid.
35. Harner in ibid.
36. Marlene Dobkin de Rios, 1984/1990, op.cit.
37. Harner, 1973, op.cit.

38. La Barre, 1989, op.cit.
39. Joseph Campbell, 1988, op.cit.
40. La Barre, 1989, op.cit.
41. Ibid.
42. Halifax, 1982, op.cit.
43. Harner, 1973, op.cit.
44. Ibid.
45. Cited by Siegel and Jarvik, 'Drug-Induced Hallucinations in Animals and Man', in *Hallucinations*, op.cit.
46. M.J. Horowitz, 'Hallucinations – An Information-Processing Approach', in *Hallucinations*, op.cit.
47. Siegel & Jarvik, 1975, op.cit.
48. Ibid.
49. Claudio Naranjo, 'Psychological Aspects of the Yagé Experience in an Experimental Setting', in *Hallucinogens and Shamanism*, op.cit.
50. Seigel and Jarvik, 1975, op.cit.
51. J.D. Lewis-Williams and T.A. Dowson, 'The Signs of All Times', in *Current Anthropology*, Vol. 29, No.2, April 1988.
52. David S. Whitley in ibid.
53. Lewis-Williams and Dowson, 1988, op.cit.
54. Campbell, 1988, op.cit.
55. J.F. Thackeray, 'On concepts expressed in southern African rock art', in *Antiquity*, Vol. 64, No.242, March 1990.
56. Harner, 1973, op.cit.
57. Kalweit, 1988, op.cit.
58. Dobkin de Rios, 1984/1990, op.cit.
59. Kalweit, 1988, op.cit.

Chapter 7: The Lines of the Lone Wild Gander

1. This is the subtitle of Eliade's great work on shamanism, op.cit.
2. Kalweit, 1988, op.cit.
3. Eliade, 1951/1964, op.cit.
4. Celia Green, *Out-of-the-Body Experiences*, Institute of Psychophysical Research, 1968.
5. Partridge, 1958/1961, op.cit.
6. Eliade, 1951/1964, op.cit.
7. Campbell, 1988, op.cit.
8. Eliade, 1951/1964, op.cit.
9. Ibid.
10. M.F. Köprülüzadé, cited in ibid.
11. Rogan Taylor, 'Who is Santa Claus?', in *Sunday Times Magazine*, December 21, 1980.
12. Pennick, 1989, op.cit.
13. La Barre in *Hallucinations*, op.cit.
14. Ibid.
15. I am grateful to Charla Devereux for this suggestion.

16. Alaistair I. McIntosh, 'Beliefs about out-of-the-body experiences among the Elema, Gulf Kamea and Rigo peoples of Papua New Guinea', in *Journal* of the Society for Psychical Research, Vol. 50, No.785, September 1980.
17. Susan J. Blackmore, *Beyond the Body* (1982), Granada edition, 1983.
18. Campbell, 1988, op.cit.
19. Lewis-Williams and Dowson, 1988, op.cit.
20. Ibid.
21. Campbell, 1988, op.cit.
22. Halifax, 1982, op.cit.
23. Ibid.
24. R. Gordon Wasson, 'The Hallucinogenic Fungi of Mexico' (1960), in *The Psychedelic Reader*, Gunther M. Weil, Ralph Metzner and Timothy Leary (eds.), University Books, 1965.
25. Harner, 1973, op.cit.
26. Weiss in ibid.
27. My first published hint was in Chapter 6 of *Lines on the Landscape*, op.cit.
28. Marlene Dobkin de Rios, 'Plant Hallucinogens, Out-of-Body Experiences and New World Monumental Earthworks', in *Drugs, Rituals and Altered States of Consciousness*, Brian M. Du Toit (ed.), A.A. Balkema, 1977.
29. Dobkin de Rios, 1984/1990, op.cit.
30. Ibid.
31. Ibid.
32. Hadingham, 1987, op.cit.
33. Eliade, 1951/1964, op.cit.
34. Kalweit, 1988, op.cit.
35. Blackmore, 1982/1983, op.cit.
36. Eliade, 1951/1964, op.cit.
37. Henry Munn, 'The Mushrooms of Language', in *Hallucinogens and Shamanism*, op.cit.
38. Erna Ferguson, *The Dancing Gods* (1932), University of New Mexico Press edition, 1988.
39. Kalweit, 1988, op.cit.
40. Mama Bernado, cited in Ereira, 1990, op.cit.
41. Ereira, 1990, op.cit.
42. Mama Bernado, cited in ibid.
43. Richard Evans Schultes and Alec Bright, 'Ancient Gold Pectorals from Colombia: Mushroom Effigies?', in *Botanical Museum Leaflets*, Vol. 27, Nos.5–6, Harvard University, 1979 (cited in Ereira, 1990).
44. Ereira, 1990, op.cit.
45. Transcription from *From the Heart of the World*, BBC TV, 4 December 1990, Alan Ereira.
46. Ereira, *The Heart of the World*, op.cit.
47. Silverman in , *The Lines of Nazca*, op.cit.
48. Halifax, 1982, op.cit.
49. Ibid.

50. Dean Sheils, 'A Cross-Cultural Study of Beliefs in Out-of-Body Experiences', in the *Journal* of the Society for Psychical Research, March, 1978, Vol. 49, No.775.
51. Partridge, 1958/1962, op.cit.
52. R. Moody, *Life After Life*, Mockingbird Books, 1975.
53. S. Grof and J. Houston, *The Human Encounter with Death*, Dutton, 1978.
54. Siegel and Jarvik, 1975, op.cit.
55. Green, 1968, op.cit.
56. See, for example, Celia Green and Charles McCreery, *Apparitions* (1968), Institute of Psychophysical Research edition, 1989.
57. Frederick Van Eeden, 'A Study of Dreams', *Journal* of the Society for Psychical Research, Vol. 26, 1913.
58. Charles T. Tart (ed.), *Altered States of Consciousness*, John Wiley, 1969.
59. Green, 1968, op.cit.
60. Keith Hearne, *The Dream Machine*, Aquarian, 1990.
61. Stephen LaBerge, *Lucid Dreams*, Ballantine, 1985.
62. Susan Blackmore, 'Dreams that do what they're told', in *New Scientist*, 6 January 1990.
63. Greg Long, *Examining the Earthlight Theory*, Centre for UFO Studies, 1990.
64. Blackmore, 1982/1983, op.cit.
65. See, for example, Kenneth M. Kensinger, 'Banisteriopsis Usage Among the Peruvian Cashinahua', in *Hallucinogens and Shamanism*, op.cit.
66. See, for instance, Montague Ullman, Stanley Krippner, with Alan Vaughan, *Dream Telepathy*, McFarland & Co., 1989.

ADDITIONAL NOTES

SEE PAGE 128

That death roads are the evolution of a basic concept of spirit ways has, in fact, been effectively confirmed by recent findings by German researcher Ulrich Magin *(The Ley Hunter*, No. 116, 1992). Inspired by the Dutch material, he checked through German archives for reference to similar features. He found something even more remarkable. In the *Handwortbuch de deutschen Aberglaubens* (de Gruyters, 1933), Magin found a reference to *Geisterwege,* or ghost paths. The entry reads:

> GHOST PATHS. These are always in the same place; on them one meets with ghosts quite often. The paths, with no exception, always run in a straight line over mountains and valley and through marshes...In the towns they pass the houses closely or go right through them. The paths end or originate at a cemetery. This idea may stem from the ancient custom of driving a corpse along a special dead man's road, therefore this way or road was believed to have the same characteristics as a cemetery, it is a place where spirits of the deceased thrive.

The source for this were dated 1901 and 1908, but Magin has now confirmed that other sources go back to at least the nineteenth century, and, of course, relate to beliefs and superstitions much earlier.

British researchers have just started the search for the UK equivalent of these German *Geisterwege* and the Dutch *Doodwegen* (which were also known as *Spokenwegen* — spook or ghost roads). They think they are to be found in the tradition of 'corpse ways' or 'church paths'. A legend exists, for instance, of a 'lost path' linking Brailles Hill in Warwickshire with Bredon Hill in Worcestershire, two prominent features 23 miles apart. This invisible road is associated in folklore with an old Warwickshire custom stating that a right-of-way was automatically established wherever a funeral party walked bearing a corpse to its burial. Physical examples of such corpse ways still fragmentarily survive in various parts of Britain, in fact. It seems that oral tradition in Cornwall, for example, remembers them as 'coffin lines', and their courses may possibly be decipherable from stone stiles in field walls, even though the paths, the 'lines', have now disappeared or been re-routed.

The research into the significance of such features is only just beginning, but already some ley hunters, myself included, are tempted to suspect strongly that at least some of Alfred Watkins' 'leys' were vestigal traces of medieval death or ghost roads, rather than remnants of Neolithic traders' routes (and *certainly* rather than nebulous 'energy lines'!). One such example could well be Watkins' Sutton Walls alignment (see Chapter 1), which had evidence of an actual track falling along it, and which links perhaps *cemeteries* rather than *churches* — it is noteworthy that the line passes through only the cemetery at Sutton St Nicholas. The idea may also clear up a mystery on one of Watkins' other leys, which involves the ancient, ruined Llanthony Abbey, in the Black Mountains on the Wales–England border. Here, Watkins found an old, hollow road running in line from a notch on a ridge to the abbey. On the same alignment, a curious groove ran up the steep mountain slope beyond Llanthony. There are in fact three of these straightish paths or grooves on the slope, but one is dominant. No one has ever been able to explain what these things were — they look for all the world like some of the Bolivian altiplano lines. I have climbed up this groove or path, and it is crudely structured with rough stones. Could it be that it marks a medieval ghost or death road leading to the abbey?

SEE PAGE 179

The whole concept of witchcraft was, however, very much a mirage conjured up by the church. Those accused of it were all too often innocent 'cunning folk', country herbalists and healers, and, to be sure, magicians. They were, indeed, a folk vestige of shamanism. Hallucinogenic ointments were certainly made for out-of-body spirit journeys. As Hans Peter Duerr put it in his *Dreamtime* (1978/1985):

> Women of this kind who journeyed about at night were quite familiar to country folk. It was known that they sometimes rubbed themselves

with mysterious salves prepared from plants. This made their bodies sink into a stupor, and their souls (or whatever) fled away into the wilderness.

So familiar, in fact, that certain old houses, in the Channel Islands, for example, would have a stone slab sticking out of their chimney stacks so passing Night Travellers could settle down for a rest. The Night Travellers were not Satanists, and Duerr points out that the hallucinogenic aspects of the 'flying' were played down by the medieval Church as it made it more difficult for the Devil to be blamed — the folk shamans had to be shown to be 'in league with the Devil', after all!

SEE PAGE 202

It appears that the Mamas did not specify that they flew during their travels in the spirit world, and it would be nice to get their full comments on this, but there can be virtually no doubt that magical flight would have to be at least one of their key ways of out-of-body locomotion, for it is the commonest sensation of out-of-body travel, and is in any case so fundamentally embedded in the traditions of shamanism, as the universality of bird symbolism demonstrates. The Sanema Indians *did* specify to anthropologist Johannes Wilbert, however, that their shamans could fly, or at least walk one foot above the ground.

232

INDEX

walking, 87, 88, 91, 112, 120, 191, 199

water, 81, 91, 92, 125, 126

Watkins, Alfred, 10, 14, 19, 20–8, 36, 39–41, 50, 64, 79

Watkins, Allen, 21, 33

Wedd, Tony, 32–3, 43, 45

Wharam, Alan, 23

Winchester, 18

witches, 98, 130, 150–1, 177–80
flying, 150–1, 231–2

women, 141, 175, 180

Wood, James G., 19

Woolhope Club, 16, 25

Worsley, Alan, 210, 214

York, 37